THE GREAT BAHAMIAN HURRICANES OF 1899 AND 1932

The Story of Two of the Greatest and Deadliest Hurricanes to Impact the Bahamas

WAYNE NEELY

iUniverse, Inc.
Bloomington

The Great Bahamian Hurricanes of 1899 and 1932
The Story of Two of the Greatest and Deadliest
Hurricanes to Impact the Bahamas

iUniverse books may be ordered through booksellers or by contacting:

iUniverse
1663 Liberty Drive
Bloomington, IN 47403
www.iuniverse.com
1-800-Authors (1-800-288-4677)

Because of the dynamic nature of the Internet, any web addresses or links contained in this book may have changed since publication and may no longer be valid. The views expressed in this work are solely those of the author and do not necessarily reflect the views of the publisher, and the publisher hereby disclaims any responsibility for them.

Any people depicted in stock imagery provided by Thinkstock are models, and such images are being used for illustrative purposes only.

Certain stock imagery © Thinkstock.

ISBN: 978-1-4759-2553-1 (sc)
ISBN: 978-1-4759-2554-8 (e)
ISBN: 978-1-4759-2555-5 (dj)

Printed in the United States of America

iUniverse rev. date: 6/5/2012

CONTENTS

DEDICATION

This book is dedicated first and foremost to all of the victims of the *Great Bahamian Hurricanes of 1899 and 1932.* It is my hope that their stories will live on for future generations of Bahamians to read about and to appreciate why these storms were regarded as 'Great Bahamian Hurricanes.'

To the Late Mr. William Holowesko, it was you having the confidence in me to lend me a 'stranger' at the time, some of your books on hurricanes and Bahamian history from your library that started me on this noble journey of documenting Bahamian history and historic Bahamian hurricanes. You may be gone but your spirit and your kindness lives on forever in these books.

To Mr. Les Brown who at a conference held here in the Bahamas through his own unique way and method reminded me to: 1) "Pass it on"; 2) "It is important how you use your down time"; 3) "Someone's opinion of you doesn't have to become a reality"; and 4) "In the time of adversity Expand!" To Dr. Myles Munroe who always reminds me to 1) "Die empty!" 2) "To pursue my purpose!" and 3) "Maximize My Potential." I listened to them and this book is the end result… Thank you Mr. Les Brown and Dr. Myles Munroe for your invaluable contribution to my life.

Dr. Martin Luther King Jr. once said, "Faith is taking the first step even when you don't see the whole staircase."

Mahatma Gandhi once said, "You must be the change you want to see in the world!" and "There are 2 types of people in this world, those that take the credit and those that actually do the work. Take my advice and follow the latter, as there is a lot less competition there."

Tyler Perry once said "There comes a time when even your dreams believe because there will come a point where that dream will take on the belief for you-Believe in your dreams and stick with it no matter what because anything you want is possible…Simply believe in it!"

PREFACE

The hurricanes of the Bahamas have often been considered either exogenous acts of God or the uncontrollable results of nature. This is because hurricanes, like any other natural hazards, only become disasters due to the vulnerability of specific social and economic structures and because of political decisions and a variety of human actions before and after their impact. So it can be said that disasters such as hurricanes, are socially produced, and like revolutions or wars, they are moments of extreme stress that can reveal the underlying structures of social and political life. A growing number of books covering many aspects of hurricanes have examined their social impacts. However, the historiography of the Bahamas and even the Caribbean has rarely approached hurricanes in this way as I have done with this book on two very destructive Bahamian hurricanes. In the history of the Bahamas, often considered a patriarchal society in which the hurricanes traditionally bore the names not of women but of the islands which they devastated, have impacted all aspects of our everyday lives.

The *Great Bahamas Hurricane of 1899* and the *Great Abaco Hurricane of 1932* holds a special place in the archives of Bahamian History. I must note here that the Great Bahamas Hurricane of 1899 is also called the San Ciriaco Hurricane in record books around the region because of the great devastation it inflicted on the island of Puerto Rico on the Saint's Day of Saint Cyriacus, before it devastated the Bahamas. This storm was the most notable storm in the 1899 North Atlantic season and was called Hurricane San Ciriaco (or the

1899 Puerto Rico Hurricane), or locally known as the Great Andros Island Hurricane of 1899 or the Great Bahamas Hurricane of 1899 in the Bahamas, which caused more than 3,800 fatalities throughout the region. For the purpose of this book, I will call it by its lesser known name *'The Great Bahamas Hurricane of 1899'* because of the great death toll and devastation occurring throughout the Bahamas. This book seeks to place these two disasters within their specific physical, social and economic contexts, and to demonstrate both how their impact were felt throughout the Bahamas and how they created conditions that influenced the subsequent history of the Bahamas.

These hurricanes which devastated the Bahamas in 1899 and 1932 were undoubtedly two of the worst natural disasters the country had experienced at the time. Even up to this day these storms are still considered among the top ten most destructive Bahamian storms of all time. These storms and the accompanying floods and strong winds caused over 352 deaths. Although the destruction was horrendous, Nassau was spared because it was not in the storms' path. Unfortunately, the islands of Abaco and Andros felt the full brunt of these storms.

The weather is a fabric that is inter-woven around every aspect of our daily lives. After writing over six books about hurricanes and weather in general, I am now even more convinced than ever that a weather connection exists within everything that we experience. Our health, our economy, our comfort, our safety, and even our politics can be tied to the weather. Amazingly, the weather is really quite easy to understand. As scientists work to unravel the mysteries of global weather and climate change it is increasingly important to establish a good base of historical data for comparison with contemporary climate conditions. My analysis of hurricane activity in the Bahamas over the many years of their occurrence is vital to this cause. Some of the historical information contained in this book can be found nowhere else in book form and some of the prior written works on these storms are inaccurate and in desperate need of revision. Many years ago I had just finished publishing my second book *'The Major Hurricanes to Affect the Bahamas'* and I was taking a signed copy of this book to a friend in the Downtown area of Nassau (Bay Street). While I was on Bay Street, I saw Mr. Paul Adderley a former

Bahamian Parliamentarian, Cabinet Minister and avid historian in passing. I informed him that my book was finally finished and it was available for sale. He said "I hope you included the 1899 Bahamas Hurricane in it" and I told him "Yes I did, but very briefly." He said that I should have gone into greater details about this hurricane, because it was perhaps one of the greatest storms that the Bahamas has ever experienced. He also suggested that I need to write an entire book on this storm. Well after five years and three books later, I finally took his useful advice. After reading this book it is my hope and desire that you will be left with no other choice but to agree with him.

Climate is generally considered to be one of the single most important resources of these islands of the Bahamas. It is one of the main reasons why last year well over 5.6 million visitors flocked to these islands to enjoy our beautiful sun, sand and sea. Some would even take up residency whether temporarily or permanently each year. This book presents the many facets of two notable Bahamian hurricanes and how they have influenced the weather and climate of the country over the years of their occurrences. In writing this book, it is imperative a clear distinction between 'weather' and 'climate' be made. The term weather describes short-term variations in the atmosphere, and is usually studied on a day-to-day basis. The term climate on the other hand, refers to the long-term conditions of the atmosphere, and is generally studied on a monthly or yearly or longer basis. Climate is not merely the description of average weather, but also includes extremes, variabilities, frequencies, periodicities and distributions of atmospheric events over time and space. Weather exerts a very strong, often controlling, effect on everyone's day-to-day activities. The effects of climate, on the other hand, influence our lifestyle, health, and often our long-term decisions we make. For example, where we live, retire and spend our vacations, what crops we grow, and how we design and build our homes are often strongly influenced by climate. For such decisions, knowledge of an area's climate is much more important than knowing what today's weather is going to be.

Hurricanes have long been a fact of life here in the Bahamas. With our extensive but lengthy, exposed coastlines jutting into the

Atlantic Ocean and reaching as far north and west as Florida and its Cays, and as far south as Cuba, and with our uniquely flat lands, shallow coastal waters, there is little wonder that these tempests have visited these islands before there was a Bahamas as we know it today. Hurricanes have literally shaped the landscape along our coast, and in a sense, the people as well. In fact, the Lucayan Indians-the first known settlers of the Bahamas believed that these islands were one big complete landmass but over the years they were separated by the howling winds and the giant waves of the hurricanes. This book discusses two of the most fearsome and violent hurricanes that have made a landfall in the Bahamas. All hurricanes have the potential to be destructive, but throughout the years several hurricanes that have visited the Bahamas were notable for a variety of factors, including high winds, massive floods or a large number of fatalities they left in their wake. In a country that is frequently visited by tropical cyclones, each generation seems to have a benchmark storm against which all others are measured. This book takes a look at two of these storms, and investigates two of the Bahamas most notable and memorable hurricanes and the impact that they had on the Bahamian society in their respective years.

The weather is the most universal of all topics, and to be quite frank how could it not be? It affects most aspects of everyone's daily lives. I am not talking about just the obvious ways-how we all check the local weather forecast before we go to sleep or upon awakening to decide what clothes to wear, what to do in your spare time, whether we'll need to allow for more travel time, or whether it will be sunny for the family picnic. Although this type of information is important, it trivializes the true impact of weather. It is quite true that the weather affects us all the time and it sometimes determines our moods. Many people I know aren't happy unless the sun is shining and the air is warm, and while I have an appreciation of a sunny, warm day, the blind acceptance that only nice weather is a sunny warm day is like saying that the only good music is a happy, optimistic song. A cloudy, cool, and breezy day can be refreshing and revitalizing, bringing energy back to the body, especially if it's been preceded by a few days of unlimited sunshine and taxing warmth. It is my favorite type of day and it is easy to see why. The sound of rain pounding down on a roof or on a windowpane and then dripping onto the concrete sidewalk with an irregular beat can be more soothing than any spa treatment. Combine that with the gentle rumbles of a distant thunderstorm, and the stage is set for a perfect night's sleep.

Technology has a way of numbing us to history. It is easy to take for granted the comforts made possible by science and engineering in recent times, easy to forget the everyday hardships experienced by the human species during most of its existence. This cultural amnesia is perhaps nowhere more evident than in our relationship with the earth's weather. In an era of satellite images, Doppler radar, super-fast computer models, and three-dimensional time-lapsed animations, when anyone with access to 24 hour cable television or the Internet can learn the five-day forecast for Nassau, Bahamas or as far east as Beijing, China. It comes as a mild shock to realize that until the mid-nineteenth century there could be no certain knowledge of whether it is raining or snowing at a location even a few miles distant. To be sure, there was a great deal of uncertain knowledge. Most pre-industrial societies accumulated a wealth of meteorological folk wisdom, and corresponding appreciation of natural indicators. Over the years with the advancement of modern technology, it has made the weather an even more topical subject.

The accuracy of forecasting hurricanes has improved tremendously over my 22 years in the meteorological field. On average, a five-day track forecast today is more accurate than a three-day forecast was in the 1970's. Better data collection and tremendous advances in computer modeling are two of the main reasons for these track improvements. Unfortunately, improved accuracy in forecasting hurricane intensity (especially rapid changes in intensity) has proven more difficult to achieve. Modern technology like the satellite and radar images have given us the opportunity to see the weather from above or to examine a cross section of a weather phenomenon like a hurricane or a thunderstorm, which none of our ancestors or early scientists could do. We can view the curl of a cold front, the symmetry of a hurricane, or the up and down drafts within an isolated thunderstorm cell in an otherwise clear sky. Modern day lifesaving weather tools such as, Doppler Radars and super computers were not available for storm tracking, and as a result, the death toll and devastation from these great hurricanes were great. There are several reasons for this high death toll and one of the most important reasons was the lack of advanced warnings and another factor was sub-standard housing on the majority of the Family Islands. Most of the fishermen were out at sea in an area known as 'the Mud' near Andros looking for sponges and many of them did not know that a storm was travelling in their area, until the storm engulfed their ships.

I have written this and my previous books with the understanding that interest in hurricanes varies from the enthusiastic, to the curious and to the unrealized. Although this book is certainly not a meteorological textbook, some hurricanes explanations are needed in order to appreciate the mysterious world of hurricanes. For example, how moisture and the uneven heating of the earth's surface and upper atmosphere in the tropics turns the atmosphere into an unending display of power, rage and fury that is unchallenged by anything humans have ever created or have imagined. Explanations are intertwined with entries throughout the book and at the back of the book there is a glossary of weather terms. The Bahamas experiences a wide variety of weather from the dramatic and dangerous to localized phenomena that are more interesting than dangerous. Hurricane history here in the Bahamas can be thought of in two ways: either as weather events that were so dramatic that they should never be forgotten, such as these two hurricanes or as weather that affected a historical event in some way such as, the Great Bahamas Hurricane of 1929 which severely impacted the sponging industry and changed the way we saw and monitored hurricanes. Although some of these major hurricanes have occurred in our lifetimes, others were defining moments for our parents, grandparents, or great-grandparents.

In the past, the science of hurricane forecasting has not always been as accurate and reliable as it is today, and mankind use to depend on local unscientific observations, birds and other animals, and recollections from the past to try and understand or forecast the weather of the future with regards to hurricanes. These ancient weather information often came to us in the form of weather wives' tales, myths and weather folklore, and although most of us don't rely on these methods anymore we still hear such things as "If the sea birds fly in from the cays in droves then it means a hurricane or storm is approaching the land" or "If a certain tree blossoms more than usual then that is a sign of a very active hurricane season up ahead." I too myself before I became a scientist often wondered whether or not these old wives tales, myths and folklore stories were indeed true. Thankfully, as a certified meteorologist, I now take a different viewpoint of our ancestors' weather insights because many of these tales simply don't stand up to the truth meter.

Most of the time nature looks kindly on us, but things can change abruptly because your home or business may be in the path of a dangerous storm. If that is the case then you may need to leave your home or business and head to a hurricane shelter or simply move out of the path of the impending storm. This book is not only about the science of hurricanes, but it is also about hurricanes themselves and their effects on us. Although we can appreciate hurricanes for what they are, from their massive size, their feeder bands or eye structure, to their majestic beauty on a satellite picture or a view from space, our appreciation of them are likely to grow with education and knowledge. Historic Bahamian hurricanes typically fall into two main categories. First, a distinctly unique or particular hurricane that is remembered for generations to come because of its extreme and historic nature, such as, Hurricane Andrew in 1992 or the Great Bahamas Hurricane of 1929. Second, a historic, political or social event in history marked or influenced by the particular storm, such as, the Great Bahamas Hurricane of 1866. This book takes a look at both types of storms. For events before the early 20th century, weather records are simply not detailed enough for the type of analysis to which we in our modern world have become accustomed. We can, however, through historical accounts, including occasional weather records, often put these events in weather perspective. For the more recent hurricane events-we have detailed hurricane records. Either way, hurricanes have played a great part in the history of the Bahamas.

We will always remember powerful Bahamian hurricanes like Andrew in 1992, which caused devastation of epic proportions to the islands of Eleuthera, Abaco and Bimini. However, some of the truly historic hurricanes happened at a much earlier time and affected many other islands of the Bahamas than this storm. Hurricane Andrew was the defining natural disaster of the early 21st century for the

Bahamas, but it was two major unnamed storms(unnamed because they occurred before tropical storms and hurricanes were assigned names), that brought unimaginable tragedy to the Bahamas at the end of the 19th century and early 20th century. On August 11th to 13th 1899 and September 5, 1932 these two notable and very destructive Bahamian hurricanes struck the Bahamas at peak intensities and resulted in the deaths of over 334 persons in 1899 and 18 persons in 1932 as they plowed through the islands of the Bahamas making these islands a wasteland of rubbles in their aftermath. During this era, the science of meteorology was in its infancy; without satellite photographs or computer models to warn of an approaching storm, residents had little or no idea of the peril awaiting the country. As often the case with hurricanes, the storm surge was the most damaging part of the storm followed by the strong winds. Many persons went out at sea on sponging and fishing trips with no idea a massive storm was approaching the Bahamas. Many of these fishermen were caught in these two storms never to be seen or heard from again. While others on land were simply washed away in their coastal homes. Many persons who fled the beach or coastal areas for stronger buildings farther inland were saved; however, many of those who stayed died. This second storm was the impetus for building codes and the building of many seawalls to protect many of the islands in the Bahamas from future storms.

FOREWORD

Wayne Neely has extensively discussed the terrible impact upon the Bahamas of the two major hurricanes which hit The islands in 1899 and 1932. Both cyclones were very intense and each tracked in a northwestward direction right along the southeast to northwest orientation of the Bahamas island chain. Both storm tracks were near ideal in their movement and intensity to cause the maximized amount of damage to the greatest number of islands.

These two hurricanes have now been largely forgotten by most people currently living on the Bahamas. But the legacy of these cyclones needs to be preserved as a reminder of the type of profound influence such hurricanes can occasionally inflict upon the Bahamas. Wayne Neely has done an excellent job in describing these cyclones' destructive impacts and the Bahamian society alterations that these cyclones caused.

Most Bahamians are young and have not lived long enough to have experienced very many hurricanes. Most have heard about global warming from rising levels of CO_2, however, Global warming stories have been very prominent in the news in the last 25 years and stories of the damage brought by US Hurricane Katrina (2005) and other unusually intense hurricanes have been used as examples of CO_2 induced future intense hurricane activity increases. This has lead, I am sure, many Bahamians to be more fearful of future hurricanes being stronger and more frequent. I and many of my colleagues have performed extensive research on this topic and do not find that CO_2 gas increases are going to change Atlantic basin hurricane activity in any significant way or make future hurricanes more intense.

So when a very destructive future hurricane hits the Bahamas, Wayne Neely's very sobering examples of the 1899 and 1932 hurricanes can be brought forward and used to show that any coming hurricanes to hit the Bahamas will likely not be more destructive than these two most destructive storms of the past.

Professor William Gray
Emeritus Professor of Atmospheric Science at Colorado State University

World renowned Professor William M. "Bill" Gray (born 1929) is Emeritus Professor of Atmospheric Science at Colorado State University (CSU), and head of the Tropical Meteorology Project at CSU's Department of Atmospheric Sciences. He is a pioneer in the science of forecasting hurricanes and one of the world's leading experts on tropical storms. In 1952, Gray received a B.S. degree in geography from George Washington University, and in 1959 a M.S. in meteorology from the University of Chicago, where he went on to earn a Ph.D. in geophysical sciences in 1964. He served as a weather forecaster for the United States Air Force, and as a research assistant in the University of Chicago Department of Meteorology. He joined Colorado State University in 1961. He has been advisor of over 70 Ph.D. and M.S. students. Gray is noted for his forecasts of North Atlantic hurricane season activity. Gray pioneered the concept of "seasonal" hurricane forecasting—predicting months in advance the severity of the coming hurricane season. Preliminary forecasts are released before the start of the hurricane season, and the forecasts are then revised as the season progresses. These predictions are so important that they help influence insurance rates throughout the United States and the rest of the region. Gray and his team have been issuing seasonal hurricane forecasts since 1984.

After the 2005 Atlantic hurricane season, Gray announced that he was stepping back from the primary authorship of CSU's tropical cyclone probability forecasts, passing the role to Philip J. Klotzbach. Gray indicated that he would be devoting more time to the issue of global warming. He does not attribute global warming to anthropogenic causes, and is critical of those who do. Gray is skeptical of current theories of human-induced global warming. He believes that humans are not responsible for the warming of the earth. Gray said those who had linked global warming to the increased number of hurricanes in recent years were in error. He cites statistics showing that there were 101 hurricanes from 1900 to 1949, in a period of cooler global temperature, compared to 83 from 1957 to 2006 when the earth warmed. Gray developed a seasonal hurricane forecasting methodology in the 1980s and began reporting his forecasts to the public. His forecasts are widely discussed in the U.S. and Regional media. Preliminary forecasts are released before the start of the hurricane season, and the forecasts are then revised as the season progresses.

INTRODUCTION

In the waning days of the summers of 1899 and 1932, a patch of bad weather-thunderstorms, wind, and rain blew off the western African coast and rumbled across the North Atlantic Ocean. As these two very powerful hurricanes approached the Bahamas in early September of 1932 and early August of 1899, they picked up a counterclockwise circulation sustained by the rotation of the earth. They also drew energy from the oceans that were warmed up for months beneath the intense summer sun, and evolved into two great Bahamian hurricanes called the 'Great Bahamas Hurricane of 1899'(San Ciriaco Hurricane of 1899') and the 'Great Abaco Hurricane of 1932'(because of the great devastation sustained by this storm on the island of Abaco). This storm struck the island of Abaco at peak intensity as a rare Category Five hurricane and became one of only two hurricanes on record to hit the Bahamas at Category Five intensity. The other was Hurricane Andrew of 1992, which was only reclassified as a Category Five hurricane ten years later. It was the time of year when such intense storms often formed in this part of the world and caused great havoc to the Bahamas and this region. These storms would strike the Bahamas with a force beyond any human imagination or standard of measurement. Their aftermaths, as you will see later, would reverberate for months and even years through the highest government offices here in the Bahamas as well as the central government of Great Britain.

A recent statement made by the American Meteorological Society noted: *"The ultimate goal of both research and operational groups is to minimize loss of life and property from hurricanes. Given the current state of the art of hurricane prediction and the recent dramatic increase in coastal population, this goal can best be accomplished in the short term through better public awareness of the hurricane problem, disaster preparedness, and coastal evacuation planning."* This statement is especially cogent here in the Bahamas, especially with regards to these two devastating hurricanes. In 1899 and 1932, the islands of the Bahamas were left reeling from the vicious onslaught of two deadly and devastating hurricanes. The 1899 hurricane remains one of the deadliest hurricanes on record in the Bahamas and the 1932 hurricane was also very deadly and devastating and was the first of two Category Five hurricanes on record to hit the Bahamas. Both of these storms were Cape Verde type hurricanes whose fury no one could match. For over twenty four hours, both of these respective storms squatted over the Bahamas laying claim to its victims. When they were finally over, there were hardly any leaves on the trees, and the country was left in shambles. During these storms, hundreds of families were forced to seek safe shelter elsewhere when their own houses began to fall to pieces. As a result, many of the sturdier residences were crammed with weeping and frightened neighbours who had lost all of their worldly possessions and were fearful for their lives. Every gust of wind striking their homes was like a battering ram, minute after minute, hour after hour, and day after day. The terror and anxiety from these storms were almost too much for a human to endure. After it was all over, the inhabitants walked out into the streets in a bewildered daze, looking and feeling as if they had just been through a war-zone. Fortunately, those on land were the lucky ones for those at sea felt the full-fledged wrath of these two merciless storms. Many of the sponge fishermen were at sea and caught the brunt of these two storms. Many succumbed to these storms at sea.

The 1899 hurricane season was an average one, with 9 tropical storms, of which 5 became hurricanes and only two became major hurricanes, and six of them impacted the Bahamas in a significant way. The 1932 hurricane season was slightly above average with 11 named storms and 4 major hurricanes, and four of them actually impacted the Bahamas in a significant way. These years were extremely active years for hurricanes making landfall in the Bahamas. Don't be surprised by the high totals because the Bahamas is one of the most active areas hit by hurricanes and tropical storms in the North Atlantic. The Bahamas on average gets brushed or hit by a hurricane once every 2.4 years, and gets hit by a major hurricane once every 12 years. The Bahamas has been brushed or hit by a tropical storm or hurricane 57 times since 1871. There are three Bahamian islands ranked in the top 10 affected by tropical systems of all cities, islands and countries in the North Atlantic Basin - Andros, Abaco and Grand Bahama. The first on the list of the most active area to get hit or brushed by a tropical storm or hurricane is Grand Cayman which is affected once every 2.21 years and since 1871 it was brushed or hit by a hurricane 62 times. The average years between direct hits are once every 6.52 years. Second on the list is Andros here in the Bahamas, which is affected once every 2.40 years and since 1871 it was brushed or hit by a tropical storm or hurricane 57 times. The average years between direct hurricane hits are once every 8.06 years. Third is Abaco, which is affected once every 1.77 years and since 1871 was brushed or hit by a tropical storm or hurricane 56 times. The average years between direct hurricane hits are once every 8.57 years. Fourth is Grand Bahama, which is affected every 2.49 years and since 1871, it was brushed or hit by a tropical storm or hurricane 55 times. The average years between direct hurricane hits are once every 6.52 years. Fifth is Cape Hatteras, North Carolina, sixth is Delray Beach, Florida, seventh is Cancun, Mexico, eighth is Hollywood, Florida, ninth is Deerfield Beach, Florida and tenth is Bermuda. Interestingly, New Providence is ranked 39th on the list, and is affected once every 2.98 years. It was brushed or hit by a tropical storm or hurricane 46 times since 1871. The average years between direct hurricane hits are once every 11.42 years.

This book on these two powerful Bahamian hurricanes are a history lesson in hurricanes and their impact on the Bahamian society, because it not only focuses on how these storms develop, what causes them to be so powerful but also the history behind them. To pen "The Great Bahamian Hurricanes of 1899 and 1932" required me to travel to the major inhabited islands of the Bahamas to interview many elderly persons who experienced the 1932 Hurricane and had heard about the 1899 Hurricane as well. While the Great Abaco Hurricane of 1932 actually never made landfall upon the continental United States, however, its effects were felt, nonetheless, throughout Florida and the eastern coast of the United States. The hurricane actually struck the Bahamas at its peak intensity, with the majority of the hurricane damage occurring on the island of Abaco. The 1932 Bahamas Hurricane only claimed 18 lives, which, while tragic, means that it was not, in fact, one of the most deadly Bahamian hurricanes ever to strike these islands. However, I included it in this book as an example of how much damage a hurricane can inflict to a land area and to property when it strikes full force, and even when you're only experiencing the peripheral effects of the storm. I am also hoping to point out just how far we've come in terms of using the latest technology to properly prepare for a hurricane.

Over the years, I have had a love affair with very destructive hurricanes that have impacted the Bahamas and the rest of the region. This love affair was ignited when I was just eight years old, when I was first told about a very deadly and destructive hurricane called the 'Great Bahamas Hurricane of 1929' by my grandparents growing up on the island of Andros. Over the recent years it has led me to teaching and sharing information about hurricanes here locally and abroad. I have focused on the understanding of hurricanes, how they form and die out, how destructive and deadly they are and how we affect them and how, ultimately, they affect us. I am continually amazed at how organized the world of hurricanes really is and what makes them work. Patterns are everywhere-in the clouds, in weather maps and satellite images and even in the oceans. This quest for knowledge and understanding has enabled me to develop a panorama which has caused me to question and rethink our knowledge base on destructive Bahamian hurricanes. Nowhere do I question it more than in the debate that has developed on global warming and climate change and their impact on hurricanes. This book looks at two of these very destructive hurricanes and the great impact they had on the Bahamian society in 1899 and 1932. Furthermore, this book looks at what we know about these hurricanes and explains the difference between the two while raising the questions about what we should be asking about them. It looks at all aspects of these hurricanes and attempts to answer many of the questions about what we know and don't know about them. Am I correct to question the conventional beliefs we had on historic Bahamian hurricanes? I say yes, but I also hope that this book will get Bahamians talking and assessing what has happened and what still is happening to our country-past, present and future with regards to Bahamian hurricanes and their impact on our society.

While tropical cyclones helps transfer heat and moisture poleward, middle-latitude cyclones on the other hand brings colder and drier air towards the equator, hurricanes and their counterparts in all locales-all within a broad class of storms known as tropical cyclones, move incredible amounts of tropical heat and moisture toward the poles. That's because these storms form much closer to the equator, over warm ocean waters, and typically do not have fronts associated with them until they reach higher latitudes and are in their waning phases. Hurricanes are noted for their circular, banded patterns, low-level inflow and upper-level outflow which all drive the hurricane's internal engine. They typically form and move westward within the trade wind easterlies near the equator, and recurve to the east only when they reach the middle latitudes. The transformation from a warm and humid air mass into one filled with towering cumulus clouds, generates an incredible amount of energy. In fact, according to the Atlantic Oceanic and Meteorological Laboratory (AMOL), an average hurricane (one with a radius of about 400 miles) can produce the equivalent of 200 times the world's electrical generation capacity each day. These storms have multi-day lifetimes, and some 70-80 occur each year around the world, truly make the hurricane the "Greatest storm on Earth."

CHAPTER ONE
FUNDAMENTALS OF A HURRICANE

Tropical cyclones are the broad class of all low-pressure systems that form in the tropics and have a closed wind circulation with sustained winds of at least 39 mph. When sustained winds reach 74 mph, the storm is classified according to its geographical location:

1. Hurricane (the North Atlantic Ocean, the Northeast Pacific Ocean east of the International Dateline or the South Pacific Ocean east of 160E);
2. Typhoon (the Northwest Pacific Ocean west of the International Dateline);
3. Severe Tropical Cyclone (the Southwest Pacific Ocean west of 160E or Southeast Indian Ocean east of 90E);
4. Severe Cyclonic Storm (the Southwest Indian Ocean).

For the ease of describing these intense tropical cyclones I will simply refer to them as hurricanes, unless there's a specific geographical focus. Once winds in a closed tropical low-pressure system reach 39 mph, the system is named either a tropical storm or tropical cyclone depending upon its location. Then, a name is assigned according to WMO's international naming conventions. These names are drawn from the Region IV naming list for the North Atlantic. Names are used to help focus attention to particular storms, especially when several storms are occurring at the same time. The names also provide easy recognition for the past historical and destructive hurricanes. Storms that are especially deadly or destructive have their names retired. Evolving from a tropical wave, through a tropical depression, to a tropical storm and finally a hurricane, tropical cyclones often capture our attention not only because of their power but also because of their wide-ranging societal, economic and physical impacts.

What distinguishes hurricanes from other types of low-pressure or another storm system is that hurricanes are 'warm-core' systems. This means that the entire storm system is compose of warm air. Middle-latitude low-pressure systems often have cold and warm sectors separated by weather fronts. Most hurricanes form over warm tropical oceans during the summer and early fall months. Peak hurricane season is usually about two months after the summer solstice. Hurricane season extends far beyond the warmest months of the year because ocean waters warm more slowly and retain their heat longer than either air or land. Scientists now realize that hurricanes are most likely to form and intensify when ocean water temperatures are at least 80°F.

Tropical cyclones are systems of large, rotating thunderstorms that form over warm tropical waters where the winds and the seas are conducive to the development and growth of these storms. There is nothing like the hurricane in the atmosphere. Even seen by remote sensors on satellites thousands of miles above earth, the uniqueness of these powerful, tightly coiled storms is clear. Hurricanes are not the largest storm systems on earth, nor the most violent—but they combine those qualities as no other phenomenon does, as if they were designed to be powerful engines of death and destruction. Due to the effects of the earth's rotation, these storms rotate in a counter clockwise direction in the northern hemisphere, and rotate clockwise in the southern hemisphere. They are found in all areas of the tropical regions of the world with the exception of the southern Atlantic Ocean (although there was a case where a tropical cyclone called Cyclone Catarina formed there in 2005 but this was a rare exception to the rule). These tropical cyclones are called hurricanes in the North Atlantic once they exceed the seventy-four-mile-per-hour threshold.

In the Northern Hemisphere, these storms are called hurricanes, a term that echoes colonial Spanish and Caribbean Indian words for evil spirits and big winds created by their gods. The word 'hurricane' has its origins in the names given to the storm gods by various tribes of local Indians within this region. Here in the Bahamas, it is certain that the Lucayan Indians who were the first people to inhabit the land we now call the Bahamas experienced the high winds, rough seas and heavy rains of these storms. Unfortunately they left no written accounts of their experiences with these storms. According to the edited abstracts taken from Spanish Priest Bartholomew de Las Casas he said that these Indians believed that the islands of the Bahamas were comprised of one giant complete landmass but had been separated by the howling winds and rough seas of the hurricane.

When the Europeans first attempted to establish permanent settlements in the Caribbean, they quickly learned about these storms when it destroyed their first built settlements in the New World on the island of Hispaniola. In the Bahamas, Christopher Columbus was lucky enough to not have encountered any storms on his first voyage, but in 1499 Vicente Yañez Pinzón captain of Columbus's ship 'the Niña' lost two ships in the fleet in the Exuma Cays due to a hurricane. Furthermore, she was the only ship to survive the famous 1495 hurricane, battered but safely returning to Spain in 1496. In 1495, Christopher Columbus encountered a hurricane near Hispaniola and it was the earliest hurricane reported by Christopher Columbus, who also encountered a tropical storm on one of his voyages to the New World. He later declared that "nothing but the service of God and the extension of the monarchy" would induce him to expose himself to such dangers from hurricanes ever again.

Fortunately, here in the Caribbean, as time passed and these European settlers learned more about their new homeland, they experienced these storms so regularly that they became accustomed to them. Eventually, they began calling them 'equinoctial storms,' as the storms normally hit in the weeks around the period of the fall equinox, which in the Northern Hemisphere occurs in late September. Now thanks in part to over four hundred years of observations and advances in technology, we now know that hurricanes can strike at any time between June and November. The peak of the season in the Bahamas is on the 11th of September of each year, and August and

September are the most active months for hurricanes to strike any part of the Bahamas. These storms are products of the tropical oceans and atmosphere: powered by heat from the sea, steered by the easterly trades and temperate westerlies, and driven by their own fierce energy. Around their tranquil core called the eyewall, winds blow with lethal velocity and the ocean develops an inundating surge. In addition, as they move ashore, tornadoes may descend from the advancing bands of the surrounding thunderstorms. Hurricanes, as poorly understood as they are today, seem to have two main benefits—first, they are a major source of rain for many tropical and subtropical land areas and second, they are responsible for redistribution heat from the equator to the poles which allow us as humans to live and survive on an otherwise very volatile planet.

A hurricane represents the most advanced stage of a tropical cyclone. A cyclone refers to those types of storms having low atmospheric pressure at the center and cyclonic or rotating wind circulation. Thus a tropical cyclone is a low pressure storm system that originates in tropical (or less often subtropical) areas. The tropics are defined as that area of the earth which lies between the Tropic of Cancer, 23.5 degrees north of the equator, and the Tropic of Capricorn, 23.5 degrees south of the equator. Hurricanes vary greatly in size, intensity, behavior and path, but they have enough characteristics in common that some generalizations can be made. A hurricane can be visualized as an organized system of thunderstorm-type clouds generally assembled into spiral bands, called rainbands. Much of the rain generated by a hurricane occurs within these spiraling bands of clouds, with rainfall between the bands generally being much less intense or even absent. Thunder and lightning are not always present, but when occurring will generally be found within those rainbands and the eyewall. There are generally from one to seven bands in a hurricane, with each band commonly 50 miles long. This accounts for the average diameter of the major area covered by a hurricane being roughly 100 miles, although diameters have ranged from less than 100 miles to over 500 miles. Tropical storm-force winds (39 to 73 miles per hour) may occur at a distance from the center of the storm that is several times the diameter of the major cloudy portion of the hurricane.

One of the most distinctive features shared by nearly all hurricanes is the eye. This central portion of the storm varies greatly in size among hurricanes, with some only 3 miles in diameter and others extending to well over 38 miles across. The average eye is about 15 to 20 miles in diameter. The winds in the eye are greatly reduced, often blowing only 15 miles per hour, and the sky may be nearly rain and cloud free. Many people who have been in the eye of a hurricane tell of finding clear blue skies above them as the eye passed over. The eye is also where the lowest atmospheric pressure and highest temperatures of the storm occur and in many cases birds are frequently trapped in the eye, often found in large numbers clinging in desperation to the rigging of ships. They are blown into the eye and trapped there as the storm intensifies, then cannot escape through the violent winds which surround the eye. As a matter of fact, several bird species have entered the United States especially Florida in this manner from the Bahamas and other Caribbean countries, including the Black Anis from Haiti, the Bahamas Honeycreeper, the Bahamas Shallow, the Cuban Cliff Swallow, several West Indian Doves and Pigeons, and most recently the Cattle Egret from the Antilles.

The eye is completely surrounded by the most intense portion of the hurricane, the eyewall. The clouds that compose this imposing feature of the storm reach heights of over 50,000 feet. The eyewall consist of very intense cumulonimbus clouds and within these clouds contains massive amounts of water vapour brought into this area by the rainbands which are forced upwards, converting the water vapour into water and in the process releasing a tremendous amount of heat. This process helps to produce the high winds and the torrential rainfall found within the hurricane. The strongest winds and the heaviest rainfall are often found within or near the eyewall. Many persons have been fooled as the eye passes them into thinking that the storm is over, individuals venture out, only to be surprised as the other side of the eyewall approaches, bringing winds of equal destruction but now blowing from the opposite direction. Together, the eye and eyewall represents the heart of a hurricane.

For a tropical disturbance to develop into a hurricane, there must be several environmental factors that must be present, and they must interact in rather specific ways. This interaction is most likely to occur in late summer/early fall, which is the main reason for the higher incidence hurricanes forming during this time. The official hurricane season for the Bahamas is June 1st, to November 30th of each year. September is especially significant, since more hurricanes have hit the Bahamas during this month than any other month and as stated before, the peak of the hurricane season in the North Atlantic is September 11th of each year. As previously mentioned, a hurricane represents the ultimate stage of a tropical cyclone. The different stages of tropical cyclone development can be described in a number of ways. The classification scheme most commonly used in this region recognizes four stages, based on form and intensity. The stages of the tropical cyclone are:

1. Tropical disturbance: no strong winds (this stage is actually a precursor to a tropical cyclone).
2. Tropical depression: some rotary circulation at the surface and sustained winds speed of less than 39 miles per hour.
3. Tropical storm: distinct rotary circulation with highest sustained wind speed of 39 to 73 miles per hour.
4. Hurricane: very pronounced rotary circulation with sustained winds of 74 miles per hour or greater.

Several factors account for this particular seasonality. Hurricanes nearly always develop from low-pressure disturbances within the trade-wind belt, the area from approximately 30 degrees north latitude to within five degrees of the equator which experiences consistent winds blowing from east to west. Several mechanisms are known to produce areas of low pressure in the trades, and these mechanisms are most prevalent during the summer and early fall. If the Bermuda or subtropical high pressure system is particularly weak and displaced south of this normal position, a condition quite common in early summer and fall, a region of low pressure may be introduced into the trade-winds belt. For example, higher-latitude low pressure systems can more easily penetrate into the tropics when the Bermuda high is displaced southward. The southern end of such systems may become trapped in the trades and provide the seeds of a hurricane.

Another mechanism generating low-pressure disturbances in the trades involves a low-pressure belt called the Intertropical Convergence Zone (ITCZ), which is located near the equator. In the summer, most frequently during the month of August, the ITCZ is at its northernmost location, about 12 degrees north latitude. A rotating low-pressure system forming where the ITCZ meets the trades can become a westward-migrating system in the trades. When this happens the conditions are favorable for the necessary rotation of the newly formed low-pressure system to be achieved.

Another extremely common type of low-pressure disturbance is an easterly wave. This is not an oceanic wave, but an atmospheric low-pressure feature, embedded in the trade winds belt, that moves east to west. The eastern portions of these waves are often very cloudy with heavy rain showers. These systems are nearly always present in abundant numbers during the hurricane season in the North Atlantic. The African continent, especially the very southern edge of the Sahara Desert, is the dominant source for easterly waves in the Atlantic during the peak of the hurricane season. In fact, it is a bit ironic that one of the driest places on earth is the birthplace for storms that have produced some of the greatest rainfall records on earth. These easterly waves in any given year often number somewhere between 50 to 70 (but can be as high as 80) per year, and are very common during May through November. Hurricanes that develop in this manner are called Cape Verde-type hurricanes.

After a hurricane develops, a tremendous amount of energy is released. A moderate hurricane is capable of taking up from the ocean approximately 15 million tons of water vapour per minute from the ocean through the process of evaporation. The amount of energy release into the atmosphere by the transformation of this vapour back into liquid by the hurricane is the major driving force of the hurricane, and a true driving force it is. An average hurricane will release in 24 hours the energy equivalent to one-half million Nagasaki-type atomic bombs or 400 20-megaton hydrogen (fusion) bombs. This energy, if converted to electricity, would satisfy the electrical needs of the United States for more than six months. This transformation of tremendous amounts of energy is why tropical cyclones are called 'heat engines.' One of the most important requirements for the growth and development of a hurricane is the need for warm oceanic waters of 80°F or higher to supply the system with a continuing supply of warm and moisture rich air to allow the system to develop and strengthen.

In the North Atlantic, there are four different types of hurricanes that influence us in some way or the other. Each is uniquely different and has unique and different characteristics that are found in that type of hurricane alone in terms of formation and strength. The first is the Cape Verde Type hurricane which as its name suggests originates off the African Coast in the vicinity of the Cape Verde Islands. Initially it moves in a westerly direction and then in a west-northwest to a northwesterly direction as it makes its way through the Caribbean, Central America, the Bahamas and the United States. Both of these hurricanes in 1899 and 1932 were regarded as Cape Verde Storms. The Cape Verde Islands is an archipelago about 400 miles off the West African Coast and are volcanic in nature. It was colonized by Portugal in the fifteenth century and became an independent country in 1975. At one point in their history, these islands served as an outpost station for the movement of African slaves on the 'Middle Passage' to the Americas. This type of hurricane forms over the Atlantic mainly during the early to mid-part of the season, June through mid-September months when the easterly waves are the most dominant weather features in the Caribbean region. This type of hurricane tend to produce the strongest hurricanes in this category because of the great distance they have in traversing the warm waters of the Atlantic before they get to any landmass giving them the time and the opportunity to strengthen before hitting some landmass in the Caribbean, North or Central America.

At the beginning and the middle of the hurricane season, storms also tend to form near the Bahamas mainly from upper-level systems or TUTT low pressure systems and this type of hurricane has come to be known as '*Bahama Busters*' according to world renowned Professor William Gray from Colorado State University. An example of this type of storm was Hurricane Katrina in 2005, which formed just east to the Bahamas from the remnants of Tropical Depression

#10 and became Tropical Depression #12. This system initially moved westward and then northwestward into the Gulf of Mexico and then over Louisiana. This type of storm tends to produce moderate to intense hurricanes and it all depends not only on the environmental factors at the time, but also how long it remains in the Gulf of Mexico before hitting any landmass on the Gulf Coast States.

Another type of hurricane is the Gulf of Mexico type, which as its name suggests originates in the Gulf of Mexico and travels northward or westward from its inception and mainly influences Latin America, and the Gulf Coast of the United States. This type of hurricane tends to be the weakest of all four types of hurricanes because of the short distance from its formation to the time it hits any land area and began the weakening or dissipating stage. Finally, there is the Western Caribbean type which forms during the early and late parts of the hurricane season and forms in the most favoured location near the Gulf of Honduras or the southern Caribbean Sea mainly in May through June, and mid-September through late November. The formations of these cyclones are due in part to the seasonal movement of the Inter-Tropical Convergence Zone, also known as the Equatorial Trough. From its inception, this type of hurricane seems to take a westward or northward movement, which normally takes a track over Central America if it moves westward or over the island of Cuba and into the Bahamas if it moves northward. The severity of which is influenced by how long the storm remains over the mountainous terrain of Cuba. One notable example of this type of storm affecting the Bahamas was Hurricane Michelle in 2001.

Hurricanes are born in low latitudes and are nurtured by warm tropical waters. They die by moving into higher latitudes with colder waters, or by leaving the water and crossing over land, or occasionally by coming under the influence of unfavorable upper-air wind flow. Hurricanes exists an average of about nine days, although life spans have varied from less than 12 hours to more than 28 days. During this time they cover about 300 to 400 miles a day, for a total of approximately 2,700 to 3,600 total miles during their lifetime. Nearly all hurricanes in the North Atlantic are eventually steered by large-scale, global wind patterns onto land or into higher latitudes, where the process of decay begins. Most of these storms recurve, that is, change direction from a predominantly west or northwest track to a more northerly and even a northeasterly direction. This recurvature, which occurs on average at about 25 degrees latitude is produced largely by clockwise moving winds around the Bermuda high pressure system in the Atlantic, and by interaction of the hurricane with the prevailing westerlies of the mid-latitudes. A hurricane will often reach its maximum intensity just before or at the point of recurvature, at which time many hurricanes slow their forward progress. Once the path of the hurricane has changed it will often increase forward speed, attaining its greatest speed soon after recurvature.

As a hurricane moves into higher latitudes while still over water, the ocean temperatures become too cold to sustain the heat engine of the storm and some would eventually become 'extra-tropical' in nature. The decaying process is especially evident once the storm moves up to oceanic regions of approximately 40 degrees latitude. Hurricane decay due to landfall is a much more complicated process. Once over land, several processes combine which together lead to the demise of the storm. Friction is involved, but to a much lesser degree than originally thought. In fact, the friction that a hurricane encounters from the extremely agitated ocean surface and tremendous amounts of spray thrown into the air is greater than the friction a hurricane would encounter over relatively flat terrain such as, the Florida Everglades.

Much more significant than friction, and the prime reason for a hurricane's demise over land, is the rapid cooling experienced by the inner core of the hurricane soon after it makes landfall. This cooling results from the loss of a hurricane's major energy source, which are heat and moisture derived from the ocean, and the conversion of water vapour into liquid water. The cooling of the inner core is immediately followed by a process called filling. During this process more air is coming in toward the central portion of the storm than is being exhausted upward through the system. The pressure in the central part of the hurricane increases, the area of maximum winds becomes more spread out and diffuse, and eventually the hurricane simply 'unravels' and dies. Some hurricanes are transformed into extratropical cyclones or combine with existing middle-latitude storms once they move into higher latitudes. Extratropical cyclones, sometimes called mid-latitude cyclones, baroclinic storms or wave cyclones, are a group of cyclones defined as synoptic scale low pressure weather systems that occur in the middle latitudes of the earth (outside of the tropics) having neither tropical nor polar characteristics, and are connected with fronts and horizontal gradients in temperature and dew point otherwise known as "baroclinic zones." When a hurricane combines with such a storm there may actually be a brief period of intensification of the hurricane, but this is often short-lived, as the cool air quickens the demise of the hurricane and it quickly dies or turns into a much weaker mid-latitude storm.

The movement of hurricanes from the lower to higher latitudes serves a very useful, in fact essential purpose in the world's climate on a global scale. Between about 35 degrees north and south of the equator, heat (shortwave radiation) from the sun absorbed by the earth and atmosphere is greater than the heat (longwave radiation) that is radiated from the earth and atmosphere back into space. If the heating that results from this imbalance is not carried away, the tropical and subtropical regions of the earth would be constantly growing warmer. Fortunately, nature has provided two mechanisms to transfer this excess energy to the higher latitudes, where there is an energy deficit, and therefore, maintain a global balance. A portion of this excess heat is carried away by ocean currents. For example, the Gulf Stream carries warmth away from the equatorial areas into coolers waters of the North Atlantic. However, most of the heat transfer is accomplished in the atmosphere. Tropical cyclones are a part of this atmospheric heat movement process. Hurricanes are therefore necessary for the earth to maintain an energy balance to support life on this planet. In this respect, these generally hated and despised storms might be viewed as 'necessary evils' of nature.

Furthermore, these storms also have other advantages in addition to helping to maintain an energy balance for the earth and that is, they provide much needed rainfall to many parched areas of the earth. A typical hurricane usually brings about 5 to 12 inches or greater of rainfall to much of the areas affected, and in the process produces over 200 billion tons of rainwater each day, an amount equal to the average annual flow of the Colorado River. Although rainfall is often a major cause of damage associated with hurricanes, the effects are not always undesirable. Over a six month hurricane season of June-November, tropical systems generally account for 45% to 60% of the seasonal rainfall in the Bahamas. Hurricanes often provide this much-needed rain to drought-stricken coastlines.

Their ocean interactions can flush bays of pollutants, restoring the ecosystem's vitality. After the record rainfall from Hurricane Claudette in 1979 in Texas, fish were being caught in the northern industrialized reaches of Galveston Bay that had vanished for several years. Finally, in cruel Darwinian fashion, weak sea life and plants perish during a hurricane, leaving only the strong to survive and reproduce. In this same manner, sometimes hurricanes 'correct' humanity's mistakes. For example, in the early 1900's non-native foliage, such as Australian pine trees, had been planted on the tip of Key Biscayne, Florida (now the Bill Baggs State Park). These non-native plants had very few natural enemies in their new environment, and quickly dominated the plant life, resulting in a loss of the natural habitat of that area. However, These Australian non-native lacked the ability to withstand hurricane-force winds because of their shallow roots, and Hurricane Andrew came along and destroyed them all in 1992. It was only then that park officials seized the rare opportunity to replant the park with native foliage.

Virtually all literal use of the word hurricane in literary works evokes violent wind. Yet some of the worst tropical cyclone catastrophes are caused not by winds but by torrential rain (e.g. Hurricane Katrina in 2005). The rainfall associated with hurricanes is both beneficial and harmful. Although the rains contribute to the water needs of the areas traversed by the hurricane, the rains are harmful when the amount is so large as to cause extensive flooding. There are about four factors that determine how much rain will fall in a given place: the amount of water vapour in the air, topography, the vertical extent and duration of the updraft. In fact, some of the most devastating floods are produced by tropical cyclones of sub-hurricane strength. The torrential rainfall which normally accompanies a hurricane can cause serious flooding. A recent and especially tragic example of this is that of Hurricane Mitch of 1998, the deadliest North Atlantic hurricane since the Great Hurricane of 1780. Floods produced by Mitch killed more than 11,000 people in Central America, and the President of

Honduras declared that Mitch destroyed 50 years of progress in that country. Whereas, the storm surge and high winds are concentrated near the eye, the rain may extend outward for hundreds of miles away from the center and may last for several days, affecting areas well after the hurricane has diminished or passed over a particular area.

An average of 10 to 15 inches of rain falls over coastal areas during the passage of a well-developed hurricane, but over 20 inches have been recorded and rain may fall at the rate of one inch an hour. In twenty-four hours a record of 32.67 inches of rain fell at Belize City in Belize from Hurricane Keith in 2000, for comparison, the average annual rainfall of Belize is about 74.4 inches. Furthermore, Hurricane Camille dumped over 760 millimeters (30 inches) of rainfall over Central Virginia, drowning 109 persons in the process with flash flooding. For comparison, the average annual rainfall of Central Virginia is about 45.22 inches. The Cedar Key Hurricane of September, 1950, poured nearly 39 inches of rain in 24 hours on Yankeetown, Florida, off the Gulf Coast. This 9-day hurricane traced an unusual double loop in the Cedar Keys area, and the coast from Sarasota northward suffered extensive wind and flood damage. The coastal area inland from Yankeetown to Tampa was flooded for several weeks. In 1963 Pacific Hurricane Season, Typhoon Gloria dumped 49.13 inches of rainfall in Baxin, Taiwan. While in the 1967 Pacific Typhoon Season 65.83 inches felled at Xinliao in Taiwan during a 24 hour period from Typhoon Carla. For comparison, the average annual rainfall of Xinliao, Taiwan is about 85 inches. However, Tropical Cyclone Denise in Foc-Foc in the La Reunion Island on the 7th and 8th of January, 1966 holds a world record of 45 inches in just 12 hours and 71.80 inches of rainfall in 24 hours in the same location for the total amount of rainfall over a particular location from a tropical cyclone. Tropical Storm Noel in 2007 over Exuma here in the Bahamas, caused heavy rainfall reaching a record level of 15 inches (380mm) during its passage.

Of all the tropical cyclone damaging agents, strong winds are perhaps the best understood of all of them. Damaging winds will accompany any hurricane, no matter what category it is. A hurricane by definition has winds of at least 74 miles per hour. This wind speed alone is enough to cause great damage to poorly constructed signage and knock over some of the sturdiest trees and other vegetation. Obviously, the stronger the hurricane (higher winds), the more potential there is for wind damage to exists. The fierce winds which blow in an anti-clockwise direction around the center of the central calm in the northern hemisphere may reach 100 to 200 mph. Wind speeds are the greatest near the surface around the central calm or eye. However, whenever a hurricane touches a landmass its wind speed is significantly reduced. The strongest winds reported in the Bahamas during the passage of a hurricane were, Hurricane Andrew in 1992(155mph), the Great Nassau Hurricane of 1926 (150mph), the Great Bahamas Hurricane of 1929(140mph), and the Great Abaco Hurricane of 1932(+155mph).

Once a hurricane makes landfall, there is a significant drop in the surface and upper level winds. Two factors accounts for this abrupt drop in wind speeds once a hurricane makes landfall. Over land a hurricane is no longer in contact with its energy source of warm ocean water. Furthermore, the increased surface roughness over land weakens the system. The land surface is rougher than the sea surface so that when a hurricane moves over land, its surface winds are slowed and blow at a greater angle across the isobars and toward the storm center. This wind shift causes the storm to begin to fill, that is, the central pressure rises, the horizontal pressure gradient weakens, and the winds slacken. The energy released in a normal hurricane is great. An average hurricane winds are so great that it is equipped with some 1.5 trillion watts of power in its winds which if converted to electricity would be equivalent to about half of the world's entire electrical generating capacity. In fact, in a single day, a hurricane can release the amount of energy necessary to supply all of the United States electrical needs for about six months. One second of a hurricane's energy is equivalent to about ten Hiroshima atomic bombs and in total, a single hurricane during its lifetime can dissipate more energy than that contained in thirty thousand atomic bombs. The hurricane which hit Galveston, Texas, in September, 1900, during its lifespan had sufficient energy to drive all the power stations in the world for four years. A large hurricane stirs up more than a million miles of atmosphere every second.

The force of the wind can quickly decimate the tree population, tear down power lines and utility poles, knock over signs, and may be strong enough to destroy some homes and buildings. Flying debris can also cause damage, and in some cases where people are caught outdoors, injuries and death can prevail. When a hurricane first makes landfall, it is common for tornadoes to form which can cause severe localized wind damage. In most cases, however, wind is a secondary cause of damage. Storm surge is normally the primary cause. The right front quadrant is strongest side of the hurricane; this is the area where there is positive convergence. In this quadrant the winds are typically the strongest, the storm surge is highest, and the possibility of tornadoes is the greatest. The right side of a hurricane is the strongest side because the wind speed and the hurricane speed-of-motion are complimentary there; meaning on this side, the wind blows in the same direction as the storm's forward motion.

On the left side, the hurricane's speed of motion subtracts from the wind speed because the main bulk of the storm is moving away from it. The storm's angle of attack is a key factor in its impact. Just as in an automobile accident, the highest level of destruction is caused by a hurricane hitting the coastline head-on. If a storm travels up the coast, with its left side brushing the seashore, the most dangerous part of the storm stays offshore and the net effect will be much less damage. The worst-case scenario would be a hurricane arriving onshore at high or spring tide. With the ocean level already at its highest point of the day, the storm surge from a Category 4 or 5 hurricane can add another 15 to 20 feet of water, with abnormally large waves breaking on top of that. Water weighs around 1,700 pounds per cubic yard, and there are very few structures that can stand up to the force a high storm surge can produce.

Violent hurricane winds may produce storm surges of up to 45 feet high at sea, and storm surges of over twenty feet may crash against the shores at speeds of up to 40 mph. Long swells may move outwards from the eye of a hurricane for more than 1,000 miles. These long swells are often the first visible signs of an approaching hurricane and are known as the *storm surge*. A storm surge, also called a *hurricane surge*, is the abnormal rise in the sea level caused by wind and pressure forces of a hurricane. It can be extremely devastating, and is in fact a major cause of damage and danger to life during the passage of a hurricane. It is estimated that 75% of all hurricane related deaths and injuries are caused by the storm surge and the remaining 20% of the 25% is simply caused by negligence. For example, persons out of curiosity venturing out into the peak of the storm and being killed by flying debris, or stepping on a live wire and getting electrocuted before the 'all-clear' is given.

The storm surge isn't just another wave pushed ahead of a storm; it acts like a gigantic bulldozer that can destroy anything in its path. Think of the storm surge as a moving wall of water weighing millions of tons. The storm surge itself is caused by the wind and pressure 'pushing' the water into the continental shelf and onto the coastline caused by a hurricane. The height of the storm surge is the difference between the observed level of sea surface and its level in the absence of the storm. In other words, the storm surge is estimated by subtracting the normal or astronomical tide from the observed or estimated storm tide. The astronomical tide is the results from the gravitational interactions between the earth, moon, and sun, generally producing two high and two low oceanic tides per day. Should the storm surge coincide with the high astronomical tide, several additional feet could be added to the water level, especially when the sun and moon are aligned, which produces the highest oceanic tides (known as syzygy).

Hurricanes have a vacuum effect on the ocean. The water is pulled toward the hurricane, causing it to 'pile up' like a small mountain. A mound of water forms under the center of a hurricane as the intensely low pressure draws water up. The shape of the shoreline and the ocean bottom has a great deal to do with a storm surge's magnitude. Over the ocean, this mound of water is barely noticeable, but it builds up as the storm approaches land. The surge's height as it reaches land depends upon the slope of the ocean floor at the coast. The more gradual the slope, the less volume of sea there is in which the surge can dissipate and further inland the water is displaced. This is why Hurricane Katrina did so much damage in 2005 and why areas like New Orleans in the United States will continue to remain vulnerable to future hurricanes. This dome of water can be up to 40 to 60 miles long as it moves onto the shoreline near the landfall point of the eye.

A cubic yard of sea water weighs approximately 1,700 pounds and this water is constantly slamming into shoreline structures, even well-built structures get quickly demolished because this water acts like a battering ram on these vulnerable shoreline structures.

The highest storm surge ever recorded was produced by the 1899 Cyclone Mahina, which caused a storm surge of over 13 meters (43 feet) at Bathurst Bay, Australia. This value was derived from reanalysis of debris sightings and eyewitness reports, as a result it is controversial within the meteorological community, but clearly a phenomenal storm surge occurred. In the Bahamas, the greatest storm surge occurred with Hurricane Andrew in 1992, which saw a storm surge of over 20 feet. In the United States, the greatest recorded storm surge was generated by 2005's Hurricane Katrina, which produced a massive storm surge of approximately 9 meters (30 feet) high in the town of Bay St. Louis, Mississippi, and in the surrounding coastal counties. Hurricane Camille came in second with 24 feet of water in 1969. The worst storm surge, in terms of loss of life, was the 1970 Bhola Cyclone, which occurred in the area of the Bay of Bengal. This area is particularly prone to tidal surges and is often referred to as the "storm surge capital of the world" which produced 142 moderate to severe storm surge events from 1582 to 1991. These surges, some in excess of eight meters (26 feet), have killed hundreds of thousands of people, primarily in Bangladesh. The Caribbean Islands have endured many devastating surges as well. These powerful hurricanes listed above caused very high storm surge. However, worldwide storm surge data is sparse. Hurricanes and the accompanying storm surge they produce can even affect the very depths of the ocean. In 1975, some meteorological and oceanographic instruments were dropped from a research reconnaissance airplane in the Gulf of Mexico, which showed that Hurricane Eloise disturbed the ocean hundreds of feet down and created underwater waves that persisted for weeks.

CHAPTER TWO

THE HISTORY BEHIND THE WORD 'HURRICANE' AND OTHER TROPICAL CYCLONE NAMES

What is a hurricane? Simply put, it is a large, violent storm that originates in a tropical region and features extremely high winds-by definition, in excess of 74 miles per hour and blow anti-clockwise about the center in the northern hemisphere. It also brings drenching rains and has the ability to spin off tornadoes. Hurricanes are storms that form between the tropics of Cancer and Capricorn in the Atlantic, Pacific and Indian Oceans. They have different names depending on where they are formed and located throughout the world. In the Atlantic they are called hurricanes, in the north-west Pacific, typhoons, in the Indian Ocean they are known as tropical cyclones, while north of Australia they are sometimes called Willy Willies. However, by any name, they are impressive to behold. To form, hurricanes need sea surface temperatures of 26.5°C or greater, abundant moisture and light winds in the upper atmosphere. Around 80 tropical storms form each year with most of them occurring in the south or south-east of Asia. The North Atlantic region accounts for only a mere 12 percent of the worldwide total of tropical cyclones. These storms are enormous creatures of nature, often between 120 and 430 miles in diameter. They may last from a few days to a week or more and their tracks are notoriously unpredictable.

A tropical cyclone is a powerful storm system characterized by a low pressure center and numerous severe thunderstorms that produce strong winds and flooding rainfall. A tropical cyclone feeds on the heat released (latent heat) when moist air rises and the water vapour it contains condenses. They are fueled by a different heat mechanism than other cyclonic windstorms such as nor'easters, European windstorms, and polar lows, leading to their classification as "warm core" storm systems. The term 'tropical' simply refers to both the geographic origin of these systems, which forms almost exclusively in tropical regions of the earth, and their formation in maritime tropical air masses. The term "cyclone" refers to a family of such storms' cyclonic nature, with anti-clockwise rotation in the northern hemisphere and clockwise rotation in the southern hemisphere. Depending on their location and strength, tropical cyclones are referred to by other names, such as, hurricanes, typhoons, tropical storms, cyclonic storms, tropical depressions and simply cyclones which all have low atmospheric pressure at their center. A hurricane consists of a mass of organized thunderstorms that spiral in towards the extreme low pressure of the storm's eye or center. The most intense thunderstorms will have the heaviest rainfall, and the highest winds occurring outside the eye, in the region known as the eyewall. In the eye itself, the air is warm, winds are light, and skies are generally clear and rain free but can also be cloudy to overcast.

Captain George Nares, a nineteenth century Scottish naval officer and polar explorer, was always on the lookout for hurricanes. "June-too soon," he wrote. "July-stand by; August-look out you must; September-remember; October-all over." Whatever you think about the dynamics of hurricanes-two things can be said about them and that is they are very unpredictable and extremely destructive. The forces of nature such as, deadly hurricanes have shaped the lives of people from the earliest times. Indeed, the first 'meteorologists' were priests and shamans of ancient communities. Whatever lifestyles these ancient people followed, they all developed beliefs about the world around them. These beliefs helped them to explain how the world began, what happen in the future, or what happened after a person died. The world of spirits was very important. Those people, who became noted for their skills at interpreting signs in the world around them, became spiritual leaders in their communities. All religions and different races of people recognized the power of the weather elements and most scriptures contain tales about or prophecies foretelling, great natural disasters sometimes visited upon a community because of the sins of its citizens. Ancient peoples often reacted to the weather in a fearful, superstitious manner. They believed that mythological gods controlled the weather elements such as, winds, rain and sun which governed their existence. When weather conditions were favorable, there would be plenty of game to hunt, fish to catch, and bountiful harvests. But their livelihood was at the mercy of the wild weather because fierce hurricanes could damage villages of flimsy huts, destroy crops and generate vast floodwaters that could sweep away livestock.

In times of hurricanes, food shortages and starvation were constant threats as crops failed and game animals became scarce when their food supplies dried up due to a hurricane. These ancient tribes as you will see later believed that their weather fortunes were inextricably linked with the moods and actions of their gods. For this reason, they spent a great deal of time and effort appeasing these mythological weather gods. Many of these ancient tribes tried to remain on favorable terms with their deities through a mixture of prayers, rituals, dances and sometimes even human sacrifices. In some cultures such as the Aztecs of Central America, they would offer up human sacrifices to appease their rain-god Tláloc. In addition, Quetzalcoatl, the all-powerful and mighty deity in the ancient Aztec society, whose name means 'Precious Feathered Serpent,' played a critical role; he was the creator of life and controlled devastating hurricanes. The Egyptians celebrated Ra, the Sun god. Thor was the Norse god of thunder and lightning, a god to please so that calm waters would grace their seafaring expeditions. The Greeks had many weather gods; however, it was Zeus who was the most powerful of them all.

The actual origin of the word 'hurricane' and other tropical cyclone names were based on the many religions, cultures, myths, and races of people. In modern cultures, 'myth' has come to mean a story or an idea that is not true. The word 'myth' comes directly from the Greek word 'mythos'(μύθος), whose many meanings include, 'word', 'saying', 'story', and 'fiction.' Today, the word 'myth' is used any and everywhere and people now speak of myths about how to catch or cure the common cold. But the age-old myths about hurricanes in this book were an important part of these people's religions, cultures, and everyday lives. Often they were both deeply spiritual and culturally entertaining and significant. For many of these ancient races, their mythology was their history and there was often little, if any distinction between the two. Some myths were actually based on historical events, such as, devastating hurricanes or even wars but myths often offer us a treasure trove of dramatic tales. The active beings in myths are generally gods and goddesses, heroes and heroines, or animals. Most myths are set in a timeless past before recorded and critical history began. A myth is a sacred narrative in the sense that it holds religious or spiritual significance for those who tell it, and it contributes to and expresses systems of thought and values. It is a traditional story, typically involving supernatural beings or forces or creatures, which embodies and provides an explanation, aetiology (*origin myths)*, or justification for something such as the early history of a society, a religious belief or ritual, or a natural phenomenon.

The United Nation's sub-body, the World Meteorological Organization estimates that in an average year, about 80 of these tropical cyclones kills up to 15,000 people worldwide and cause an estimate of several billion dollars' worth of property damage alone. Meteorologists have estimated that between 1600 to today, hurricanes have caused well over 200,000 deaths in this region alone and over 8 million deaths worldwide. Hurricanes, Typhoons and Cyclones are all the same kind of violent storms originating over warm tropical ocean waters and are called by different names all over the world. From the Timor Sea to as far as northwestern Australia they are called Cyclones or by the Australian colloquial term of 'Willy-Willies' from an old Aboriginal word (derived from whirlwind). In the Bay of Bengal and the Indian Ocean, they are simply called Cyclones (an English name based on a Greek word meaning "coil" as in "coil of a snake" because the winds that spiral within them resembles the coil of a snake) and are not named even to this day.

They are called Hurricanes (derived from a Carib, Mayan or Taínos/Arawak Indian word) in the Gulf of Mexico, Central and North

America, the Caribbean and Eastern North Pacific Oceans (east of the International Dateline). A Hurricane is the name given to these intense storms of tropical origin, with sustained winds exceeding 64 knots (74 miles per hour). In the Indian Ocean all the way to Mauritius and along the Arabian Coasts they are known as 'Asifa-t.' In Mexico and Central America hurricanes are also known as El Cordonazo and in Haiti, they are known as Tainos. While they are called Typhoons [originating from the Chinese word 'Ty-Fung' (going back to as far as the Song (960-1278) and Yuan (1260-1341) dynasties) translated to mean 'Big or Great Wind'...] in the Western North Pacific and in the Philippines and the South China Sea (west of the International Dateline) they are known as 'Baguios' or 'Chubasco'(or simply a Typhoon). The word Baguio was derived from the Philippine city of Baguio, which was inundated in July, 1911, with over 46 inches of rain in a 24-hour period. This amount stood as the world record for rainfall in a 24-hour period until Tropical Cyclone Denise in Foc-Foc in the La Reunion Island on the 7th and 8th of January, 1966 replaced this record with over 71.80 inches of rainfall in 24 hours from a tropical cyclone. Also, in the scientific literature of the 1600s, including the book *Geographia Naturalis* by geographer Bernhardus Varenius, the term whirlwind was used, but this term never achieved region or worldwide acceptance as a name for a hurricane.

In Japan they are known as 'Repus,' or by the more revered name of a Typhoon. The word "taifū" (台風) in Japanese means *Typhoon*; the first character meaning "pedestal" or "stand"; the second character meaning wind. The Japanese term for "divine wind" is Kamikaze(神風). The Kamikaze, were a pair or series of typhoons that were said to have saved Japan from two Mongol invasion fleets under Kublai Khan which attacked Japan in 1274 and again in 1281. The latter is said to have been the largest attempted naval invasion in history whose scale was only recently eclipsed in modern times by the D-Day invasion by the allied forces into Normandy in 1944. This was the term that was given to the typhoon winds that came up and blew the Mongol invasion fleet off course and destroyed it as it was poised to attack Japan.

On October 29, 1274, the first invasion began. Some 40,000 men, including about 25,000 Mongolians, 8,000 Korean troops, and 7,000

Chinese seamen, set sail from Korea in about 900 ships to attack Japan. With fewer troops and inferior weapons, the Japanese were far outmatched and overwhelmed and were sure to be defeated. But at nightfall just as they were attacking the Japanese coastal forces, the Korean sailors sensed an approaching typhoon and begged their reluctant Mongol commanders to put the invasion force back at sea or else it would be trapped on the coast and its ships destroyed at anchor by this typhoon. The next morning, the Japanese were surprised and delighted to see the Mongol fleet struggling to regain the open ocean in the midst of a great typhoon. The ships sadly, were no match for this great storm, and many foundered or were simply dashed to bits and pieces on the rocky coast. Nearly 13,000 men perished in this storm mostly by drowning. This Mongol fleet had been decimated by a powerful typhoon as it was poised to attack Japan.

With the second storm, even as Kublai Khan was mounting his second Japanese offensive, he was waging a bitter war of conquest against southern China, whose people had resisted him for 40 years. But finally, in 1279, the last of the southern providences, Canton, fell to the Mongol forces, and China was united under one ruler for the first time in three hundred years. Buoyed by success, Kublai again tried to bully Japan into submission by sending his emissaries to the Japanese asking them to surrender to his forces. But this time the Japanese executed his emissaries, enraging him even further and thereby paving the way for a second invasion. Knowing this was inevitable; the Japanese went to work building coastal fortifications, including a massive dike around Hakozaki Bay, which encompasses the site of the first invasion.

The second Mongol invasion of Japan assumed staggering proportions. One armada consisted of 40,000 Mongols, Koreans, and north Chinese who were to set sail from Korea, while a second, larger force of some 100,000 men was to set out from various ports in south China. The invasion plan called for the two armadas to join forces in the spring before the summer typhoon season, but unfortunately the southern force was late, delaying the invasion until late June 1281. The Japanese defenders held back the invading forces for six weeks until on the fifteenth and sixteenth of August, history then repeated itself when a gigantic typhoon decimated the Mongol fleet poised to attack Japan again.

As a direct result of these famous storms, the Japanese came to think of the typhoon as a 'divine wind,' or 'kamikaze,' sent by their gods to deliver their land from the evil invaders. Because they needed another intervention to drive away the Allied fleet in WWII, they gave this name to their Japanese suicide pilots as nationalist propaganda. In the Japanese Shinto religion, many forces of nature are worshipped as gods, known as 'kami' are represented as human figures. The Japanese god of thunder is often depicted as a strong man beating his drum. The Japanese called it Kamikaze, and the Mongols never ever returned to attack Japan again because of their personal experiences with these two great storms. In popular Japanese myths at the time, the god Raijin was the god who turned the storms against the Mongols. Other variations say that the god Fūjin or Ryūjin caused the destructive kamikaze. This use of *kamikaze* has come to be the common meaning of the word in English.

Whatever name they are known by in different regions of the world, they refer to the same weather phenomena a *'Tropical Cyclone.'* They are all the same severe tropical storms that share the same fundamental characteristics aside from the fact that they rotate clockwise in the southern hemisphere and counterclockwise in the northern hemisphere. However, by World Meteorological Organization International Agreement, the term tropical cyclone is the general term given to all hurricane-type storms that originate over tropical waters. The term cyclone, used by meteorologists, refers to an area of low pressure in which winds move counterclockwise in the northern hemisphere around the low pressure center and are usually associated with bad weather, heavy rainfall and strong wind speeds. Whereas, a tropical cyclone was the name first given to these intense circular storms by Englishman Captain Henry Piddington (1797-1848) who was keenly interested in storms affecting India and spent many years collecting information on ships caught in severe storms in the Indian Ocean. He would later become the President of the Marine Courts of Inquiry in Calcutta, India and used the term tropical cyclone to refer to a tropical storm which blew the freighter *'Charles Heddles'* in circles for nearly a week in Mauritius in February of 1845. In his book '*Sailor's Hornbook for the Laws of Storms in All Parts of the World*,' published in 1855, he called these storms cyclones, from the Greek word for coil of a snake. He called these storm tropical cyclones because it expressed sufficiently what he described as the 'tendency to move in a circular motion.'

The word cyclone is from the Greek word 'κύκλος', meaning 'circle' or Kyklos meaning 'coils of the snake', describing the rotating movement of the storm. An Egyptian word 'Cykline' meaning to 'to spin' has also been cited as a possible origin. In Greek mythology, Typhoeus or Typhōn was the son of Tartarus and Gaia. He was a monster with many heads, a man's body, and a coiled snake's tail. The king of the gods and god of the sky and weather, Zeus, fought a great battle with Typhoeus and finally buried him under Mount Etna. According to legend, he was the source of the powerful storm winds which caused widespread devastation, loss of many lives and numerous shipwrecks. The Greek word 'typhōn' meaning 'whirlwind' comes from this legend, another possible source for the origin of the English word 'typhoon.' The term is most often used for cyclones occurring in the Western Pacific Ocean and Indian Ocean. In addition, the word is an alteration of the Arabic word, tūfān, meaning hurricane, and the Greek word, typhōn, meaning violent storm and an Egyptian word 'Cykline' meaning to 'to spin.'

The history of the word typhoon presents a perfect example of the long journey that many words made in coming to the English Language vocabulary. It travelled from Greece to Arabia to India, and also arose independently in China, before assuming its current form in our language. The Greek word typhōn, used both as the name of the father of the winds and a common noun meaning "whirlwind, typhoon," was borrowed into Arabic during the Middle Ages, when Arabic learning both preserved and expanded the classical heritage and passed it on to Europe and other parts of the world. In the Arabic version of the Greek word, it was passed into languages spoken in India, where Arabic-speaking Muslim invaders had settled in the eleventh century. Thus the descendant of the Arabic word, passing into English through an Indian language and appearing in English in forms such as touffon and tūfān, originally referred specifically to a severe storm in India.

The modern form of typhoon was also influenced by a borrowing from the Cantonese variety of Chinese, namely the word 'Ty-Fung', and respelled to make it look more like Greek. 'Ty-Fung', meaning literally "great wind," was coincidentally similar to the Arabic borrowing and is first recorded in English guise as tuffoon in 1699. The Cantonese tai-fung and the Mandarin ta-feng are derived from the word jufeng. It is also believed to have originated from the Chinese word 'jufeng.' 'Ju' can mean either 'a wind coming from four directions' or 'scary'; 'feng' is the generic word for wind. Arguably the first scientific description of a tropical cyclone and the first appearance of the word jufeng in the literature is contained in a Chinese book called Nan Yue Zhi (Book of the Southern Yue Region), written around A.D. 470. In that book, it is stated that *"Many Jufeng occur around Xi'n County. Ju is a wind (or storm) that comes in all four directions. Another meaning for Jufeng is that it is a scary wind. It frequently occurs in the sixth and seventh month (of the Chinese lunar calendar; roughly July and August of the Gregorian calendar). Before it comes it is said that chickens and dogs are silent for three days. Major ones may last up to seven days and minor ones last one or two days. These are called heifeng (meaning black storms/winds) in foreign countries."*

European travellers to China in the sixteenth century took note of a word sounding like typhoon being used to denote severe coastal windstorms. On the other hand, typhoon was used in European texts and literature around 1500, long before systematic contact with China was established. It is possible that the European use of this word was derived from Typhon, the draconian earth demon of Greek Legend. The various forms of the word from these different countries coalesced and finally became typhoon, a spelling that officially first appeared in 1819 in Percy Bysshe Shelley's play 'Prometheus Unbound.' This play was concerned with the torments of the Greek mythological figure Prometheus and his suffering at the hands of Zeus. By the early eighteenth century, typhon and typhoon were in common use in European literature, as in the famous poem *Summer* by Scottish poet James Thomson (1700-1748):

Beneath the radiant line that grits the globe,
The circling Typhon, whirled from point to point.
Exhausting all the rage of all the sky,
And dire Ecnephia, reign.

In Yoruba mythology, *Oya*, the female warrior, was the goddess of fire, wind and thunder. When she became angry, she created tornadoes and hurricanes. Additionally, to ward off violent and tropical downpours, Yoruba priests in southwestern Nigeria held ceremonies around images of the thunder and lightning god Sango to protect them from the powerful winds of hurricanes. In ancient Egyptian legend, Set was regarded as the god of storms. He was associated with natural calamities like hurricanes, thunderstorms, lightning, earthquakes and eclipses. In Iroquois mythology, Ga-oh was the wind giant, whose house was guarded by several animals, each representing a specific type of wind. The Bear was the north wind who brought winter hurricanes, and he was also capable of crushing the world with his storms or destroying it with his cold air. In Babylonian mythology, Marduk, the god of gods, defeated the bad tempered dragon goddess Tiamat with the help of a hurricane. When the other gods learned about Tiamat's plans to destroy them, they turned to Marduk for help. Armed with a bow and an arrow, strong winds and a powerful hurricane, Marduk captured Tiamat and let the hurricane winds fill her jaws and stomach. Then he shot an arrow into her belly and killed her and then became the lord of all the gods.

The Meso-American and Caribbean Indians worshipped many gods. They had similar religions based on the worship mainly agricultural and natural elements gods, even though the gods' names and the symbols for them were a bit different. People asked their gods for good weather, lack of hurricanes, abundant crops and good health or for welfare. The main Inca god was the creator god *Viracocha*. His assistants were the gods of the earth and the sea. As farming occupied such an important place in the region, the 'Earth mother' or 'Earth goddess' was particularly important. The Aztecs, Mayas, Taínos and other Indians adopted many gods from other civilizations. As with the Mayans, Aztecs and Taínos, each god was connected with some aspects of nature or natural forces and in each of these religions, hurricanes or the fear of them and the respect for them played a vital part of their worship. The destructive power of storms like hurricanes inspires both fear and fascination and it is no surprise that humans throughout time have tried to control these storms. Ancient tribes were known to make offerings to the weather gods to appease them. People in ancient times believed that these violent storms were brought on by angry weather gods. In some cultures, the word for hurricane means 'storm god', 'evil spirit', 'devil' or 'god of thunder and lightning.'

The word *hurricane* comes to us via the early Spanish explorers of the New World, who were told by the Indians of this region of an evil god capable of inflicting strong winds and great destruction on their lives and possessions. The natives of the Caribbean and Central America had a healthy respect for hurricanes and an uncanny understanding of nature. In the legends of the Mayan civilizations of Central America and the Taínos of the Caribbean, these gods played an important role in their Creation. According to their beliefs and myths, the wicked gods Huracán, Hurrikán, Hunraken, and Jurakan annually victimized and savagely ravaged their homes, inflicting them with destructive winds, torrential rainfall and deadly floods. These natives were terrified whenever these gods made an appearance. They would beat drums, blew conch shells, shouted curses, engage in bizarre rituals and did everything possible to thwart these gods and drive them away. Sometimes they felt they were successful in frightening them off and at other times their fury could not be withstood and they suffered the consequences from an angry weather god. Some of these natives depicted these fearsome deities on primitive carvings as a hideous creature with swirling arms, ready to release his winds and claim its prey.

There are several theories about the origin of the word *Hurricane*; some people believe it originated from the Caribbean Arawak-speaking Indians. It is believed that these Indians named their storm god 'Huracán' and over time it eventually evolved into the English word *Hurricane*. Others believed that it originated from the fierce group of cannibalistic Indians called the Caribs, but according to some historians this seems like the least likely source of this word. Native people throughout the Caribbean Basin linked hurricanes to supernatural forces and had a word for these storms which often had similar spellings but they all signified death and destruction by some evil spirit and the early European colonial explorers to the New World picked up the native names. Actually, one early historian noted that the local Caribbean Indians in preparation for these storms often tied themselves to trees to keep from being blown away from the winds of these storms. According to one early seventeenth-century English account, Indians on St. Christopher viewed 'Hurry-Cano' as a "tempestuous spirit." These ancient Indians of this region personalized the hurricane, believing that it was bearing down on them as punishment by the gods for something they had done-or not done. These days, there is more science and less superstition to these powerful storms of nature called hurricanes. Yet we humanize hurricanes with familiar names, and the big ones become folkloric and iconic characters, their rampages woven into the histories of the Caribbean, North and Central American coastal towns and cities.

A next popular theory about the hurricane's origin is that it came from the Mayan Indians of Mexico who had an ancient word for these storms, called 'Hurrikán' (or 'Huracán'). Hurrikán was the Mayan god of the storm. He was present at all three attempts to create humanity, in which he did most of the actual work of creating human beings under the direction of Kukulkán (known by the Aztec name Quetzalcoatl) and Tepeu. Unlike the other Creators, Hurrikán was not heavily personified by the Mayans and was generally considered to be more like the winds and the storms themselves. In the Mayan language, his name means "one legged". The word *hurricane* is derived from Hurrikán's name. Hurrikán is similar to the Aztec god Tlaloc. In Mayan mythology, 'Hurrikán' ("one legged") was a wind, storm and fire god and one of the creator deities who participated in all three attempts of creating humanity. 'Hurrikán' was the Mayan god of big wind, and his image was chiseled into the walls of the Mayan temples. He was one of the three most powerful forces in the pantheon of deities, along with Cabrakán (earthquakes) and Chirakán (volcanoes). He also caused the Great Flood after the first humans angered the gods. He supposedly lived in the windy mists above the floodwaters and repeated "earth" until land came up from the seas. In appearance he has one leg, the other being transformed into a serpent, a zoomorphic snout or long-nose, and a smoking object such as a cigar, torch holder or axe head which pierces a mirror on his forehead.

Actually, the first human historical record of hurricanes can be found in the ancient Mayan hieroglyphics. A powerful and deadly hurricane struck the Northern Yucatán in 1464 wiping out most of the Mayan Indian population of that area. According to Mayan mythology, the Mayan rain and wind god, Chac, sent rain for the crops. But he also sent hurricanes, which destroyed crops and flooded villages. The Mayans hoped that if they made offerings to Chac (including human sacrifices), the rains would continue to fall, but the hurricanes would cease. Every year the Mayans threw a young woman into the sea as a sacrifice to appease the god Hurrikán and a warrior was also sacrificed to lead the girl to Hurrikán's underwater kingdom. Also, one of the sacrifices in honour of this god was to drown children in wells. In some Maya regions, Chac the god of rain and wind was so important that the facades of their buildings were covered with the masks of Chac. In actual fact, at its peak, it was one of the most densely populated and culturally dynamic societies in the world but still they always built their homes far away from the hurricane prone coast.

By customarily building their major settlements away from the hurricane-prone coastline, the Mayan Indians practiced a method of disaster mitigation that, if rigorously applied today, would reduce the potential for devastation along coastal areas. The only Mayan port city discovered to date is the small to medium sized city of Tulum, on the east coast of the Yucatán Peninsula south of Cancun. Tulum remained occupied when the Spaniards first arrived in the sixteenth century and its citizens were more prepared for the storms than for the Spaniards. As the many visitors to these ruins can see, the ceremonial buildings and grounds of the city were so skillfully constructed that many remain today and withstanding many hurricanes. The Indians of Guatemala called the god of stormy weather 'Hunrakán.' Of course, the Indians did not observe in what period of the year these hurricanes could strike their country; they believed that the devil or the evil spirits sent them whenever they pleased. Their gods were the uncontrollable forces of nature on which their lives were wholly dependent, the sun, the stars, the rains and the storms.

The Taínos were generally considered to be part of the Taíno-Arawak Indians who travelled from the Orinoco-Amazon region of South America to Venezuela and then into the Caribbean Islands of the Dominican Republic, Haiti, the Bahamas, Jamaica, Puerto Rico, and as far west as Cuba. Christopher Columbus called these inhabitants of the western hemisphere 'Indians' because he mistakenly thought he had reached the islands on the eastern side of the Indian Ocean. The word 'Taíno' comes directly from Christopher Columbus because they were the indigenous set of people he encountered on his first voyage to the Caribbean and they called themselves 'Taíno' meaning 'good' or 'noble' to differentiate themselves from their fierce enemies-the Carib Indians. This name applied to all the Island Taínos including those in the Lesser Antilles. These so-called Indians were divided into innumerable small ethnic groups, each with its own combination of linguistic, cultural, and biological traits.

Locally, the Taínos referred to themselves by the name of their location. For example, those in Puerto Rico referred to themselves as Boricua which means 'people from the island of the valiant noble lords' their island was called Borike'n meaning 'Great land of the valiant noble lord' and those occupying the Bahamas called themselves 'Lucayo' or 'Lucayans' meaning 'small islands.' Another important consequence of their navigation skills and their canoes was the fact that the Taínos had contact with other indigenous groups of the Americas, including the Mayas of Mexico and Guatemala. What is the evidence to suggest that the Taínos had contact with the Mayan culture? There are many similarities between the Mayan god, 'Hurrikán' and Taíno god 'Huracán' also, similarities in their ballgames, and similarities in their social structure and social stratification. Furthermore, the Meso-Indians of Mexico also flattened the heads of their infants in a similar fashion to the Island based Taínos and their relatives.

The Taíno Indians believed in two supreme gods, one male, and the other female. They also believed that man had a soul and after death he would go to a paradise called *Coyaba* where the natural weather elements such as droughts and hurricanes would be forgotten in an eternity of feasting and dancing. In the Taíno Indians culture, they believed in a female zemí (spirit) named Guabancex who controlled hurricanes among other things but when angered she sent out her herald Guataba to order all the other zemis to lend her their winds and with this great power she made the winds and the waters move and cast houses to the ground and uprooted trees. Representations of Guabancex portrayed her head as the eye of the storm, with twisting arms symbolizing the swirling winds. The international symbol that we use today for hurricanes was derived from this zemi. The various likenesses of this god invariably consist of a head of an indeterminate gender with no torso, two distinctive arms spiraling out from its sides. Most of these images exhibit cyclonic (counterclockwise) spirals. The Cuban ethnologist Fernando Ortiz believes that they were inspired by the tropical hurricanes that have always plagued the Caribbean. If so, the Taínos discovered the cyclonic or vortical nature of hurricanes many hundreds of years before the descendents of European settlers did. How they may have made this deduction remains a mystery to this day.

The spiral rain bands so well known to us from satellites and radars were not officially 'discovered' until the meteorological radar was developed during World War II, and they are far too big to be discerned by eye from the ground. It is speculated that these ancient people surveyed the damage done by the hurricane and, based on the direction by which the trees fell, concluded that the damage could only have been done by rotating winds. Or perhaps they witnessed tornadoes or waterspouts, which are much smaller phenomena whose rotation is readily apparent, and came to believe that all destructive winds are rotary. They also believed that sickness, or misfortunes such as devastating hurricanes were the works of malignant or highly displeased zemis and good fortune was a sign that the zemis were pleased. To keep the zemis pleased, great public festivals were held to propitiate the tribal zemis, or simply in their honour. On these occasions everyone would be well-dressed in elaborate outfits and the cacique would lead a parade beating a wooden drum. Gifts of the finest cassava were offered to the zemis in hopes that the zemis would protect them against the four chief scourges of the Taínos existence: fire, sickness, the Caribs and most importantly devastating hurricanes.

The language of the Taínos was not a written one, and written works from them are very scarce. Some documentation of their lifestyles may be found in the writings of Spanish priests such as, Bartholomew de Las Casas in Puerto Rico and the Dominican Republic during the early 16th century. Some of the Taíno origin words were borrowed by the Spanish and subsequently found its way into the English Language, and are modern day reminders of this once proud and vigorous race of people. These words include; avocado, potato, buccaneer, cay, manatee, maize, guava, *barbacoa* (barbecue), *cacique* (chief), jamaca (hammock), Tabacú (tobacco), caniba (cannibal), *canoa* (canoe), Iguana (lizard), and *huracán* or *huruká* (hurricane). Interestingly, two of the islands in the Bahamas, Inagua and Mayaguana both derived their names from the Lucayan word 'Iguana.' Bimini (meaning "two small islands" in English), another island here in the Bahamas also got it's name from these Indians; however most of the other islands here in the Bahamas were also given Indian names but they have been changed over the many years and centuries by various groups of people who settled or passed through the Bahamas. For example, the Lucayans called Exuma-*Yuma*, San Salvador was called *Guanahani*, Long Island was called *Samana*, Cat Island was called *Guanima*, Abaco was called *Lucayoneque,* Eleuthera was called *Cigateo*, Rum Cay was called *Manigua* and Crooked Island was called *Saomere*. Christopher Columbus when he came to the Bahamas and landed on Guanahani he renamed it San Salvador, Manigua he renamed it Santa Maria de la Concepcion, Yuma he renamed it Fernandina, Saomete he renamed it Isabella and the Ragged Island chain he renamed Islas de Arenas. However, for the early Spanish explorers, the islands of the Bahamas were of no particular economic value, so therefore they established only temporary settlements mainly to transport the peaceful Indians to be used as their slaves in East Hispaniola and Cuba to mine the valuable deposits of gold and silver and to dive for pearls.

Jurakán is the phonetic name given by the Spanish settlers to the god of chaos and disorder that the Taíno Indians in Puerto Rico (and also the Carib and Arawak Indians elsewhere in the Caribbean) believed controlled the weather, particularly hurricanes. From this we derive the Spanish word *huracán* and eventually the English word *hurricane*. As the spelling and pronunciation varied across various indigenous groups, there were many alternative names along the way. For example, many West Indian historians and indigenous Indians called them by the various names including, Juracán, furacan, furican, haurachan, herycano, hurachano, hurricano, and so on. The term makes an early appearance in William Shakespeare's King Lear (Act 3, Scene 2). Being the easternmost of the Greater Antilles, Puerto Rico is often in the path of many of the North Atlantic tropical storms and hurricanes which tend to come ashore on the east coast of the island. The Taínos believed that Juracán lived at the top of a rainforest peak called El Yunque (literally, the anvil but truly derived from the name of the Taíno god of order and creation, Yuquiyú) from where he stirred the winds and caused the waves to smash against the shore.

In the Taíno culture, it was said that when the hurricane was upon them, these people would shut themselves up in their leaky huts and shouted and banged drums and blew shell trumpets to keep the evil spirits of the hurricane from killing them or destroying their homes and crops. According to Taíno legend, the goddess Atabei first created the Earth, the sky, and all the celestial bodies. The metaphor of the sacred waters was included because the Taínos attributed religious and mythical qualities to water. For example, the goddess, Atabei, was associated with water. She was also the goddess of water. Yocahú, the supreme deity, was also associated with water. Both of these deities are called *Bagua*, which is water, the source of life. This image of water as a sacred entity was central to their beliefs. They were at the mercy of water for their farming. Without rain, they would not be able to farm their *conucos*.

These Indians prayed to the twin gods of rain and fair weather so that they would be pleased and prayed to these gods to keep the evil hurricane away from their farms and homes. To continue her (Atabei) work, she bore two sons, Yucaju and Guacar. Yucaju created the sun and moon to give light, and then made plants and animals to populate the Earth. Seeing the beautiful fruits of Yucaju's work, Guacar became jealous and began to tear up the Earth with powerful winds, renaming himself Jurakan, the god of destruction. Yucaju then created Locuo, a being intermediate between a god and a man, to live in peaceful harmony with the world. Locuo, in turn, created the first man and woman, Guaguyona and Yaya. All three continued to suffer from the powerful winds and floods inflicted by the evil god Jurakán. It was said that the god Jurakán, was perpetually angry and ruled the power of the hurricane. He became known as the god of strong winds, hence the name today of hurricane. He was feared and revered and when the hurricanes blew, the Taínos thought they had displeased Jurakán. Jurakán would later become *Huracán* in Spanish and *Hurricane* in English.

The origin of the name "Bahamas" is unclear in the history of these islands. Some historians believe it may have been derived from the Spanish word *baja mar*, meaning lands of the *'shallow seas'*; or the Lucayan Indian word for the island of Grand Bahama, *ba-ha-ma* meaning *'large upper middle land.'* The seafaring Taíno people moved into the uninhabited Southeastern Bahamas from the islands of Hispaniola and Cuba sometime around 1000-800 A.D. These people came to be known as the Lucayans. According to various historians, there were estimated reports of well over 20,000 to 30,000+ Lucayans living in the Bahamas at the time of World famous Spanish Explorer Christopher Columbus's arrival in 1492. Christopher Columbus's first landfall in the New World was on an island called San Salvador which is generally accepted to be present-day San Salvador (also known as Watlings Island) in the Southeastern Bahamas. The Lucayans called this island Guanahaní but Columbus renamed it as San Salvador (Spanish for "Holy Saviour"). However, Columbus's discovery of this island of San Salvador is a very controversial and debatable topic among historians, scientists and lay-people alike. Even to this day, some of them still suggest that Columbus made his landfall in some other islands in the Bahamas such as, Rum Cay, Samana Cay, Cat Island and some even suggested he landed as far south as the Turks and Caicos Islands. However, it still remains a matter of great debate and mystery within the archeological and scientific community. Regrettably, that question may never be solved, as Columbus's original log book has been lost for centuries, and the only evidence is in the edited abstracts made by Father Bartholomew de Las Casas.

In the Bahamas, Columbus made first contact with the Lucayans and exchanged goods with them. The Lucayans-a word that meant 'meal-eaters' in their own language, from their dependence upon cassava flour made from bitter manioc root as their staple starch food. They were sub-Taínos of the Bahamas and believed that all of their islands were once part of the mainland of America but had been cut off by the howling winds and waves of the hurricanes and they referred to these storms as huruká. The Lucayans (the Bahamas being known then as the Lucayan Islands) were Arawakan People who lived in the Bahamas at the time of Christopher Columbus landfall on October 12, 1492. Sometime between 1000-800 A.D. the Taínos of Hispaniola pressured by over-population and trading concerns migrated into the southeastern islands of the Bahamas. The Taínos of Cuba moved into the northwestern Bahamas shortly afterwards. They are widely thought to be the first Amerindians encountered by the Spanish.

Early historical accounts describe them as a peaceful set of people and they referred to themselves as 'Lucayos,' 'Lukku Kairi' or 'Lukku-Cairi' meaning 'small islands' or 'island people' because they referred to themselves by the name of their location. The Lucayans spoke the Ciboney dialect of the Taíno language. This assumption was made from the only piece of speech that was recorded phonetically and has been passed down to us. Las Casas informs us that the Arawaks of the Greater Antilles and Lucayans were unable to understand one another, *'here'*(in Hispaniola), he wrote *'they do not call gold 'caona' as in the main part of the island, nor 'nozay' as on the islet of Guanahani(San Salvador) but tuob.'* This brief hint of language difference tends to reinforce the theory that the Bahama Islands were first settled by people coming from eastern Cuba of the sub-Taíno culture.

Before Columbus arrived to the Bahamas, there were about 20,000 to 30,000+ Lucayans living here, but because of slavery, diseases such as smallpox and yellow fever (to which they had no immunity), and other hardships brought about by the arrival of the Europeans, by 1517, they were virtually non-existent. As a matter of fact, when Spanish Conquistador Ponce de Leon visited these islands in 1513 in search of the magical 'Fountain of Youth,' he found no trace of these Lucayan Indians, with the exception of one elderly Indian woman. These Indians of the Caribbean and Central America lived in one of the most hurricane prone areas of the earth; as a result most of them built their temples, huts, pyramids and houses well away from the hurricane prone coastline because of the great fear and respect which they had for hurricanes.

Many early colonists in the Caribbean took solace by displaying a Cord of Saint Francis of Assisi, a short length of rope with three knots with three turns apiece, in their boats, churches and homes as a protective talisman during the hurricane season. Various legends and lore soon developed regarding Saint Francis and his connection with nature, including tropical weather and hurricanes. According to tradition, if these residents untied the first knot of the cord, winds would pick up but only moderately. Winds of 'half a gale' resulted from untying the second knot. If all three knots were untied, winds of hurricane strength were produced. Today, some descendants of African slaves in the West Indies still tie knots in the leaves of certain trees and hang them in their homes to ward off hurricanes.

Similar accounts also emerged from encounters with the Carib Indians. In old historical accounts these Indians were referred to by various names such as, *'Caribs' 'Charaibes' 'Charibees'* and *'Caribbees'* and they were a mysterious set of people who migrated from the Amazon jungles of South America. They were a tribe of warlike and cannibalistic Indians who migrated northwards into the Caribbean in their canoes overcoming and dominating an earlier race of peaceful set of people called the Arawaks. While Columbus explored all parts of the West Indies, his successors colonized only those parts inhabited by the Arawak or Taíno Indians, avoiding the Carib inhabited islands because they lacked gold but most importantly because the Carib Indians were too difficult to subjugate. Ironically, the region became known as the Caribbean, named after these fierce Indians. Their practice of eating their enemies so captured the imagination of the Europeans that the Caribbean Sea was also named after these Indians. The English word 'cannibal' is derived from one of the terms, 'Caniba' used by the Arawaks to refer to the Caribs eating the flesh of their enemies. Their raids were made over long distances in large canoes and had as one of their main objectives was to take the Arawak women as their captives, wives and slaves. While on the other hand, the captured Arawak men were tortured and killed and then barbecued and eaten during an elaborate ceremony because it was believed that if they did this, they would obtain their enemies personal power and control their spirits. The French traveller Charles de Rochefort wrote that when these Caribs Indians heard the thunder clap, they would *"make all the haste they can to their little houses, and sit down on low stools about the fire, covering their faces and resting their heads on their hands and knees, and in that posture they fall a weeping and say...Maboya is very angry with them: and they say the same when there happens a Hurricane."*

The Caribs were terrified of spilling fresh water into the sea because they believed that it aroused the anger of hurricanes. They had no small stone gods but believed in good and powerful bad spirits called 'Maboya' which caused all the misfortunes of their lives. They even wore carved amulets and employed medicine men to drive the evil Maboya away. When a great and powerful storm began to rise out of the sea, the Caribs blew frantically into the air to chase it away and chewed manioc bread and spat it into the wind for the same purpose. When that was no use, they gave way to panic and crouched in their communal houses moaning, with their arms held over their heads. They felt that they were reasonably safe there because they fortified their houses with corner posts dug deep into the ground. They also believed that beyond the Maboya were great spirits, the male sun, and the female moon. They believed that the spirits of the stars controlled the weather. They also believed in a bird named Savacou which was sent out by the angry Maboya to call up the hurricane, and after this task was finished this bird would then be transformed into a star.

According to a noted English Historian John Oldmixon of the late 1600's and early 1700's, he reported that the Carib Indians excelled in forecasting hurricanes. Writing about a hurricane which occurred in 1740 on the island of St. Christopher he said:- *"Hurricanes are still frequent here, and it was some time since the custom of both the English and French inhabitants in this and the other Charibbees-Islands, to send about the month of June, to the native Charibbees of Dominica and St. Vincent, to know whether there would be any hurricanes that year; and about 10 or 12 Days before the hurricane came they constantly sent them word, and it was rarely failed."*

According to Carib Indians 'Signs or Prognosticks,' a hurricane comes *"on the day of the full change, or quarters of the moon. If it will come on the full moon, you being in the change, then observe these signs. That day you will see the skies very turbulent, the sun more red than at other times, a great calm, and the hills clear of clouds or fogs over them, which in the high-lands are seldom so. In the hollows of the earth or wells, there will be great noise, as if you were in a great storm; the stars at night will look very big with Burs about them, the North-West sky smelling stronger than at other times, as it usually does in violent storms; and sometimes that day for an hour or two, the winds blows very hard westerly, out of its usual course. On the full moon you have the same signs, but a great Bur about the moon, and many about the moon, and many about the sun. The like signs must be taken notice of on the quarter-days of the moon."*

According to several elderly Carib Indians, who stated that hurricanes had become more frequent in the recent years following the arrival of the Europeans to the Caribbean, which they viewed as punishment for their interactions with them. In fact, as early as 1630s, English colonists reported that Carib Indians knew when storms would strike by the number of rings that appeared around the moon: three rings meant the storm would arrive in three days, two rings meant two days and one ring meant the storm would arrive in one day. Of course, the connection between such signs and the onset of hurricanes was indeed a very unreliable way to predict the onset of hurricanes. The Carib Indians while raiding islands in the Caribbean would kill off the Arawak men and take the Arawak women as wives and mothers to their children. Actually, when the Europeans came to the Caribbean, they surprisingly found that many Carib women spoke the Taíno language because of the large number of female Taíno captives among them. So it is speculated that a word like 'hurricane' was passed into the Carib speech and this was how these fierce people learned about the terror of these savage storms. Native Indians of the West Indies often engaged in ritual purifications and sacrifices and offered songs and dances to help ward off hurricanes.

An Aztec myth tells that when the gods created the world, it was dark and cold. The youngest of the gods sacrificed himself to create a sun. But it was like him, weak, dim and feeble. Only when more powerful gods offered themselves did the sun blaze into life and shine brightly on them. However, there was one disadvantage, and that was that these gods needed constant fuel, human lives and the Aztecs obliged. They offered tens of thousands of human sacrifices a year, just to make sure that the sun rose each morning and to prevent natural disasters such as, devastating hurricanes from destroying their communities and villages. Tlaloc was an important deity in Aztec religion, a god of rain, fertility, and water. He was a beneficent god who gave life and sustenance, but he was also feared for his ability to send hurricanes, hail, thunder and lightning, and for being the lord of the powerful element of water. In Aztec iconography he is usually depicted with goggle eyes and fangs. He was associated with caves, springs and mountains. He is known for having demanded child sacrifices. The Aztec god Tezcatlipoca (meaning Lord of the Hurricane) was believed to have special powers over the hurricane winds, as did the Palenque god Tahil (Obsidian Mirror) and the Quiché Maya sky god Huracán. The Aztec god Tezcatlipoca was feared for his capricious nature and the Aztecs called him Yaotl (meaning 'Adversary'). Tonatiuh was the Aztec Sun god and the Aztecs saw the sun as a divinity that controlled the weather, including hurricanes and consequently, all human life form. The Aztecs of Mexico, in particular built vast temples to the sun God Tonatiuh, and made bloody sacrifices of both human and animal, to persuade him to shine brightly on them and in particular not send any destructive hurricanes their way and to allow prosperity for their crops. When they built these temples, they were constructed according to the earth's alignment with the sun but most importantly they were always constructed with hurricanes in mind and away from the hurricane prone coastline.

The Aztec people considered Tonatiuh the leader of Tollán, their heaven. He was also known as the fifth sun, because the Aztecs believed that he was the sun that took over when the fourth sun was expelled from the sky. Mesoamerican creation narratives proposed that before the current world age began there were a number of previous creations, the Aztecs account of the five suns or world ages revealed that in each of the five creations the earth's inhabitants found a more satisfactory staple food than eaten by their predecessors. In the era of the first sun, which was governed by Black Tezcatlipoca, the world was inhabited by a race of giants who lived on acorns. The second sun, whose presiding god was a serpent god called Quetzatzalcóatl was believed to be the creator of life and in control of the vital rain-bearing winds, and he saw the emergence of a race of primitive humans who lived on the seeds of the mesquite tree.

After the third age, which was ruled by Tláloc, in which people lived on plants that grew on water, such as the water lily, people returned to a diet of wild seeds in the fourth age of Chalchiúhtlicue. It was only in the fifth and current age, an age subject to the sun god Tonatiuh that the people of Mesoamerica learned how to plant and harvest maize. According to their cosmology, each sun was a god with its own cosmic era. The Aztecs believed they were still in Tonatiuh's era and according to their creation mythology, this god demanded human sacrifices as a tribute and without it he would refuse to move through the sky, hold back on the rainfall for their crops and would send destructive hurricanes their way. It is said that some 20,000 people were sacrificed each year to Tonatiuh and other gods, though this number however, is thought to be highly inflated either by the Aztecs, who wanted to inspire fear in their enemies, or the Spaniards, who wanted to speak ill of the Aztecs. The Aztecs were fascinated by the sun so they worshiped and carefully observed it, and had a solar calendar second only in accuracy to the Mayans.

It was Captain Fernando de Oviedo who gave these storms their modern name when he wrote *"So when the devil wishes to terrify them, he promises them the 'Huracan,' which means tempest."* The Portuguese word for them is Huracao which is believed to have originated from the original Taíno word Huracán. The Native American Indians had a word for these powerful storms, which they called 'Hurucane' meaning 'evil spirit of the wind.' When a hurricane approached the Florida coast, the medicine men of the North American Indians worked frantic incantations to drive the evil hurricane away. The Seminole Indians of Florida were actually, the first to flee from a storm, citing the blooming of the Florida Everglades saw grass. They believed that only 'an atmospheric condition' such as a major hurricane would cause the pollen to bloom on the sawgrass several days before a hurricane's arrival, giving the native Indians an advanced warning of the impending storm.

Many other sub-culture Indians had similar words for these powerful storms which they all feared and respected greatly. For example, The Galibi Indians called these hurricanes Yuracan and Hyroacan. The Quiche people of Guatemala believed in the god Huraken for their god of thunder and lightning. Giuana Indians called them Yarukka and other similar Indian names were Hyrorokan, aracan, urican, huiranvucan, Yurakon, Yuruk or Yoroko. As hurricanes were becoming more frequent in the Caribbean, many of the colonists and natives of this region had various words and spellings all sounding phonetically similar for these powerful storms. The English called them, 'Hurricanes', 'Haurachana', 'Uracan', 'Herocano', 'Harrycane', 'Tempest', and 'Hyrracano.' The Spanish called them, 'Huracán'and 'Furicane'and the Portuguese called them, 'Huracao' and 'Furicane.' The French had for a long time adapted the Indian word called 'Ouragan' and the Dutch referred to them as 'Orkan.' These various spellings were used until the word 'hurricane' was finally settled on in the English Language. Among the Caribbean, Central and South American peoples the word 'hurricane' seems to have always been associated with evil spirits and violence.

Christopher Columbus on his first voyage managed to avoid encountering any hurricanes but it wasn't until some of his later voyages that he encountered several hurricanes that disrupted these voyages to the New World. Based on his first voyage before encountering any hurricanes, Columbus concluded that the weather in the New World was benign: *"In all the Indies, I have always found May-like weather,"* he commented. Although sailing through hurricane-prone waters during the most dangerous months, he did not have any serious hurricane encounters on his early voyage. However, on his final voyages, Christopher Columbus himself weathered at least three of these dangerous storms. Columbus provided the earliest account of a hurricane in a letter written to Queen Isabella in 1494. In this letter he wrote, *"Eyes never beheld the seas so high, angry and covered by foam. We were forced to keep out in this bloody ocean, seething like a pot of hot fire. Never did the sky look more terrible; for one whole day and night it blazed like a furnace. The flashes came with such fury and frightfulness that we all thought the ships would be blasted. All this time the water never ceased to fall from the sky."*

By June of 1494, the small town of Isabella, founded by Columbus on Hispaniola, became the first European settlement destroyed by a hurricane. The Spaniards who accompanied Columbus on his four voyages to the New World took back to Europe with them a new concept of what a severe storm could be and, naturally, a new word of Indian origin. It seems that the Indian word was pronounced 'Furacán' or 'Furacánes' during the early years of discovery and colonization of America. Peter Martyr, one of the earliest historians of the New World, said that they were called by the natives 'Furacanes,' although the plural is obviously Spanish. The Rev. P. du Tertre, (1667) in his great work of the middle of the seventeenth century, wrote first 'ouragan', and later 'houragan.'

After 1474 some changes in the Spanish language were made. For instance, words beginning with 'h' were pronounced using the 'f consonant.' The kingdoms of Aragon and Castile were united in 1474, before the discovery of America, and after that time some changes in the Spanish language were made. One of them involved words beginning with the letter 'h.' In Aragon they pronounced such words as 'f'. As Menéndez Pidal said, 'Aragon was the land of the 'f', but the old Castilian lost the sound or pronunciation, so that Spanish Scholar Nebrija (Nebrija wrote a grammar of the Castilian language, and is credited as the first published grammar of any Romance language) wrote, instead of the lost 'f', an aspirated 'h.' Menéndez wrote concerning the pronunciation of the word 'hurricane' and its language used by Fernando Colón, son of Christopher Columbus "Vacillation between 'f' and 'h' is very marked predominance of the 'h.' And so, the 'h' became in Spanish a silent letter, as it still is today." Father Bartholomew de Las Casas, referring to one of these storms wrote: *"At this time the four vessels brought by Juan Aguado were destroyed in the port (of Isabella) by a great tempest, called by the Indians in their language 'Furacán.' Now we call them hurricanes, something that almost all of us have experienced at sea or on land..."* In fact, Las Casas, outraged by the brutal treatment of the Indians on Hispaniola, declared that the wrath of the hurricane which struck Hispaniola was the judgment of God on the city and the men who had committed such sins against humanity. All other European languages coined a word for the tropical cyclone, based on the Spanish 'Huracán.' Gonzalo Fernandez de Oviedo (Oviedo y Valdes, 1851, Book VI, Ch. III) is more explicit in his writings concerning the origin of the word 'hurricane.' He says: *"Hurricane, in the language of this island, properly means an excessively severe storm or tempest; because, in fact, it is only a very great wind and a very great and excessive rainfall, both together or either these two things by themselves."* Oviedo further noted that the winds of the *'Huracán'* were so *"fierce that they topple houses and uproot many large trees."*

Even in the English Language the word 'hurricane' evolved through several variations, for example, William Shakespeare mentioned it in his play 'King Lear' where he wrote *"Blow, winds, and crack your cheeks! Rage! Blow! You catracts and hurricanes, spout till you have drench'd out steeples, drown'd the cocks!"* Girolamo Benzoni, in 1565 in his Book *History of the New World* he mentioned his encounter with a hurricane in Hispaniola which at the time he referred to it as *'Furacanum'*: *"In those days a wondrous and terrible disaster occurred in this country. At sunrise such a horrible, strong wind began that the inhabitants of the island thought they had never seen or heard anything like it before. The raging storm wind (which the Spaniards called Furacanum) came with great violence, as if it wanted to spit heaven and earth apart from one another, and hurl everything to the ground...The people were as a whole so despairing because of their great fear that they run here and there, as if they were senseless and mad, and did not know what they did...The strong and frightful wind threw some entire houses and capitals including the people from the capital, tore them apart in the air and threw them down to the ground in pieces. This awful weather did such noticeable damage in such a short time that not three ships stood secure in the sea harbour or came through the storm undamaged. For the anchors, even if they were yet strong, were broken apart through the strong force of the wind and all the masts, despite their being new, were crumpled. The ships were blown around by the wind, so that all the people in them were drowned. For the most part the Indians had crawled away and hidden themselves in holes in order to escape such disaster."*

As stated earlier, Christopher Columbus did not learn on his first voyage, the voyage of discovery, of the existence of such terrible 'tempests' or 'storms.' He had the exceptional good fortune of not being struck by any of them during this voyage. The Indians, while enjoying pleasant weather had no reason to speak about these storms to a group of strangers who spoke a language which they could not understand. Naturally, Columbus did not say one word about these awful storms in his much celebrated letter *"The letter of Columbus on the Discovery of America."* However, on his second voyage things were quite different. After arriving on November 3, 1493, at an island in the Lesser Antilles which he named Dominica, Columbus sailed northward and later westward, to Isabella Hispaniola, the first city in the New World, at the end of January, 1494. Then in June of that year, 1494, Isabella was struck by a hurricane, the first time that European men had seen such a terrible storm. Surely, for the first time, they heard the Taíno Indians, very much excited; extending their arms raised upward into the air and shouting: *"Furacán! Furacán!"* when the storm commenced. We can indeed say that it was that moment in history, when the word *'Hurricane'* suddenly appeared to the Europeans. Columbus was not at that time in Isabella because he was sailing near the Isle of Pines, Cuba. So his companions of the ships *Marigalante* and *Gallega* were the first white men to hear these words, which were of Indian origin and about a phenomenon of the New World. Knowledge of 'Furacanes,' both the word and the terrifying storms it described, remained limited to Spanish speakers until 1555, when Richard Eden translated Columbus's ship report and other Spanish accounts of the New World, making it the first time it appeared in the English vocabulary.

In October of 1495, probably in the second half of the month, another hurricane struck Isabella, which was much stronger than the first. It finally gave Columbus, who was there at the time, the opportunity of knowing what a hurricane was and of its destructive abilities. It also gave him the opportunity of hearing the Indians shouting the same word with fear and anxiety on their faces, on the account of these terrible storms of the tropics, which they believed were caused by evil spirits. Columbus reported in his log: *"The tempest arose and worried me so that I knew not where to turn; eyes never beheld the seas so high, angry, and covered with foam...Never did the sky look more terrible. The people were so worn out, that they longed for death to end their terrible suffering."* Christopher Columbus would later declare that *"nothing but the service of God and the extension of the monarchy"* would induce him to expose himself to such danger from these storms ever again. *'The Niña'* was the only vessel which was the smallest, oldest and the most fragile at the time but amazingly withstood that hurricane, the two other ships of Columbus, *'The San Juan'* and *'The Cordera,'* were in the harbour and were lost or badly damaged by this hurricane. Columbus gave orders to have one repaired and another ship known as *India* constructed out of the wreck of the ones which had been destroyed, making it the first ship to be built in the Caribbean by Europeans.

In 1502 during his fourth voyage, Columbus warned the Governor Don Nicolas de Orvando of Santo Domingo of an approaching hurricane, but he was ignored; as a result a Spanish treasure fleet set sailed and lost 21 of 30 ships with 500 men. Columbus had a serious disagreement with the bureaucrats appointed by Spain to govern the fledgling colonies in the Caribbean to extract gold, pearl and other precious commodities from the native Indians. Among the more unfriendly of these exploiters was Don Nicolas de Orvando, the Governor of Hispaniola, with whom Columbus had been forbidden to have any contact with by the request of his Spanish sovereigns. But as Columbus approached Santa Domingo, he recognized the early signs of an approaching hurricane, such as large ocean swells and a veil of cirrostratus clouds overhead. Concerned for the safety of his men and ships, he sent a message to Governor Orvando begging him to be allowed to seek refuge in Santa Domingo Harbour. Columbus had observed that the Governor was preparing a large fleet of ships to set sail for Spain, carrying large quantities of gold and slaves, and warned him to delay the trip until the hurricane had passed. Refusing both the request and the advice, Orvando read Columbus's note out loud to the crew and residents, who roared with laughter at Columbus's advice. Unfortunately, the laughter was very short-lived and Orvando's ships left port only to their own demise when 21 of the 30 ships were lost in a hurricane between Hispaniola and Puerto Rico. An additional four of them were badly damaged but fortunately they were able to return to port where they too eventually sunk. Only one ship, the *Aguja*, made it to Spain, and that one, no doubt to Orvando's intense distress, was carrying what little remained of Columbus's own gold.

Meanwhile, Columbus, anticipating strong winds from the north from this hurricane, positioned his fleet in a harbour on the south side of Hispaniola. On the 13th of June, the storm hit with ferocious northeast winds. Even with the protection of the mountainous terrain to the windward side, the fleet struggled. In Columbus's own words, *"The storm was terrible and on that night the ships were parted from me. Each one of them was reduced to an extremity, expecting nothing save death; each one of them was certain the others were lost."* The anchors held only on Columbus's ship; the others were dragged out to sea, where their crews fought for their lives. Nevertheless, the fleet survived with only minimal damage. Almost 18 months later, Columbus returned to Santo Domingo, only to discover that it had been largely destroyed by the hurricane.

When the Europeans first attempted to create settlements in the Caribbean and the Americas, they quickly learned about these storms. As time passed and these settlers learned more about their new homeland, they experienced these storms on such a regular basis that they became accustomed to them. Eventually, they began calling them equinoctial storms, as the storms would normally hit in the weeks around the period of the fall equinox, which in the northern hemisphere occurs in late September. English explorers and privateers soon contributed their own accounts of encounters with these storms. In 1513 Juan Ponce de León completed the first recorded cruise along the Florida coast and came ashore near present-day St. Augustine to claim Florida for Spain. Famous for his unsuccessful search for the magical Fountain of Youth, he might have discovered Florida earlier had it not been for the ravages of hurricanes. In August of 1508, he was struck by two hurricanes within two weeks. The first drove his ship onto the rocks near the Port of Yuna, Hispaniola, and the second left his ship aground on the southwest coast of Puerto Rico. Soon after Hernando Cortés found treasures of gold and silver in the newly discovered lands of West, expeditions to retrieve the riches of the New World for Spain began in earnest. In 1525 Cortés lost the first ship he sent to Mexico in a severe hurricane, along with its crew of over seventy persons. Famous English explorer Sir John Hawkins wrote his own encounters with these storms. Sir John Hawkins wrote that he left Cartagena in late July 1568 *"Hoping to have escaped the time of their stormes...which they call Furicanos."* Hawkins did not leave soon enough, and he and his ships were bashed by an *"extreme storme"* as he referred to it, lasting several days.

English Explorer Sir Francis Drake encountered several major hurricanes while sailing the dangerous seas of the Americas and the Atlantic Ocean and in most cases these encounters changed the course of West Indian and American history. Sir Francis Drake, who travelled the seas of the globe in quest of glory and plunderage, nearly lost his ships in the fleet on the Outer Banks of Carolina. One of his most famous encounters was with a major hurricane which occurred while he was anchored near the ill-fated Roanoke colony in present day North Carolina in June of 1586. His ships were anchored just off the banks while he checked on the progress of Sir Walter Raleigh's colonists on Roanoke Island. The hurricane lasted for three days, scattering Drake's fleet and nearly destroying many of his ships. There was no greater thorn in the side of the Spanish than Francis Drake. His exploits were legendary, making him a hero to the English but a simple pirate to the Spaniards and for good reasons because he often robbed them of their valuable treasures. To the Spanish, he was known as *El Draque*, "the Dragon"; "Draque" is the Spanish pronunciation of "Drake." As a talented sea captain and navigator, he attacked their fleets and took their ships and treasures. He raided their settlements in America and played a major role in the defeat of the greatest fleet ever assembled, the "Spanish Armada."

No other English seaman brought home more wealth or had a bigger impact on English history than Drake. At the age of 28 he was trapped in a Mexican port by Spanish war ships. He had gone there for repairs after an encounter with one of his first major hurricanes at sea. Drake escaped but some of the sailors left behind were so badly treated by the Spanish that he swore revenge. He returned to the area in 1572 with two ships and 73 men. Over the next fifteen months he raided Spanish towns and their all important Silver train across the isthmus from Panama. Other English accounts reported ships damaged or lost in storms characterized by extreme wind and rain, some of which were definitely hurricanes. The English (including Drake and Hawkins) had a great respect for hurricanes, to such an extent that, as the hurricane season was understood to be approaching, more and more pirates went home or laid up their ships in some sheltered harbour until the last hurricane had passed and was replaced by the cool air of old man winter.

Probably those that first discovered the period of the year in which hurricanes developed were Spanish priest, officers of the navy or army, or civilians that had lived for a long time in the Caribbean. By the end of the sixteenth century they should have already known the approximate period that these hurricanes occurred. The Roman Catholic Church knew early on that the hurricane season extended at least from August to October because the hierarchy ordered that in all of the churches in the Caribbean to say a special prayer to protect them from these deadly hurricanes. The prayer which had to be said was: *'Ad repellendas tempestates,'* translated to mean *'for the repelling of the hurricanes or tempests.'* It was also ordered that the prayer should be said in Puerto Rico during August and September and in Cuba in September and October. This indicates that it was known that hurricanes were more frequent in those islands during the months mentioned. Eventually, West Indian colonists through first hand experiences with these storms gradually learned that hurricanes struck the Caribbean within a well-defined season. Initially, those early colonists believed that hurricanes could strike at any time of the year, but by the middle of the seventeenth century most of them recognized that there was a distinct hurricane season. This was because the hurricanes simply occurred too frequent within a particular time period for them to remain strange and unusual in their eyes. Numerous letters and reports written by colonists specifically discussed the period between July and October as the *'time of hurricanes.'*

The geography of hurricanes challenged the concept of these storms as 'national judgments or divine favor' by which God spoke to a specific group of people or country. Individual storms routinely struck various islands colonized by different European powers. For example, in 1707 a hurricane devastated the English Leeward Islands, the Dutch Islands of Saba and St. Eustatius, and the French Island of Guadeloupe. In 1674, a Dutch attack on the French Islands was thwarted by a hurricane, which also caused significant damage in the English Leeward Islands and in Barbados. The presence of hurricanes made colonists question their ability to transform the hostile environment of the Caribbean and by extension their ability to establish successful and stable societies here. But hurricanes raised other questions as well: What caused them? What forces gave rise to such powerful and dangerous storms? For some-probably a significant majority during the first several decades of the seventeenth century-they believed that these storms came directly from the hands of God. They interpreted hurricanes as 'wondrous events,' divine judgments for human sins. Others linked hurricanes to various natural processes, including shifting wind patterns. The explosion of various natural processes, including shifting wind patterns, the explosion of various chemicals in the atmosphere, and the celestial movement of the planets and stars.

CHAPTER THREE

THE NAMING OF HURRICANES

ATLANTIC TROPICAL CYCLONE NAMES

2012	2013	2014	2015	2016	2017
Alberto	Andrea	Arthur	Ana	Alex	Arlene
Beryl	Barry	Bertha	Bill	Bonnie	Bret
Chris	Chantal	Cristobal	Claudette	Colin	Cindy
Debby	Dorian	Dolly	Danny	Danielle	Don
Ernesto	Erin	Edouard	Erika	Earl	Emily
Florence	Fernand	Fay	Fred	Fiona	Franklin
Gordon	Gabrielle	Gustav	Grace	Gaston	Gert
Helene	Humberto	Hanna	Henri	Hermine	Harvey
Isaac	Ingrid	Ike	Ida	Igor	Irene
Joyce	Jerry	Josephine	Joaquin	Julia	Jose
Kirk	Karen	Kyle	Kate	Karl	Katia
Leslie	Lorenzo	Laura	Larry	Lisa	Lee
Michael	Melissa	Marco	Mindy	Matthew	Maria
Nadine	Nestor	Nana	Nicholas	Nicole	Nate
Oscar	Olga	Omar	Odette	Otto	Ophelia
Patty	Pablo	Paloma	Peter	Paula	Philippe
Rafael	Rebekah	Rene	Rose	Richard	Rina
Sandy	Sebastien	Sally	Sam	Shary	Sean
Tony	Tanya	Teddy	Teresa	Tomas	Tammy
Valerie	Van	Vicky	Victor	Virginie	Vince
William	Wendy	Wilfred	Wanda	Walter	Whitney

Information Courtesy of NOAA.

Hurricanes are the only weather disasters that have been given their own iconic names, such as, Hurricane Andrew, Gilbert, Katrina, Camille or Mitch. No two hurricanes are the same but like people; they share similar characteristics but yet still they have their own unique stories to tell. The naming of storms or hurricanes has undergone various stages of development and transformation. Initially, the word 'Hurricane' accompanied by the year of occurrence was used, for example, *'the Great Hurricane of 1780'* which killed over 22,000 persons in Martinique, Barbados and St. Eustatius. Another example was *'the Great Storm of 1703'* whose incredible damage of the British Isles was expertly detailed by Robinson Crusoe's author, Daniel Defoe. The naming scheme was substituted by a numbering system (e.g. Hurricane #1, #2, #3 of 1929 etc...) however; this became too cumbersome and confusing, especially when disseminating information about two or more storms within the same geographical area or location.

For the major hurricanes of this region, they were often named after the particular country or city they devastated. This was especially true for severe hurricanes which made their landing somewhere in the Caribbean. Three notable examples were, *'the Dominican Republic Hurricane of 1930'* which killed over 8,000 persons in the Dominican Republic, *'the Pointe-a-Pitre Hurricane of 1776'* which devastated the country of Guadeloupe and killed over 6,000 persons and devastated it's largest city and economic capital of Pointe-a-Pitre. Third was *'the Great Nassau Hurricane of 1926'* which devastated the city of Nassau in the Bahamas during the 1926 North Atlantic hurricane season. In some cases they were even named after the holiday on which they occurred, for example, *'the Great Labour Day Hurricane of 1935.'* The Great Labour Day Hurricane of 1935 was the strongest tropical cyclone during the 1935 North Atlantic hurricane season. This compact and intense hurricane caused extensive damage in the Bahamas and the upper Florida Keys. To this day, *the Great Labour Day Hurricane of 1935* is the strongest and most intense hurricane on record to ever have struck the United States in terms of barometric pressure. *The Great Labour Day Hurricane of 1935* was one of the strongest recorded hurricane landfalls worldwide. It was the only hurricane known to have made landfall in the United States with a minimum central pressure below 900 Mbar; only two others have struck the United States with winds of Category 5 strength on the Saffir-Simpson Scale. It remains the third-strongest North Atlantic hurricane on record, and it was only surpassed by Hurricane Gilbert (888Mbar) in 1988 and Hurricane Wilma (882Mbar) in 2005. In total, at least 408 people were killed by this hurricane.

In some cases they were named after the ship which experienced that particular storm. Two notable examples were: - *'The Racer's Storm of 1837'* and *'The Sea Venture Hurricane of 1609.'* The *1837 Racer's Storm* was a very powerful and destructive hurricane in the 19th century, causing 105 deaths and heavy damage to many cities on its 2,000+ mile path. *The Racer's Storm* was the 10th known tropical storm in the 1837 North Atlantic hurricane season. *The Racer's Storm* was named after the British war ship *HMS Racer* which encountered the storm in the extreme northwest Caribbean on September 28th. Another example was *The Sea Venture Hurricane of 1609*. In July 28th of 1609, a fleet of seven tall ships, with two pinnaces in tow carrying 150 settlers and supplies from Plymouth, England to Virginia to relieve the starving Jamestown colonists was struck by a hurricane while en route there. They had been sent by the Virginia Company of London to fortify the Jamestown settlement. Sir George Somers mission was to resupply the six hundred or so pioneers who a year before had settled in the infant British colonial settlement of King James's Town, sited in one of the estuaries south of the Potomac River. *The Sea Venture* was grounded at Bermuda which for some time was called *Somers Island* after the ship's captain, Admiral Sir George Somers. After being struck by this hurricane, *The Sea Venture* sprung a leak and everyone on board worked frantically to save this ship and their lives by trying to pump the water out of the hull of the ship. They tried to stem the flow of water coming into the ship by stuffing salt beef and anything else they could find to fit into the leaks of the ship. After this proved futile most of the crew simply gave up hope, falling asleep where they could, exhausted and aching from their relentless but futile efforts. But just as they were about to give up and face the grim reality that they would be loss to the unforgiving Atlantic Ocean, they spotted the island of Bermuda. Somers skillfully navigated the floundering *Sea Venture* onto a reef about half a mile to the leeward side of Bermuda. They used the ship's long boat to ferry the crew and passengers ashore.

The passengers of the shipwrecked *Sea Venture* became Bermuda's first inhabitants and their stories helped inspire William Shakespeare's writing of his final play *'The Tempest'* making it perhaps the most famous hurricane in early American history. *"And another storm brewing,"* William Shakespeare wrote in *The Tempest. "I hear it sing in the wind."* Most of those venturing to the New World had no knowledge of the word or the actual storm. The lead ship, the three-hundred-ton *Sea Venture*, was the largest in the fleet and carried Sir Thomas Gates, the newly appointed governor of the colony, and Sir Georges Somers, admiral of the Virginia Company. It is interesting to note that Shakespeare did not name his play *'The Hurricane.'* He actually did know the word *"hurricano"* because it appears in two earlier plays, *King Lear* and *Troilus and Cressida.* Maybe he recognized that such a title would be confusing and unfamiliar to most of his audience, so he chose a more familiar word 'Tempest' instead. Though the island was uninhabited, Spaniards had visited Bermuda earlier and set ashore wild pigs. The shipwrecked passengers fed on those wild pigs, fish, berries and other plentiful game on the island. Although they yearned to stay in that island paradise, they managed to make two vessels *Patience* and the *Deliverance* out of what was left of the *Sea Venture* and ten months later they set sailed for Jamestown. However, some persons remained on the island and became the first colonists of that island, including Admiral Sir George Somers who initially left with the other Jamestown passengers but eventually returned and died on that island.

In some instances, hurricanes were named after important persons within this region; one such storm was, the *'Willoughby Gale of 1666.'* The word *'gale'* during these colonial times was often interchanged with the word 'hurricane' but they often meant the same thing-a hurricane and not the official term we now use today for the definition of a 'meteorological gale.' This storm was named after the British Governor of Barbados, Lord Francis Willoughby who lost his life aboard the flagship *Hope* along with over 2,000 of his troops in his fleet in this hurricane. He was appointed Governor of Barbados by Charles II in May of 1650 and attempted to negotiate the strained politics of that island, which also experienced a division between the Royalists and Parliamentarians. His last act on behalf of the English Crown came in July 1666 when, having learned of the recent French seizure of St. Kitts, he formed a relief force of two Royal Navy Frigates, twelve other large vessels (including commandeered merchant ships), a fire ship, and a ketch, bearing over 2,000 men.

Lord Willoughby had planned to proceed north to Nevis, Montserrat, and Antigua to gather further reinforcements before descending on the French. Leaving Barbados on July 28, his fleet waited for the French just off the coast of Martinique and Guadeloupe, where he sent a frigate to assault the harbour and ended up capturing two French merchant vessels on August 4. This success could not be exploited however, as that night most of his force was destroyed by a strong hurricane, including the flagship *Hope*, from which Willoughby drowned in this ship during the storm. This hurricane occurred in 1666 and was a very intense storm which struck the islands of St. Kitts, Guadeloupe, and Martinique. The fleet was actually caught by surprise by this hurricane after leaving Barbados en-route to St. Kitts and Nevis to aid the colonists there to help battle against the French attacks. After the storm, only two vessels from this fleet were ever heard from again and the French captured some of these survivors. All of the vessels and boats on the coast of Guadeloupe were dashed to pieces. For a period in the late seventeenth century, some colonists referred to especially powerful and deadly hurricanes as "Willoughby Gales." Personal names were also used elsewhere in this region, for example, *'Saxby's Gale'* which occurred in Canada in 1869, and was named after a naval officer who was thought to have predicted it.

Another example was, the *Daniel Defoe Hurricane of 1703* which occurred in November of 1703 and moved from the Atlantic across to southern England. It was made famous by an obscure political pamphleteer, Daniel Defoe. It was six years before he wrote the world famous book *Robinson Crusoe*. At the time the hurricane struck, he needed money so the storm gave him the idea of collecting eye-witness accounts of the storm and publishing it in a pamphlet. He printed and sold this pamphlet under the very strange and exceptionally long title of *'The storm or collection of the Most Remarkable Casualties and Disasters which happened in the late Dreadful Tempest both by Sea and Land.'* In total, around 8,000 sailors lost their lives, untold numbers perished in the floods on shore, and 14,000 homes, 400 windmills and 16,000 sheep were destroyed. Some of the windmills burned down, because they turned so fast in the fierce winds that friction generated enough heat to set them on fire. The damage in London alone was estimated to have cost £2 million (at 18th century prices).

An additional example was, the *Benjamin Franklin Hurricane of October 1743,* which affected the Northeastern United States and New England, brought gusty winds and rainy conditions as far as Philadelphia, and produced extensive flooding in Boston. This was the first hurricane to be measured accurately by scientific instruments. John Winthrop, a professor of natural philosophy at Harvard College, measured the pressure and tides during the storm passage. This storm, which wasn't particularly powerful but was memorable because it garnered the interest of future patriot and one of the founders of the United States, Benjamin Franklin, who believed the storm was coming in from Boston. He was wrong, because it was actually going to Boston. From this information, he surmised that the storm was travelling in a clockwise manner from the southwest to northeast. Putting two and two together, Franklin concluded that the low pressure system was causing the storm to move in this manner.

One aspect of the Earth's general circulation is that storms are not stationary; they move, and in somewhat predictable ways. Until the mid-eighteenth century, it had been generally assumed that storms were born, played out, and died in a single location and that they did not move across the Earth's surface. Benjamin Franklin had planned to study a lunar eclipse one evening in September 1743, but the remnants of this hurricane ruined his evening. This was a big disappointment to him, because he had been looking forward to this lunar eclipse that this storm had obscured. His curiosity aroused, Franklin gathered additional details about the storm by reading the Boston newspapers and learned that the storm had moved up the Atlantic seaboard and against the surface winds. He learned that this hurricane struck Boston a day later, sending flood tides sweeping over the docks, destroying boats, and submerging waterfront streets. In the succeeding months he collected additional reports from travellers and newspapers from Georgia to Nova Scotia, and satisfied himself that at least in this part of the world, storms have a tendency to take a northeasterly path up the Atlantic Coast. Thus science took the first step toward a basic understanding of hurricanes and their movements.

Benjamin Franklin is also popularly known for his off the wall weather experiment years later where during a thunderstorm, in 1752, he carried out a dangerous experiment to demonstrate that a thunderstorm generates electricity. He flew a kite, with metal objects attached to its string, high in the sky into a thunderstorm cloud (Cumulonimbus). The metal items produced sparks, proving that electricity had passed along the wet string. After discovering that bolts of lightning were in fact electricity, with this knowledge Franklin developed the lightning rod to allow the lightning bolt to travel along the rod and safely into the ground. This discovery by Franklin is still used even to this day all over the world. A year later after Benjamin Franklin's famous kite flight, Swedish physicist G.W. Richmann conducted a similar experiment following Franklin's instructions to the letter, and as fate would have it, he was struck by a lightning which killed him instantly. Sailing home from France on the fifth of September, 1789, after his great years as a US Ambassador, Benjamin Franklin experienced a storm which may have been the same storm which devastated Dominica. He was eighty years old and suffering from "the Stone" but was busy observing the temperatures of the sea water, which would eventually lead to his discovery of the Gulf Stream.

Finally, there was the *Alexander Hamilton Hurricane of 1772*, which he experienced growing up as a boy living in the Caribbean on the island of St. Kitts in the Leeward Islands. This was an extremely powerful and deadly hurricane. He later on in life became the confidential aide to George Washington and his greatness rests on his Federalist influence on the American Constitution and much as on his financial genius as the first United States Secretary of the Treasury. Today he is featured on the U.S. ten dollar bill and he is one of two non-presidents featured on currently issued U.S. bills. The other is

Benjamin Franklin who is found on the U.S. $100 bill. A westward moving hurricane hit Puerto Rico on August 28. It continued through the Caribbean, hitting Hispaniola on the 30th and later Jamaica. It moved northwestward through the Gulf of Mexico, and hit just west of Mobile, Alabama on the 4th. Many ships were destroyed in the Mobile area, and its death toll was very severe. In Pensacola, it destroyed most of the wharves. The most devastation occurred in the vicinity of Mobile and the Pasca Oocola River. All shipping at the Mouth of the Mississippi was driven into the marshes; this included the ship *El Principe de Orange* from which only 6 survived.

This storm was famously described by Alexander Hamilton, who was living on the island of St. Croix at the time, and wrote a letter about it to his father in St. Kitts. The letter was so dramatic and moving that it was published in newspapers locally on the island and first in New York and then in other states (please see my book- *'Rediscovering Hurricanes'* for a complete copy of this letter), and the locals on St. Kitts raised enough money to have him brought to America to receive a formal education to make good use of his intellectual abilities. This was because, this letter created such a sensation that some planters of St. Kitts, in the midst of the hurricane devastation, took up a collection to send him to America for better schooling because they saw in him great potential. By 1774 he was a student at King's College, now Columbia University, in New York. On St. Kitts, the damage was considerable and once again, many houses were flattened, and there were several fatalities and many more injuries. Total damage from this storm alone was estimated at £500,000 on St. Kitts. The second storm struck just three days later causing even more significant damage to the few remaining houses on this island already battered by the previous storm in 1772.

Several claimants have been put forth as the originators of the modern tropical cyclone 'naming' system. However, it was forecaster Clement Lindley Wragge, an Australian meteorologist who in 1887 began giving women's names, names from history and mythology and male names, especially names of politicians who offended him to these storms before the end of the 19th century. He was a colourful and controversial meteorologist in charge of the Brisbane, Australia Government weather office. He initially named the storms after mythological figures, but later named them after politicians he didn't like. For example, Wragge named some of these storms using biblical names such as, Ram, Raken, Talmon, and Uphaz or the ancient names of Xerxes and Hannibal. Wragge even nicknamed one storm Eline, a name that he thought was reminiscent of *'dusty maidens with liquid eyes and bewitching manners.'* Most ingeniously, he gained a measure of personal revenge by naming some of the nastiest storms with politicians' names such as, Drake, Barton, and Deakin. By properly naming a hurricane, he was able to publicly describe a politician (perhaps a politician who was not too generous with the weather-bureau appropriations) as *'causing great distress'* or *'wandering aimlessly about the Pacific.'* By naming these storms after these hated politicians he could get a degree of revenge on them without suffering any repercussions from them. During his last days in office, he fought with the Australian Government over the right to issue national forecasts and he lost, and was fired in 1902.

For a while, hurricanes in the West Indies were often named after the particular Saint's Day on which the hurricane occurred. As Christianity took hold in the West Indies, the naming system of storms here in the Caribbean was based on the Catholic tradition of naming these storms with the 'Saint' of the day (e.g. San Ciprian on September 26th). This system for naming them was haphazard and not really a system at all. Powerful hurricanes hitting especially the Spanish speaking islands of the Caribbean got Catholic Saints' names. According to Historian Alejandro Tapia, the first hurricane to be named with the Saint of the day was the *Hurricane of San Bartolomé* which devastated Puerto Rico and the Dominican Republic on August 24th and 25th of 1568. The earlier tropical cyclones were simply designated by historians' years later after their passages.

One example of a great storm named after a Saint of the day was, *'Hurricane San Felipe'* which struck Puerto Rico on 13th September 1876. Another example was *'Hurricane San Felipe the Second'* which occurred strangely enough on the very same date 52 years later on 13th September of 1928 and was responsible for well over 3,433 deaths. Another hurricane which was named the *'Hurricane of Santa Elena'* struck Puerto Rico on 18th August, 1851 and caused massive casualties. Then there was the *'Hurricane of Santa Ana'* (in English,

Saint Anne) which struck Puerto Rico and Guadeloupe on 26th July of 1825, the date of the feast in honour of the Mother of the Blessed Virgin, which killed over 1,300 persons. In addition, there was the *'Hurricane of San Ciriaco'* which killed 3,369 persons in Puerto Rico on 8th August of 1899 (feast day of Saint Cyriacus) and remains one of the longest duration tropical storms(28 days) to hit the Caribbean or anywhere in the world.

The tradition of naming storms after the Saint of the day officially ended with Hurricane Betsy in 1956 which is still remembered as the *'Hurricane of Santa Clara.'* However, years later with the passage of Hurricane Donna in 1960, the storm was recognized as the *'Hurricane of San Lorenzo.'* At this time, only the major hurricanes were given names so most storms especially the minor storms before 1950 in the North Atlantic never received any kind of special designation. This is why this hurricane in 1899 was never named but was simply referred to as 'The Great Bahamas Hurricane of 1899' after the country it devastated. The word 'Great' simply meant that the hurricane was a powerful storm and that it had sustained winds of 136 mph or greater and a minimum central pressure of 28.00 inches or less (see later chapter on the classification of hurricanes).

Later, latitude-longitude positions were used. At first they listed these storms by the latitude and longitude positions where they were first reported. This was cumbersome, slow, open to error and confusing. For example, a name like *'Hurricane 12.8°N latitude and 54.7°W longitude'* was very difficult to remember, and it would be easy to confuse this storm with another that was seen two months later, but almost at the same location. In addition, this posed another significant problem, in the 1940's when meteorologists began airborne studies of tropical cyclones, ships and aircrafts communicated mainly in Morse code. This was fine for the letters of the alphabet, but it was awkward at dealing with numbers because it was slow and caused confusion among its users.

In this region, these early storms were often referred to as *Gales, Severe Gales, Equinoctial Storms,* or *Line Storms.* The latter two names referred to the time of the year and the location from which these storms were born (referring to the Equatorial line). Gauging the strength and fury of a seventeenth or eighteenth-century storm was quite a difficult task because at the time these colonists had no means of measuring the wind speeds of a hurricane. Contemporaries recognized a hierarchy of winds ranging from *'a stark calm'* to *'a small Gale'* to *'a Top-Sail Gale'* to *'a fret of wind'* and *'a Tempest'*-later replaced by the word 'hurricane'-but such terms offered little help in interpreting the power of hurricanes or differentiating lesser tropical storms from hurricanes. Furthermore, increased development of the built environment over time meant that the potential for damage, even from minor storms, increased as well, making damage estimates a questionable foundation for judging the power of storms.

Experience has shown that using distinctive names in communications is quicker and less subject to error than the cumbersome latitude-longitude identification methods. The idea was that the names should be short, familiar to users, easy to remember and that their use would facilitate communications with millions of people of different ethnic races threatened by the storm. This was because a hurricane can last for a week or more, and there can be more than one storm at a time, so weather forecasters starting naming these storms so that there would be absolutely no confusion when talking about a particular storm. Names are easier to use and facilitate better communications among individuals and meteorologists with language barriers within the same geographical region, such as within the Caribbean, Central America and North America.

The first U.S. named hurricane (unofficially named) was Hurricane George which was the fifth storm in 1947 season. George had top winds of 155 mph as it came ashore around midday on September 17 between Pompano Beach and Delray Beach. The second hurricane unofficially named was Hurricane Bess (named for the outspoken First Lady of the USA, Bess Truman, in 1949). The third storm was nicknamed by the news media 'Hurricane Harry' after the then President of the United States Harry Truman. United States Navy and Air Force meteorologists working in the Pacific Ocean began naming tropical cyclones during World War II, when they often had to track multiple storms. They gave each storm a distinctive name in order to distinguish the cyclones more quickly than listing their positions when issuing warnings.

Towards the end of World War II, two separate United States fleets in the Pacific lacking sufficient weather information about these storms were twice badly damaged when they sailed directly into them resulting in massive causalities. Three ships were sunk, twenty one were badly damaged, 146 planes were blown overboard, and 763 men were lost. One of the results that came out of these tragedies was the fact that all US Army and Navy planes were then ordered to start tracking and studying these deadly storms, so as to prevent similar disasters like those ones from occurring again. During World War II this naming practice became widespread in weather map discussions among forecasters, especially Air Force and Navy meteorologists who plotted the movements of these storms over the wide expanses of the Pacific Ocean. Using the convention of applying 'she' to inanimate objects such as vehicles, these military meteorologists beginning in 1945 in the Northwest Pacific started naming these storms after their wives and girlfriends. However, this practice didn't last too long for whatever reason, but my guess is that those women rejected or took offense to being named after something that was responsible for so much damage and destruction. Another theory was that this practice was started by a radio operator who sang "Every little breeze seems to whisper Louise" when issuing a hurricane warning. From that point on that particular hurricane and future hurricanes were referred to as Louise, and the use of female names for hurricanes became standard practice.

An early example of the use of a woman's name for a storm was in the best selling pocketbook novel "Storm" by George R. Stewart, published by Random House in 1941, and has since been made into a major motion picture by Walt Disney further promoting the idea of naming storms. It involved a young meteorologist working in the San Francisco Weather Bureau Office tracking a storm, which he called *Maria*, from its birth as a disturbance in the North Pacific to its death over North America many days later. The focus of the book is a storm named Maria, but pronounced 'Ma-Rye-Ah.' Yes, the song in the famous Broadway show *Paint Your Wagon* named "They Call the Wind Maria" was inspired by this fictional storm. He gave it a name because he said that he could easily say 'Hurricane Maria' rather than, *'the low pressure center which at 6pm yesterday was located at latitude one-seventy four degrees east and longitude forty-three degrees north'* which he considered too long and cumbersome. As Stewart detailed in his novel, *'Not since at any price would the Junior Meteorologist have revealed to the Chief that he was bestowing names-and girls' names-upon those great moving low-pressure areas.'* He unofficially gave the storms in his book women names such as, Lucy, Katherine and Ruth after some girls he knew because he said that they each had a unique personality. It is not known whether George Stewart was indeed the inspiration for the trend toward naming hurricanes which came along later in the decade, but it seems likely.

In 1950 military alphabet names (e.g. Able, Baker, Charley, Dog, Easy, Fox etc...) were adopted by the World Meteorological Organization (WMO) and the first named Atlantic hurricane was Able in 1950. The Joint Army/Navy (JAN) Phonetic Alphabet was developed in 1941 and was used by all branches of the United States military until the promulgation of the NATO phonetic alphabet in 1956, which replaced it. Before the JAN phonetic alphabet, each branch of the armed forces used its own phonetic alphabet, leading to difficulties in inter-branch communications. This naming method was not very popular, and caused a lot of confusion because officials soon realized that this naming convention would cause more problems in the history books if more than one powerful Hurricane Able made landfall and caused extensive damage and death to warrant retirement. This was because hurricanes that have a severe impact on the lives or the economy of a country or region are remembered for generations after the devastation they caused, and some go into weather history, so distinguishing one storm name from another is essential for the history books.

The modern naming convention came about in response to the need for unambiguous radio communications with ships and aircrafts. As air and sea transportation started to increase and meteorological observations improved in number and quality, several typhoons, hurricanes or cyclones might have to be tracked at any given time. To help in their identification, in 1953 the systematic use of only regular women names were used in alphabetical order and this lasted until 1978. The 1953's Alice was the first real human-named storm. At the time they named them after women because these meteorologists reasoned that people might pay more attention to a storm if they envisioned it as a tangible entity, a character, rather than just a bundle of wind. But the use of only women names eventually was rejected as sexist and forecasters finally went with both male and female names. Beginning in 1960, four semi-permanent sets of names were established, to be re-cycled after four years. This list was expanded to ten sets in 1971, but before making it through the list even once; these sets were replaced by the now familiar 6 sets of men and women names.

This naming practice started in the Eastern Pacific in 1959 and in 1960 for the remainder of the North Pacific. It is interesting to note that in the Northwest Pacific Basin the names, by and large, are not personal names. While there are a few men and women names, the majority of the Northwest Pacific tropical cyclone names generally reflect Pacific culture and the names consists of flowers, animals, birds, trees, or even foods while some are just descriptive adjectives. In addition, the names are not allotted in alphabetical order but are arranged by the contributing nation with the countries being alphabetized. For example, the Cambodians have contributed Naki (a flower), Krovanh (a tree) and Damrey (an elephant). China has submitted names such as Yutu (a mythological rabbit), Longwang (the dragon king and god of rain in Chinese mythology), and Dainmu (the mother of lightning and the goddess in charge of thunder). Micronesian typhoon names include Sinlaku (a legendary Kosrae goddess) and Ewiniar (the Chuuk Storm god). Hurricanes in the central Pacific have name lists for only four years and use Hawaiian names.

In the North Atlantic Basin in 1979, gender equality finally reached the naming process of hurricanes when thousands of sexism complaints written to the WMO and feminists groups in the USA and worldwide urged the WMO to add men's names, hence both men and women names were used alternately and this practice is still in use today. That year would also herald the practice of drawing up list of names in advance of the hurricane season and today an alphabetical list of 21 names is used. Hurricane Bob was the first North Atlantic storm named after a man in the 1979 hurricane season, however it was not retired (it would eventually be retired in the 1991 hurricane season). Hurricane David was the second storm named after a man and it was the first male storm to be retired in the North Atlantic Region. This was due to the great death toll and substantial damage it inflicted to the countries of Dominica, the Dominican Republic and the Bahamas during the last week of August and the first week of September in 1979.

Since 1979, the naming list now includes names from non-English speaking countries within this region, such as Dutch, French and Spanish names which also have a large presence here in the Caribbean. This is done to reflect the diversity of the different ethnic languages of the various countries in this region, so the names of Spanish, French, Dutch, and English persons are used in the naming process. The names of storms are now selected by a select committee from member countries of the World Meteorological Organization that falls within that particular region of the world, and we here in the Caribbean comes under Region IV for classification purposes. This committee meets once a year after the hurricane season has passed and before the beginning of the new hurricane season to decide on which names that are to be retired and to replace those names with a new set of names when and where necessary.

The practice of giving different names to storms in different hurricane basins has also led to a few rare circumstances of name-changing storms. For example, in October of 1988, after Atlantic Hurricane Joan devastated Central America, it proceeded to move into the Pacific and became Pacific tropical storm Miriam. Hurricane Joan was a powerful hurricane which caused death and destruction in over a dozen countries in the Caribbean and Central America. Another example was Hurricane Hattie, which was a powerful Category 5 hurricane that pounded Central America on Halloween during the 1961 North Atlantic hurricane season. It caused $370 million in damages and killed around 275 persons. Hattie is the only hurricane on record to have earned three names (Hattie, Simone, Inga) while crossing into different basins twice. Hattie swept across the Caribbean and came ashore in the town of Belize City, British Honduras (now called Belize), on October 31. It was a strong Category 4 hurricane at landfall, having weakened from a Category 5 hurricane just offshore. After making landfall, its remnants crossed over into the Pacific and attained tropical storm status again under the name Simone. In a remarkable turn of events, after Simone itself made landfall, its remnants crossed back over to the Gulf of Mexico, where the storm became Tropical Storm Inga before dissipating. However, it is debatable whether Inga in fact formed from the remnants of Simone at all.

It is interesting to note here that the letters Q, U, X, Y, and Z are not included in the hurricane list because of the scarcity of names beginning with those letters. However, in other regions of the world some of these letters are used, for example; only "Q" and "U" are omitted in the Northeastern Pacific Basin. When a storm causes tremendous damage and death, the name is taken out of circulation and retired for reasons of sensitivity. It is then replaced with a name of the same letter and of the same gender and if possible, the same language as the name being retired (e.g. neither Hurricane Andrew in 1992 nor Hurricane Katrina in 2005 will ever be used again). Since 1950, there were 76 hurricanes which had their names retired. The list includes one tropical storm, Allison of 2001, which caused billions in damage from its heavy rains.

The name used the most (at least with the same spelling is Arlene (seven times), while Frances and Florence have been used seven and six times respectively. However, considering different spellings of the same name, Debbie/Debby has been used seven times, and Anna/Ana has been used eight times. The first name to be called into use five times was Edith, but that name hasn't been used since 1971. After the 1996 season, Lilly has the distinction of being the first 'L' name to be used three times, while Marco is the first 'M' name to be used more than once. The name Kendra was assigned to a system in the 1966 hurricane season, but in post-season analysis it was decided it had not been a bona fide tropical storm. This storm marked the birth of reclassification of storms in the post-hurricane season (Hurricane Andrew was a storm that was reclassified from a Category four hurricane to a Category five hurricane in the off season).

In only three years (2005, 1995, 2010) have names beginning with the letter 'O' and beyond have been used, but there have been several other years in which more than 14 storms have been tracked such as: 1887-19 storms, 1933-21 storms, 1936-16 storms, 1969-18 storms, 1995-19 storms, 2005-28 storms and 2010-19 storms. The 2010 Atlantic hurricane season has been extremely active, being the most active season since 2005. It must be noted that the 2010 season ties the record with the 1995 North Atlantic hurricane season and the 1887 North Atlantic hurricane season for the third most named storms (19). Furthermore, 2010 also ties the record with the 1969 North Atlantic hurricane season and 1887 for the second most hurricanes (12). The first three of these years were well before the naming of storms began, but 1969 requires an explanation. This was early in the era of complete satellite coverage, and forecasters were still studying the evolution of non-tropical systems (sub-tropical) into warm-core, tropical-type storms. Several systems that year were not named as tropical because they began at higher latitudes and were initially cold-cored.

Formal classification of subtropical(hybrid type) cyclones and public advisories on them began in 1972, and a few years later, a review was made of satellite imagery from the late 60's and early 70's and several of these systems were included as tropical storms. In fact, two of the storms added in 1969 were hurricanes, so 1969 now stands as having 12 hurricanes. Today, subtropical storms are named using the same list as tropical storms and hurricanes. This makes sense because subtropical cyclones often take on tropical characteristics. Imagine how confusing it would be if the system got a new name just because it underwent internal changes. There is no subtropical classification equivalent to a hurricane. The assumption is that once a storm got that strong it would have acquired tropical characteristics and therefore be called a hurricane or would have merged with an extratropical system in the North Atlantic and lost its name altogether. For example, on October 24, 1979, a subtropical storm briefly reached hurricane strength as it neared Newfoundland, Canada. It quickly combined with another low-pressure system but it was never named.

Whenever a hurricane has had a major impact, any country affected by the storm can request that the name of the hurricane be 'retired' by agreement of the World Meteorological Organization (WMO). Prior to 1969, officially, retiring a storm name actually meant that it cannot be reused for at least 10 years, to facilitate historic references, legal actions, insurance claim activities, etc... and to avoid public confusion with another storm of the same name. But today these storms are retired indefinitely and if that happens, a gender furious hurricane destructive storms that often become household names in the regions or countries they affected. When that list of names is exhausted, the Greek Alphabet (Alpha, Beta, Gamma, Delta, Epsilon, Zeta, Eta, Theta, Iota, Kappa and Lambda) is used. It must be noted that so far this list has only been used once in either the Pacific or the Atlantic Basins, which was in the North Atlantic hurricane season of 2005. It is important to note here that there were a few subtropical storms which used the Greek Alphabet in the 1970's but they were really not truly tropical in nature.

If a storm forms in the off-season, it will take the next name on the list based on the current calendar date. For example, if a tropical cyclone formed on December 29th, it would take the name from the previous season's list of names. If a storm formed in February, it would be named from the subsequent season's list of names. Theoretically, a hurricane or tropical storm of any strength can have its name retired; retirement is based entirely on the level of damage and death caused by a storm. However, up until 1972 (Hurricane Agnes), there was no Category 1 hurricane which had its name retired, and no named tropical storm had its name retired until 2001 (Tropical Storm Allison). Allison is the only tropical storm to have its name retired without ever having reached hurricane strength. This is at least partially due to the fact that weaker storms tend to cause less damage, and the few weak storms that have had their names retired caused most of their destruction through heavy rainfall rather than winds.

While no request for retirement has ever been turned down, some storms such as Hurricane Gordon in 1994 caused a great deal of death and destruction but nonetheless was not retired as the main country affected-Haiti did not request retirement. Hurricane Gordon in 1994 killed 1,122 persons in Haiti, and 23 deaths in other nations. Damage in the United States was estimated at $400 million, and damages in Haiti and Cuba were severe. Despite the tremendous damage caused, the name 'Gordon' was not retired and was reused in both the 2000 and 2006 North Atlantic hurricane seasons. As stated before, since 1950, 76 storms have had their names retired. Of these, two (Carol and Edna) were reused after the storm for which they were retired but were later retroactively retired, and two others (Hilda and Janet) were included on later lists of storm names but were not reused before being retroactively retired. Before 1979, when the first permanent six-year storm names list began, some storm names were simply not used anymore. For example, in 1966, 'Fern' was substituted for 'Frieda,' and no reason was cited.

In the North Atlantic Basin in most cases, a tropical cyclone retains its name throughout its life. However, a tropical cyclone may be renamed in several situations. First, when a tropical storm crosses from the Atlantic into the Pacific, or vice versa, before 2001 it was the policy of National Hurricane Center (NHC) to rename a tropical storm which crossed from Atlantic into Pacific, or vice versa. Examples included Hurricane Cesar-Douglas in 1996 and Hurricane Joan-Miriam in 1988. In 2001, when Iris moved across Central America, NHC mentioned that Iris would retain its name if it regenerated in the Pacific. However, the Pacific tropical depression developed from the remnants of Iris was called Fifteen-E instead. The depression later became Tropical Storm Manuel. NHC explained that Iris had dissipated as a tropical cyclone prior to entering the eastern North Pacific Basin; the new depression was properly named Fifteen-E, rather than Iris. In 2003, when Larry was about to move across Mexico, NHC attempted to provide greater clarity: *"Should Larry remain a tropical cyclone during its passage over Mexico into the Pacific, it would retain its name. However, a new name would be given if the surface circulation dissipates and then regenerates in the Pacific."* Up to now, it is extremely rare for a tropical cyclone to retain its name during the passage from Atlantic to Pacific, or vice versa.

Second, storms are renamed in situations where there are uncertainties of the continuation of storms. When the remnants of a tropical cyclone redevelop, the redeveloping system will be treated as a new tropical cyclone if there are uncertainties of the continuation, even though the original system may contribute to the forming of the new system. One example is the remnants of Tropical Depression #10 reforming into Tropical Depression #12 from the 2005 season which went on to become the powerful and deadly Hurricane Katrina. Another example was a storm which had the most names as stated earlier; in 1961 there was one tropical storm which had three lives and three names. Tropical Storm Hattie developed off the Caribbean Coast of Nicaragua on October 28, 1961, and drifted north and west before crossing Central America at Guatemala. It re-emerged into the Pacific Ocean on November 1 and was re-christened Simone. Two days later it recurved back towards the coastline of Central America and crossed over into the Atlantic via Mexico, re-emerging into the Gulf of Mexico as Inga.

CHAPTER FOUR

THE CLASSIFICATION OF HURRICANES

THE SAFFIR-SIMPSON HURRICANE DAMAGE-POTENTIAL SCALE

Saffir-Simpson Scale for Hurricane Classification				
Strength	Wind Speed (Kts)	Wind Speed (MPH)	Pressure (Millibars)	Pressure
Category 1	64- 82 kts	74- 95 mph	>980 mb	28.94 "Hg
Category 2	83- 95 kts	96-110 mph	965-979 mb	28.50-28.91 "Hg
Category 3	96-113 kts	111-130 mph	945-964 mb	27.91-28.47 "Hg
Category 4	114-135 kts	131-155 mph	920-944 mb	27.17-27.88 "Hg
Category 5	>135 kts	>155 mph	919 mb	27.16 "Hg
Tropical Cyclone Classification				
Tropical Depression	20-34kts			
Tropical Storm	35-63kts			
Hurricane	64+kts or 74+mph			

It must be noted that the Classification by central pressure came to an end in the 1990s, and wind speed alone is now used. These estimates of the central pressure that accompany each category are for reference only.

The Saffir-Simpson Hurricane Damage Potential Scale is a classification used for most western hemisphere tropical cyclones which exceed the intensities of "tropical depressions" and "tropical storms," and thereby become hurricanes. The scale divides hurricanes into five categories distinguished by the intensities of their sustained winds. Hurricanes are ranked according to strength and by the amount of damage they cause. The weakest hurricane is designated a Category 1 status with maximum sustained winds from 74 mph to 95 mph and an average storm surge of 4 to 5 feet above sea level. In contrast, a Category 5 hurricane has maximum sustained winds of greater than 155 mph and a storm surge of greater than 18 feet. Storm surge depends on many factors such as, the shape of the continental shelf just offshore, whether the hurricane makes landfall at high or low tide, and the location of the offshore and onshore winds relative to the eye of the hurricane.

As a result of the difficulty in relating the different and varying factors or characteristics of a hurricane to the destruction potential, the Saffir-Simpson Damage Potential Scale was developed in 1969 and completed in 1971. The scale was introduced to the general public in 1973, and saw widespread use after Neil Frank replaced Simpson at the helm of the National Hurricane Center in 1974. This scale was named for Herbert Saffir a civil engineer in Coral Gables, Florida and Robert Simpson, a meteorologist and the then Director of the National Hurricane Center in Miami, Florida. It has been used for well over 37 years to estimate the relative damage potential of a hurricane due to wind and storm surge. The initial scale was developed by Mr. Herbert Saffir (who at the time was well known as the father of the Miami's building codes) while working on commission from the United Nations to study low-cost housing in hurricane-prone areas. While performing the study, Saffir realized that there was no simple scale for describing the likely effects of a hurricane. Knowing the usefulness of the Richter Magnitude Scale in describing earthquakes, he devised a similar 1-5 scale based on wind speed that showed expected damage to structures. Saffir looked at the scale from an engineering point of view because he was well-versed in Miami's Building Codes. Saffir then gave the scale to the National Hurricane Center, and Simpson added in the likely effects of storm surge and flooding. Simpson became the Director of the National Hurricane Center in 1968 and he was already one of the world's leading authorities on tropical cyclones and a veteran of numerous Air Force and Navy flights into these hurricanes. Simpson later recalled that the National Hurricane Center at the time was having difficulty telling disaster agencies how much damage to expect from particular storms.

Using a mixture of structural engineering and meteorology, they constructed the Saffir-Simpson Damage Potential Scale because both men had first-hand experiences with hurricanes. It does not take into account rainfall or location, which means that a Category 3 hurricane which hits a major city will likely do far more damage than a Category 5 hurricane which hits a rural area. The Saffir-Simpson Scale classifies hurricanes into Categories 1,2,3,4, and 5, depending on the barometric pressure, wind speed, and storm surge and destruction. A Category 1 hurricane, for example, would inflict minimal damage, mainly to shrubbery, trees, foliage, unanchored structures, mobile homes, small craft, and low-lying areas that could become flooded. Whereas, a Category 5 hurricane would cause catastrophic damage, such as blown down trees, power lines, and poles; overturned vehicles; torn down or blown away buildings; complete destruction of mobile or manufactured homes and massive flooding. According to Robert Simpson, there is no reason for a Category 6 on the Saffir-Simpson Scale because it is designed to measure the potential damage of a hurricane to man-made structures. If the speed of the hurricane is above 156 mph, then the damage to a building will be "serious no matter how well it's engineered." However, the result of new technologies in construction leads some to suggest that an increase in the number of categories is necessary. This suggestion was emphasized after the devastating effects of the 2005 Atlantic hurricane season. During that record year Hurricane Emily, Hurricane Katrina, Hurricane Rita, and Hurricane Wilma all became Category 5 hurricanes. A few newspaper columnists and scientists have brought up the idea of introducing a Category 6 and amending the scale to include the risk of flooding but in most cases it is often rebuffed.

The practical usefulness of the Saffir-Simpson Scale is that it relates properties of the hurricane to previously observed damage.

Until the Saffir-Simpson Damage Potential Scale was developed, hurricanes were referred to as, *Great (or Extreme) Hurricanes, Severe Hurricanes, or Minor, Minimal or Major Hurricanes.* A Minor Hurricane had maximum winds of 74 mph and a minimum central pressure of 29.40 inches. A Minimal hurricane had maximum winds of between 75 to 100 mph and a minimum central pressure of between 29.03 to 29.39 inches. A Major hurricane had winds between 101 to 135 mph and a minimal central pressure of 28.01 to 29.02 inches. An Extreme or Great hurricane had winds of 136 mph or over and a minimum central pressure of 28.00 inches or less. However, these terms are no longer used but may appear in historical materials now and then. It is important to note that when dealing with narrative descriptions of historical events, these determinations must be somewhat subjective. For the purposes of this book, these categories will be any storm causing devastating damage through either wind action or storm surge. Some authors over the years have used the word or terminology 'extreme' very loosely to describe the worst of these events but I will refrain from using that terminology. The word 'extreme' in my opinion would imply the 'peak' or 'maximum' of a very powerful and destructive storm. For this book, I prefer to use the more acceptable and more appropriate word of 'Great' to label these very destructive and powerful storms but I will mention it when it is only necessary. It is important to note that tropical storms are named but are not assigned a Saffir-Simpson category number.

Only a few Atlantic hurricanes have made landfall with winds estimated to have reached the rarefied extreme of 200 mph, at least in gusts. These includes, the Great Labour Day Hurricane of 1935 which passed over the Florida Keys (inspiring the classic Humphrey Bogart movie *Key Largo*); Hurricane Camille, which came ashore at Pass Christian, Mississippi in 1969, and Hurricane Andrew in 1992, which struck the lower Florida Peninsula. Some top wind speeds from some of these powerful Atlantic storms will never ever be known because in most cases the instruments were destroyed before they measured the worst of their respective winds. This is because very few anemometers are capable of accurately measuring the winds of a Category 5 hurricane. The list of Category 5 Atlantic hurricanes encompasses 32 tropical cyclones that reached the extremely rare

Category 5 intensity on the Saffir-Simpson Hurricane Scale within the Atlantic Ocean (north of the equator), the Caribbean Sea and Gulf of Mexico. They are the most catastrophic hurricanes that can form on planet Earth. They are relatively rare in the North Atlantic Ocean, and generally occur only about once every three years on average in the North Atlantic basin. Only four times-in the 1960, 1961, 2005 and 2007 hurricane seasons-have multiple Category 5 hurricanes formed. Only in 2005 have more than two Category 5 storms formed, and only in 2007 has more than one made landfall at Category 5 strength.

Tropical cyclones are ranked according to their maximum winds using several scales and methods depending on which area of the world they are located. These scales are provided by several bodies, including the World Meteorological Organization, the U.S. Joint Typhoon Warning Center, the National Hurricane Center in Miami, and the Bureau of Meteorology in Australia. The National Hurricane Center uses the Saffir-Simpson Scale for hurricanes in the eastern Pacific and Atlantic Basins. Australia uses a different set of tropical cyclone categories for their region. Many basins have different names of hurricane/typhoon/cyclone strength. The United States National Hurricane Center, the main governing body for hurricanes in the North Atlantic region classifies hurricanes of Category 3 and above as *Major Hurricanes*. Whereas, the U.S. Joint Typhoon Warning Center classifies typhoons with wind speeds of at least 150 mph (67 m/s or 241 km/h, equivalent to a strong Category 4 storm) as *Super Typhoons*. The term 'major hurricane' supplants the previously used term of *Great Hurricane* which was used throughout the 1950's and the 1960's.

The use of different definitions for maximum sustained winds creates additional confusion into the definitions of cyclone categories worldwide. The Saffir-Simpson Hurricane Scale is used only to describe hurricanes forming in the Atlantic Ocean and Northern Pacific Ocean east of the International Date Line. Other areas use their own classification schemes to label these storms, which are called 'cyclones' or 'typhoons' depending on the area where they occur around the world. The Australian Bureau of Meteorology uses a 1-5 scale called *Tropical Cyclone Severity Categories*. Unlike the

Term	Meaning
Cyclone (Generic term for a low-pressure system Tropical Cyclone)	Cyclone is a generic term to refer to a low-pressure system. Typhoons and other types of low pressure systems are all cyclones. The direction of rotation is opposite in the northern hemisphere and the southern hemisphere, but other essential features of a cyclone are shared in both hemispheres.
Tropical Cyclone	Tropical cyclone is in general a cyclone formed in the tropical areas. However, the word "tropical" does not refer to the place of formation, and it actually refers to the structure of a cyclone. This means that a cyclone with the structure of a tropical cyclone is called a "tropical cyclone" regardless of the place. Typhoons, hurricanes and others are all "intense" tropical cyclones, so they are regarded as same meteorological phenomena (classification of intensity). A unique convention for tropical cyclones is that each tropical cyclone is named.
Extratropical Cyclone	Extratropical cyclone literally means a cyclone outside of the tropical areas. Most of the low pressure systems that pass around Japan belong to this type. Just like a tropical cyclone, this term also does not refer to the place of formation, but refers to the structure of a cyclone. The fundamental difference between a tropical cyclone and this type is that the former consists of warm air only, while the latter consists of both cold air and warm air. This difference also leads to the different source of energy for intensification. Finally, we often see a tropical cyclone transformed into an extratropical cyclone, but the inverse is extremely rare.
Typhoon	Typhoon is a tropical cyclone located in the western north Pacific basin (between 100E and 180E in the northern hemisphere). The category of a typhoon is decided by the maximum sustained winds, but please note that the typhoon in Japanese standard and the typhoon in international standard is not the same. Finally, among tropical cyclones in the world, the typhoon is the most frequent and the strongest tropical cyclone. Typhoons are named.
Hurricane	Hurricane is a tropical cyclone located in the north Atlantic, eastern or central north Pacific (east of 180E (180W) in the northern hemisphere), eastern south Pacific (east of 160E in the southern hemisphere). The category of a hurricane follows the same international standard as the typhoon based on the maximum sustained wind. When a hurricane reaches the 180E (180W) degree line and enters into the basin of the typhoon, it starts to be called a typhoon. Hurricanes are named.
Cyclone(Abbreviation of a tropical cyclone)	Cyclone is a generic term for a cyclonic system, but the same word is also used as an abbreviation of 'tropical cyclone' as long as a special term to represent a tropical cyclone does not exist. In northern Indian ocean (west of 100E), the term "cyclonic storm" is used, and in southern Indian ocean, around Australia, and in the southern Pacific ocean, the term "tropical cyclone" is in use. If a typhoon moves westward to pass 100E, then it starts to be called as a cyclone. It seems that the first tropical cyclone in the south Atlantic in 2004 is called either a cyclone or a hurricane. Cyclones are named.
Willy-Willy	Willy-Willy is often introduced as the name of a tropical cyclone around Australia, but it seems that it actually means something like a dust devil, and has little relationship with a tropical cyclone.

*Unfortunately, there are at least two definitions of this term in widespread use. Most countries (including us here in the Bahamas) use the World Meteorological Organization's definition, which is a ten-minute sustained average wind at an elevation of ten meters. But the United States uses a one-minute average, which is almost always higher.

Saffir-Simpson Scale, severity categories are based on the strongest wind gusts and not sustained winds. Severity categories are scaled somewhat lower than the Saffir-Simpson Scale. A Category 1 storm features gusts less than 126 km/h (78 mph), with a severity Category 2 tropical cyclone, being roughly equivalent to a Saffir-Simpson Category 1 hurricane, while gusts in a Category 5 cyclone are at least 280 km/h (174 mph).

The U.S. Joint Typhoon Warning Center classifies West Pacific typhoons as tropical cyclones with wind speeds greater than 73 mph (118 km/h). Typhoons with wind speeds of at least 150 mph (67 m/s or 241 km/h, equivalent to a strong Category 4 hurricane) are dubbed *Super Typhoons.* In the Southwestern Indian Ocean: (1) a "tropical depression" is a tropical disturbance in which the maximum of the average wind speed is 28 to 33 knots (51 to 62 km/h); (2) a "moderate tropical storm" is a tropical disturbance in which the maximum of the average wind speed is 34 to 47 knots (63 to 88 km/h); (3) a "severe tropical storm" is a tropical disturbance in which the maximum of the average wind speed is 48 to 63 knots (89 to 117 km/h); (4) a "tropical cyclone" is a tropical disturbance in which the maximum of the average wind speed is 64 to 89 knots (118 to 165 km/h); (5) an "intense tropical cyclone" is a tropical disturbance in which the maximum of the average wind speed is 90 to 115 knots (166 to 212 km/h); and (6) a "very intense tropical cyclone" is a tropical disturbance in which the maximum of the average wind speed is greater than 115 knots (greater than 212 km/h).

The Beaufort Wind Scale was a scale that was developed by Sir Francis Beaufort in 1805 of the British Navy and was based solely on human observation. The Beaufort Wind Scale is now universally used around the world by seamen and lay persons alike. In 1805-06 Commander Francis Beaufort (Later Admiral Sir Francis Beaufort) devised a descriptive wind scale in an effort to standardize wind reports in ship's logs. As a result of this scale we have hurricane winds starting at 64 knots. His scale divided wind speeds into 14 Forces (later reduced to thirteen) with each Force assigned a number, a common name, and a description of the effects such a wind would have on a sailing ship. Since the worst storm an Atlantic sailor was likely to run into was a hurricane that name was applied to the top

Force on the scale. During the 19th century, with the manufacture of accurate anemometers, actual numerical values were assigned to each Force Level, but it wasn't until 1926 (with revisions in 1939 and 1946) that the International Meteorological Committee (predecessor of the World Meteorological Organization) adopted a universal scale of wind speed values. It was a progressive scale with the range of speed for Forces increasing as you go higher. Thus, Force 1 is only 3 knots in range, while the Force 11 is 8 knots in range and Force 12 starts out at 64 knots (74 mph). There is nothing magical in this number, and since hurricane force winds are a rare experience, chances are the committee which decided on this number didn't do so because of any real observations during a hurricane.

Indeed the Smeaton-Rouse wind scale in 1759 pegged hurricane force winds at 70 knots (80 mph). Just the same, when a tropical cyclone has maximum winds of approximately these speeds we do see the mature structure (eye, eyewall, spiral rainbands) begin to form, so there is some unity with setting hurricane force winds in this neighbourhood. For example, if whole trees moved and resistance was felt while walking against the wind and the waves produced white foam with streaks on it then the observer would categorize it as a gale. In the 1800's and early 1900's Bahamian fishermen used this Beaufort Wind Scale almost exclusively to gauge the intensity of a storm. If a tropical storm or hurricane was in the vicinity of the Bahamas, many Bahamians (especially the older ones) would say that 'gale was travelling.' Even in historical records in the Bahamas, many of these storms were simply referred to as 'gales' or 'severe gales' rather than hurricanes or tropical storms. This often resulted in many of these storms going unreported or under-reported because a gale in meteorological terms simply meant that these storms had sustained wind speeds of between 34 to 47 knots (39 to 54 mph) as opposed to 64 knots (74 mph) or greater for a hurricane. Although the traditional definition of a hurricane is Beaufort Force 12 winds ('air filled with foam, sea completely white with driving spray, visibility greatly reduced'), nowadays the Saffir-Simpson Scale is used, especially in this region of the world. It is a scale which is used as a quick means of informing not only meteorologists, but also the public, of the relative intensity of an approaching storm.

In Meteorology as in nature, the elements always try to achieve a perfect balance but thankfully they never do. For example, a hurricane's main objective is a simple one, to take heat from the equator to the poles and likewise, the cold front's objective is similarly to take cold air from the poles to the equator but thankfully none of them ever gets to achieve their objectives so they continue trying in this never ending cycle and the result is life here on Earth as we know it today. The sun is our only source of heat on a global scale. Around 70% of the Earth's surface is covered in water-mostly the oceans. Since water holds heat energy better than the land, our tropical oceans are extremely efficient in storing energy transmitted by the sun. So the heat generated by the sun and stored in the oceans is the first major ingredient for fueling hurricanes. Hurricanes form over tropical waters where the winds are light, the humidity is high in a deep layer, and the surface water temperature is warm, typically 26.5 degrees Celsius or greater over a vast area, often between latitudes 5 degrees to 25 degrees north or south of the equator. Over the tropical and subtropical North Atlantic and North Pacific oceans these conditions prevail in the summer and early fall; hence, the hurricane season normally runs from June through November. At this time the water is hot enough to create atmospheric convection that casts moisture 10 miles up into the atmosphere.

These extremely hazardous weather systems occur most commonly across the low-latitude Northwest Pacific and its 'downstream' land areas, where on average just over a third of the global total of such storms develop. In an average year there are approximately 80 of these Tropical Cyclones which form over warm tropical oceans with 48 of them becoming hurricanes and 20 of them becoming intense hurricanes. Many residents within this region perceive the North Atlantic Ocean basin a prolific producer of hurricanes because of the worldwide publicity these storms generate. In reality, the North Atlantic is generally only a marginal basin in terms of hurricane activity. Every tropical ocean except the South Atlantic and Southeast Pacific contains hurricanes; several of these tropical oceans produce more hurricanes annually than the North Atlantic. Hurricanes are generally a summer phenomenon, but the length of the hurricane season varies in each basin, as does the peak of activity. The Northeast

Pacific averages 17%, the Northwest Pacific averages just over 33%, while the North Atlantic typically sees about 12% of the world's total of tropical cyclones, while the other regions accounts for the remaining 38%(the percentages may vary from year to year and basin to basin but these are just conservative averages) of the world total of hurricanes. Additionally, most basins use a 10-minute average of sustained wind speeds to determine intensity, as recommended by the WMO, but this is not the case in the North Atlantic and Northeastern Pacific regions, where 1-minute averages, almost always higher, are used.

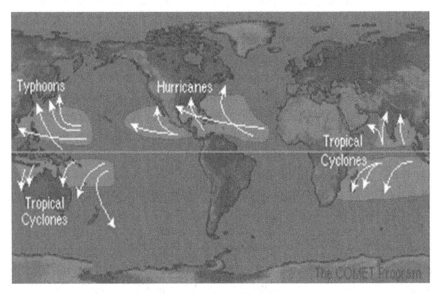

(Courtesy of www.comet.ucar.edu)

- **Northern Atlantic Ocean:** The most-studied of all tropical basins and accounts for approximately 12% of the world's total tropical cyclones. Tropical cyclone formation here varies widely from year to year, ranging from twenty eight to one per year with an average of around ten. The United States Atlantic and Gulf Coasts, Mexico, Central America, the Caribbean Islands, and Bermuda are frequently affected by storms in this basin. Venezuela, the south-east of Canada and Atlantic "Macaronesian" islands are also occasionally affected. Many of the more intense Atlantic storms are Cape Verde-Type hurricanes, which forms off the west coast of Africa near the Cape Verde Islands. On rare occasions, a hurricane can reach the European mainland such as, Hurricane Lili, which dissipated over the British Isles in October of 1996 and Tropical Storm Vince in September 2005, which made landfall on the southwestern coast of Spain in the record breaking 2005 North Atlantic hurricane season. In an average year, about 10 storms form in this basin with 6 of them becoming hurricanes and of that total 2 of them becoming intense hurricanes. In this basin, the hurricane season runs from June 1 to November 30 with the peak of the season occurring around September 10.

- **Northeastern Pacific Ocean:** This is the second most active basin in the world accounting for approximately 17% of the world's total tropical cyclones, and the most compact (a large number of storms for such a small area of ocean). Storms that form here can affect western Mexico, Hawaii, northern Central America, and on extremely rare occasions, California and Arizona. There is no record of a hurricane ever reaching California; however, to some meteorologists, historical records in 1858 indicate that there was a storm which struck San Diego with winds of over 75 mph. In an average year, about 17 storms form in this basin with 10 of them becoming hurricanes and of that total 5 of them becoming intense hurricanes. In this basin, the hurricane season runs from May 15 to November 30 with the peak of the season occurring around August 25.

- **Northwestern Pacific Ocean:** Tropical cyclone activity in this region frequently affects China, Japan, Hong Kong, the Philippines, and Taiwan, but also many other countries in Southeast Asia, such as Vietnam, South Korea, and parts of Indonesia, plus numerous Oceanian islands. This is by far the most active basin, accounting for over 33% of all tropical cyclone activity in the world. The coast of China sees the most land falling tropical cyclones worldwide. The Philippines receives an average 18 typhoon landings per year. Rarely does a typhoon or an extratropical storm reach northward to Siberia, Russia. In an average year, about 27 storms form in this basin with 17 of them becoming hurricanes and of that total 8 of them becoming intense hurricanes. It is interesting to note that in this basin, the hurricane season occurs year-round with the peak of the season occurring around September 1 and the minimum occurring in February.

- **Northern Indian Ocean:** This basin is sub-divided into two areas, the Bay of Bengal and the Arabian Sea, with the Bay of Bengal dominating (5 to 6 times more activity). This basin's season has an interesting and rare double peak season; one in April and May before the onset of the monsoons, and another in October and November just after the monsoons. Tropical cyclones which form in this basin has historically cost the most lives — most notably, the November, 1970 Bhola Cyclone killed approximately 300,000 to 500,000 persons mainly in Bangladesh and coastal India from drowning. Nations affected by this basin include India, Bangladesh, Sri Lanka, Thailand, Myanmar, and Pakistan. Rarely, a tropical cyclone formed in this basin will affect the Arabian Peninsula. This basin accounts for about 12% of the worlds' total of tropical cyclones. In an average year about 5 storms form in this basin with 2 of them becoming hurricanes and of that total 1 becoming an intense hurricane. In the North Indian basin, storms are most common from April to December 30, with peaks in May 15 and November 10.

- **Southwestern Pacific Ocean:** Tropical activity in this region largely affects Australia and Oceania. On rare occasions, tropical storms reach the vicinity of Brisbane, Australia and into New Zealand, usually during or after extratropical transition. This basin accounts for about 11% of the worlds' total of tropical cyclones. In an average year about 10 storms form in this basin with 5 of them becoming hurricanes and of that total 2 of them becoming intense hurricanes. In this basin, the hurricane season runs from October 15 to May 1 with the peak of the season occurring around March 1.

- **Southeastern Indian Ocean:** Tropical activity in this region affects Australia and Indonesia. According to the Australian Bureau of Meteorology, the most frequently hit portion of Australia is between Exmouth and Broome in Western Australia. This basin accounts for about 7% of the worlds' total of tropical cyclones. In an average year about 7 storms form in this basin with 3 of them becoming hurricanes and of that total 1 becoming an intense hurricane. In this basin, the hurricane season runs from October 15 to May 1 with the peak of the season occurring January 15 and February 25.

- **Southwestern Indian Ocean:** This basin is often the least understood, due to a lack of historical data. Cyclones forming here impact Madagascar, Mozambique, Mauritius, Reunion, Comoros, Tanzania, and Kenya. This basin accounts for about the remaining 8% of the worlds' total of tropical cyclones. In an average year about 10 storms form in this basin with 5 of them becoming hurricanes and of that total 2 of them becoming intense hurricanes. In this basin, the hurricane season runs from October 15 to May 15 with the peak of the season occurring January 15 and February 20.

A hurricane is a circular, cyclonic system with a diameter anywhere from 100 to 500 miles extending upwards to heights of 40,000 to 50,000 feet. They draw their energy from latent heat from the warm tropical seas and they are generally smaller than middle-latitude cyclones, which on the other hand depend on the tropics-to-pole temperature gradient for their energy. At the base of the hurricane, air is sucked in by the very low pressure at the center and then spirals inward. Once within the hurricane structure itself, air rises rapidly to the top and spirals outward. It is this rapid upward movement of great quantities of moisture rich air that produces the enormous amounts of rain during a hurricane. A hurricane consists of huge swirl of clouds rotating around a calm center-the eye-where warm air is sucked down. Clouds, mainly cumulonimbus clouds are arranged in bands around the eye, the tallest forming the wall of the eye. The eyewall as it is commonly called is the area of highest surface winds in the tropical cyclone. It is composed of many strong updrafts and downdrafts. The mechanisms by which the eyewall and the eye are formed are not very well understood but it is generally thought that the eye feature is a fundamental component of all rotating fluids.

Hurricanes have very strong pressure gradients with isobars that decrease in value toward the center of the very low pressure. The strong pressure gradients are the main reason behind the powerful winds of the hurricane. In addition, the resulting latent heat of condensation that is released provides the power to drive the storm. High pressure air in the upper atmosphere (above 30,000 feet/9,000m) over the storm's center also removes heat from the rising air, further driving the air cycle and the hurricane's growth. As high pressure air is sucked into the low-pressure center of the storm, wind speeds increase. At the center of the hurricane is the eye of the storm, which is an area of calm, usually warm and humid, but rainless air. Spiral rain bands and these bands of heavy convective showers that spiral inward toward the storm's center surround hurricanes. Cumulus and Cumulonimbus clouds ascend and lightning develop. Although a great deal of time, money and effort has been spent on studying the development, growth, maturity and tracks of hurricanes, much is still not known about these mysterious but powerful storms. For example, it is still not possible to predict the exact track of a hurricane with pinpoint accuracy, even though it can be tracked with weather radars and studied through reconnaissance aircrafts, computer models and weather satellites. Furthermore, meteorologists can list factors that are favorable for development of a hurricane or list pre-conditions that are necessary for the formation of a hurricane but they can't say with a degree of certainty or pin-point accuracy that in a certain situation or scenario that a hurricane will definitely develop and travel along a particular path. However numerical weather predictions models are becoming more accurate and precise in trying to predict the movement and strength of these storms. In actual fact, meteorologists from all around the world have come to rely on the accuracy of these models to help predict the movement and strength of these storms thereby improving the hurricane forecast of these dangerous storms.

CHAPTER FIVE
THE SISAL INDUSTRY OF THE BAHAMAS DURING THE GREAT BAHAMAS HURRICANE OF 1899

SISAL PLANTATION. [Photo : J. O. Sands, Nassau]

A Sisal Plantation with white helmeted overseers in North Andros (Courtesy of the Department of Archives, Nassau, Bahamas).

The year 1899 was a mixed blessing for the Bahamas. It was an era in which the economy alternatively flourished and declined along with an era of improved communications and one which saw the beginning of a social awakening. It was also a time of hardship and suffering which eventually led to large scale migration of Bahamians to the United States. The years immediately preceding the late 1890s were difficult ones for the Bahamas. The boom period during the Blockade running era (1861-65) had come to an end. Industry and agriculture were in severe decline and poverty was rampant. The year 1870 marked the beginning of a kind of reconstruction with the introduction of new industries and rebuilding of old ones. The sponge industry, one of the Colony's oldest, flourished during this period, the peak years being the 1890s. The pineapple industry also experienced a boom period during this time as well with a total of 665,332 dozen pineapples valuing £56,061 being exported in 1892. Furthermore, pineapple factories were opened in Nassau by J.S. Johnson Company and in Eleuthera by C.T. Sands. These companies exported the reserved fruit all over the world.

Unlike pineapple and sponging, the salt industry reported a significant decline during this period. The salt decline was due partly to the high U.S. import tariffs and unavailability of new salt markets. Many new industries were introduced during this period. The most prominent one was the sisal industry and had a marked effect on the Bahamas if only for a short period of time. But why was sisal introduced? Fruits and vegetables crop production had been tried but had all failed. This was due to natural elements such as, the weather, poor quality soil and poor shipping which saw what crops had been grown deteriorate whilst waiting for delayed ships and the inefficiency of the local workers. What was needed was a crop that was resilient to the weather (especially droughts and hurricanes) and would not deteriorate with long storage. Sisal was the ideal crop. Sisal prefers to grow in Limestone areas where the bedrock is exposed and has only a thin covering of soil and requires only several years to reach its maturity. The leaves contain long slender fibers extending just under the surface. The plant is in fact an Agave and was first discovered in the Yucatan in Mexico. The word 'sisal' is derived from the port in Yucatan where the fiber was exported. Therefore sisal became the commercial term for the fiber.

Demographic statistics tells an interesting story of the incipient metropolitan dominance in the Bahamas. The population of the Bahamas in 1899 was around 50,000 people, and approximately 11,000 of whom lived in Nassau and only fractionally less on Andros, Eleuthera (including Harbour Island and Spanish Wells) and some of the major other islands. One hundred years later the population of New Providence had increased 500% while the population of Eleuthera and adjacent islands remained just about the same. The population in the rest of the Bahamas for the next hundred years also remained fairly constant except for Grand Bahama which, because of the development of Freeport, enjoyed rapid growth in the second half of the century. In 1899, the sea itself was by no means unproductive, yet little of its abundance could be exported with ease. The exceptions were turtle shells, ambergris, and an occasional pearl. On land, the sisal and hemp industry developed in the late 1880's and 1890's also became an important industry in the Bahamas. For 30 years (1889-1919), sisal plantations throughout a few select islands of the Bahamas provided a much needed boost to the economy of these impoverish islands. Industrialists established sisal companies such as, the Munroe Fibre Company, Sisal Fibre Company and the Bahamas Fibre Company on Andros, Grand Bahama, Abaco and a few other islands.

In 1899 Great Inagua became one of the main sisal growing areas in the Bahamas. Two sisal companies called 'Bahama Fiber' and 'Standard Sisal Hemp,' cultivated thousands of acres of land on this island. Inagua sisal was used mainly as a binder twine for grain harvest in the United States. The industry failed after the production of fiber in Mexico increased. Plantation owners were no longer able to compete because the American buyers considered the Mexican product a superior fiber. Foreign investors also tried Cotton and cattle rearing during this era. During the latter part of the 19th century, Great Inagua was certainly the shipping capital of the Bahamas. Mathew Town the capital of Great Inagua was named after George B. Mathew, who was Governor of the Bahamas from 1844-1848. Thanks in part to sisal and salt, Mathew Town was the first planned town in the country and the colony's first port of entry. This port town was port of call for Hamburg American and Royal Netherlands Lines. Hundreds of Bahamians who migrated to the island were engaged as stevedores and sailors aboard the ships and as contract workers on the Panama Canal, Mahogany Industries of Central America, and the Mexican railway.

A lady in Chas. J. Kelly's Lumber Yard drying sisal on several lines in Downtown Nassau.

The first plants of the sisal tree from which rope was made were introduced by the Colonial Secretary C.R. Nesbitt in 1845. It reached its peak in the late 1800's and the early 1900's where well over 400 tons of sisal was exported annually. Unfortunately, the acquisition of the Philippine Islands by the United States, steep competition elsewhere and infertile soils led to the decline of the Bahamian sisal industry. The Philippines had privileged access to the American market and the Bahamas was unable to compete. The large Bahamian estates, many of them badly located on unsuitable and nutrient lacking soils with an insufficient labour force, fell into bankruptcy and the mills closed. Produced uneconomically on smallholdings and beaten crudely by hand in salt water, the quality and price of the Bahamian Fibre declined even further. The government ordinances supervising the production and grading the sisal became a dead letter and the Bahamian product became far inferior to those grown in vast quantities in the Philippines, Mexico, India and East Africa, where these plants grew more readily, were superior in quantity and quality, and the labour costs were significantly cheaper. By the 1920s, the sisal industry in the Bahamas was dead. Worldwide, by the late 1930's it came to an end with the introduction of synthetic nylon which was much cheaper to produce and more versatile than the natural sisal plant.

A Sisal Plantation with three white helmeted overseers on a North Andros Plantation (Courtesy of the Department of Archives, Nassau, Bahamas).

The sisal and hemp industry began in 1887 when Sir Ambrose Shea originally from New Foundland came to the Bahamas to take up residence as the newly appointed Governor (1887-94). He immediately became attracted to our local plant called by its scientific name of *agave rigida sisilana* but commonly known as *sisal*. The fibre had to be extracted from the leaves of the plant and had many uses as a finished product such as, to make rope, rugs, hats and handbags. Forty two years prior to that, the sisal plant was introduced to the

Bahamas from the Yucatan by the then Colonial Secretary Mr. C.R. Nesbit. He had the fibre extracted from the long green leaves and sent to England for assessment. A favourable report was received, and over the years this sisal plant became a briefly vibrant industry even though in the long term it became an unprofitable and lack luster industry in the Bahamas. Initially, the statistics really looked very impressive but in the long term it simply wasn't for a number of reasons. The healthy plant if properly trimmed and cared for would live for over fourteen years. It was also resilient plants which grew like weeds and produce thousands of offspring. The plant after four years began to be productive that required a semi-annual harvest which would yield anywhere from one-half to a ton of fibre for each acre under production.

It was little doubt in anyone's mind that Governor Shea looked on sisal as a sort of magic plant which would completely transform the Bahamian economy. He travelled to Canada, Newfoundland and England to look for potential investors for the sisal finished product. He also had a commission set up and sent some of the members to Yucatan in Mexico on an investigative and fact finding mission and they came back and reported that we had similar soil and climate conditions like that of Mexico where the sisal plant was successfully being grown. The Bahamas plant was of a darker green hue, and there were no thorns along the hedges of the leaf, but in other respects it resembled the Yucatan variety. The most suitable land in the Bahamas is that called coppice land. After four years of growth, or less in very favourable conditions, the leaves are fit for cutting. They weigh from 5 to 21 pounds and are scraped by machines or by hand which takes off all the vegetable matter, leaving only the fibre, which emerges white and clean, and is hung out across posts and rails to dry in the sun. When thoroughly dried it is placed under pressure and packed in bales of 350 to 500 pounds in weight, and is then ready for export.

Governor Shea realistically recognized that efficient production demanded large plantations and factories, and therefore required substantial investors. But production was labour intensive at a time when most suitable land areas were in the Out Islands which at the time were relatively under populated. Each stage in the production of sisal required a fair amount of workers, not to mention the large labour force needed for clearing and preparing the land, planting, tending the plants, and cutting and carrying the leaves to the factory and the bales of sisal hemp to the dock. The Governor was a really good salesman and travelled to Canada, Newfoundland and England to drum up support for potential investors to come to the Bahamas and invest in sisal. The proposition he sold the potential sisal investors was an irresistible one. In addition, he had legislation passed to encourage the cultivation of the fibre plant in 1889 and convinced the Out Islanders at a series of town meetings that the systematic cultivation of sisal, which at the time was considered a pest or nuisance weed could radically transform the Bahamian economy. There was significant amount of land available and plenty of labourers. Sisal was grown in Andros, Savannah Sound, Eleuthera, Long Island, Rum Cay, Cat Island, Inagua and Abaco. On Great Abaco, there were three large sisal plantations and several small farms, owned by American and British Companies. On Little Abaco, a wealthy London company had acquired 10,000 acres and had planted nearly 2,000 acres. A sisal plantation was established south of Marsh Harbour. Several large plantations were founded on Little Abaco Island. Sisal processing mills were also located at Marsh Harbour, Hope Town, Guana Cay, Coco Plum Creek and Sandy Point.

Large acres of Crown Land were sold on leased on favorable or easy terms. Tracts of available Crown Land would cost only sixteen shillings an acre and after only four years it could produce an annual profit of £10 could be expected from each acre planted out. In addition to that, a bounty of £4 and 10 shillings was offered for each ton of fibre exported during the first seven years. This large profit margin was achieved because one of the chief markets for sisal was the United States and it did not produce its own supply and charged no import duty, and that current market prices were high enough to make it a worthwhile venture. Furthermore, to prevent a glut on the market, only 100,000 acres of land would be sold to investors during the first ten years. Within a year amazingly the entire 100,000 acres had been taken up. It got such a good response and the general satisfaction was so great that many of the investors agreed to forego the bounty offered by the Government. In addition, acts were passed in 1889 placing a 20% duty on imports of foreign sisal and offering a bounty

of one cent per pound of hemp produced up to 1895. Attracted by these attractive terms and by the fact that the U.S. did not levy import duties on hemp, groups of English Capitalists initially established plantations on San Salvador and Andros. Prominent among them was the Rt. Hon. Joseph Chamberlain, Secretary of State for the Colonies who had sent his son Neville to manage the estate.

Bales of Sisal in Nassau Harbour being prepared for shipping abroad (Courtesy of the Department of Archives, Nassau, Bahamas).

By 1891, there were approximately 48,000 acres (inclusive of the 20,000 acres leased by Joseph Chamberlain), had been set aside for sisal cultivation with more than 6,000 acres already planted. In 1888, approximately 10,000, young plants were planted on new grounds on Harbour Island in Eleuthera alone. The next year the total sisal plants for the entire island of Eleuthera was 80,000 to 100,000 and 17 bales of 1½ tons of fibre were shipped from the district to Nassau for the English market. Industrial machines had been imported to clean the fibre but much of it was still done by hand. In 1892, with exports of 150 to 200 tons expected, Shea stated that the sisal industry in the Bahamas was now a full-fledged and viable industry with great prospects. In fact, by 1899 during the year of this great hurricane, about 400 tons of sisal was exported annually. By 1893, 70,000 acres of Crown Land had been acquired for the industry, of which nearly 12,000 acres were already under cultivation. Small shipments were being made and there was still tremendous confidence in the industry. In the spring of 1894 when Governor Shea visited the Chamberlain plantation in North Andros he was very much impressed by what he saw. He reported that over 5,000 acres of land was already under cultivation. Furthermore, he noted that this industry revitalized and transformed the entire population of North Andros. Socially and morally he was able to transform this island and its people as well. He managed to control the excessive drinking among the people, closed unlicensed grog shops, and had opened a general store and savings bank for the people. As a result of these changes he said that he noticed a significant positive change in the moral and demeanor of the people.

There was a concern that some Bahamians who owned no land would be left out of the rewards offered by this package and would prefer to grow their own sisal rather than work for a wage on one of the larger plantations. However, that was taken into consideration when they allowed each head of the family, in this category to be granted 10 acres at the old price of five shillings per acre, to be paid from the proceeds of the first harvest. These grants were independent of the 100,000 acre limit. This had a positive impact on the industry because soon after this took place the sisal plant was growing everywhere and many families went full force into the business. Within a few years fourteen mills were busy at work harvesting and processing the sisal plant and the amounts invested in the production, harvesting and shipping of the sisal product was huge. One English company put £150,000 into several plantations. The Chamberlain family invested £50,000 in a plantation in Andros but this massive investment was considered small when comparing it to the expected returns. For example, Mr. Joseph Chamberlain, the future Secretary of State for the colonies, might have calculated that with 5000 of his 7000 acres planted out, he would recover his initial investment deposit in five years, at the first cuttings, and each year thereafter he would receive almost equal to his capital investment. His actual estimate of a thirty percent return must have seemed very conservative. Sisal was indeed an incredible prospect. It rapidly over took citrus and pineapples and quickly climbed to second place, just behind sponging, in economic importance. The fibre cost about £12 a ton to produce and as long as the market price remained steady at £20-£25, a good commercial profit could be made. The labourers were comprised of mostly Nassauvians and their pay was £1.40 per month.

An Out Island sloop loaded with sisal has come to Nassau to sell their sisal.

Between 1898 and 1902 the effect of the Spanish-American War (which cut off supplies from Cuba, Puerto Rico and the Philippines) and the Boer War (which produced a large surge in demand by the British army) sky-rocketed the price up to £38 a ton and no less than 20,000 acres were planted. The Spanish-American War was a conflict in 1898 between Spain and the United States that saw the Americans attack Spain's Pacific possessions which led to involvement in the Philippine Revolution and ultimately to the Philippine-American War. On April 25, 1898 the United States declared war on Spain following the sinking of the Battleship Maine in Havana Harbour on February 15, 1898. The war ended with the signing of the Treaty of Paris on December 10, 1898. As a result Spain lost its control over the remains of its overseas empire--Cuba, Puerto Rico, the Philippines Islands, Guam, and other islands. This war had a significant impact on the sisal industry in the Bahamas and eventually the Bahamas had to compete with the Philippines on an uneven footing. Fourteen mechanical mills in Andros, Abaco and Eleuthera were established to clean the fibre, and by 1902 production had been raised to nearly 1,000 tons, valued at £37,574.

Initially, this war had a positive impact on the Bahamas sisal industry when the disruption of the production of sisal in Cuba and the Philippines led to a false positive spur in the production and worldwide increase in the demand of sisal and hemp at end of the War. It was unfortunately only a brief benefit for the Bahamian sisal industry because after the war the Americans took over and revitalized the Cuban and Philippines sisal industries, which led to a slump, followed by a steady slide even further below profitable levels for the sisal. At the best of times, most sisal workers depended on almost completely on wage employment, and very few chanced growing sisal for themselves. Even then, wages were commonly paid in credit tokens, redeemable at company stores, rather than in cash. Unfortunately, when the market declined, so too did payments. There were significant cut backs in levels of payments and when this happened, their large debts owed to their employers further increased. As a result, it was no longer worthwhile or even profitable for even the most industrious Bahamian sisal farmer to grow sisal. Virtually no sisal workers became small freeholders under the terms of Governor Shea's land allotment scheme, and the miserable conditions under which those who couldn't escape were forced to live and work under similar conditions as those in the sponge industry at the hands of the Greeks.

As quickly did the sisal boom began so did the end. Sisal proved to be the most disappointing of all of the agricultural crops at the time because so much hope and promise had been attached to the success of this crop. The Chamberlain experience was typical in fate as the others. Rt. Hon. Joseph Chamberlain, Secretary of State for the Colonies had sent his son, Neville, later on he became the Prime Minister of Great Britain, to supervise his Andros Fibre Company. Planting began in 1892 and by April 1895, 6000 acres of former pine and scrub land had been brought into cultivation. The impact that it had on the local economy was quite noticeable, a new harbour was expanded and improved, new roads and railways built and new houses sprung up everywhere. A railway had been laid out from the coast for several miles into the forest as a cheap and reliable means to transport the sisal from the plantation in the Pine Barrens to the boat for shipping. However, in 1896, when the first plants were four years old and should have shown long and dark-green leaves, ready for harvesting, Neville Chamberlain noted that they were yellowish and stunted *"as bad as can be."* He wrote to his father, *"I no longer see a chance of making the investment pay. Practically nothing going on here-I confess I do not feel very sanguine about the future."* Finally, a year later he threw in the towel and conceded, *"I no longer see any chance of making the investment pay."* The sisal plant simply could not grow in the very rocky and infertile soils of the Bahamas. In 1940, Neville Chamberlain told his successor Winston Churchill that the tribulations he had suffered as Prime Minister of Britain reminded him of the tough times and disappointments he had endured as a young man trying to make a success of his father's sisal plantation in Andros.

Sisal products being sold at the local Straw Market in Downtown, Nassau (Courtesy of the Department of Archives, Nassau, Bahamas).

Making rope out of the sisal plant on a sisal plantation in Abaco (Courtesy of the Albert Lowe Museum-Used with permission).

In 1902, C.N. Mooney of the Baltimore Geographical Society wrote that *"the fibre industry of the Bahamas promises to become of great importance,"* but in fact the short lived boom for sisal was over. The Philippines were more than rejuvenated with American capital and the world price for sisal took a nose dive. As a result, the large Bahamian plantations, many of them badly located on unsuitable and infertile soils and an insufficient labour force fell into bankruptcy and the mills closed. Only J.S. Johnson in New Providence managed to continue to struggle on. Produced uneconomically on smallholdings and beaten crudely by hand in salt water, the quality and price of Bahamian fibre declined even further. The Government ordinances supervising the production and grading of the sisal became a dead letter and the Bahamian product became far inferior to that grown in vast quantities in India and East Africa. Although in 1923 over 2,000 tons were exported, the price per ton was less than half that of 1902. Plantation owners soon discovered that they could not compete with growers in other countries such as, Mexico, Africa, India and the

Philippines where the plants grew more luxuriantly in better soils, abundant rainfall and the labour was significantly cheaper. All of the large plantations failed and went out of business or moved elsewhere to another country. By 1946, although the world price soared again to £38 per ton, they could barely muster an insignificant 165 tons for export. The impact of this was disastrous to the local Bahamian economy. The closure of the Andros Fibre company resulted in 800 people being left unemployed. Throughout the Bahamas, thousands of others who had become accustomed to a daily wage were likewise affected, and those who were not attracted to the sponging industry could see no prospects of employment before them so they were forced to return to their previous subsistence agriculture to support their families. The final nail in the coffin for the sisal industry was the gradual substitution of synthetic fibre for natural fibres in the making of rope from the 1930s onwards.

CHAPTER SIX
THE BOOTLEGGING INDUSTRY IN THE BAHAMAS DURING THE GREAT ABACO HURRICANE OF 1932

Boxes and barrels of liquor in Nassau Harbour being prepared for shipping abroad during the Bootlegging era (Courtesy of the Department of Archives, Nassau, Bahamas).

In December 1919, *The Volstead Act*, a wartime measure, was passed by the United States Congress as the Eighteenth Amendment of the Constitution. Actually the official Act was known as the *National Prohibition Act,* known informally by the more popular term as the *Volstead Act.* One of the most famous periods of rum-running began in the United States with the Eighteenth Amendment (ratified January 16, 1919 by 287 votes in favor of this Act and 100 votes against it) and the Volstead Act (passed October 28, 1919) which was introduced by Representative Andrew Volstead(R-MN). Prohibition began on January 16, 1920, when the Eighteenth Amendment went into effect. While the Eighteenth Amendment to the United States Constitution prohibited the production, sale, and transport of 'intoxicating liquors,' it did not define what was 'intoxicating liquors' or provide penalties. It granted both the federal government and the states the power to enforce the ban by what was termed 'appropriate legislation.' A bill to do so was introduced in United States Congress in 1919. The bill was vetoed by President Woodrow Wilson, largely on technical grounds because it also covered wartime prohibition, but his veto was overridden by the House on the same day, October 28, 1919, and by the Senate one day later. The three distinct purposes of the Act were, first, to prohibit intoxicating beverages, second, to regulate the manufacture, sale, or transport of intoxicating liquor (but not consumption), and third to ensure an ample supply of alcohol and promote its use in scientific research and in the development of fuel, dye and other lawful industries and practices, such as religious rituals. It stipulated further that 'no person shall manufacture, sell, barter, transport, import, export, deliver, or furnish any intoxicating liquor except as authorized by this act.' It did not specifically prohibit the use of intoxicating liquors. The act defined intoxicating liquor as any beverage containing more than 0.5% alcohol by volume and superseded all existing Prohibition laws in effect in states that had such legislation.

The Act contained a number of exceptions and exemptions. Many of these were used to evade the law's intended purpose. For example, the Act allowed a physician to prescribe whiskey for his patients, but limited the amount that could be prescribed. Subsequently, the House of Delegates of the American Medical Association voted to submit to Congress a bill to remove the limit on the amount of whiskey that could be prescribed and questioning the ability of a legislature to determine the therapeutic value of any substance. The Act called for trials for anyone charged with an alcohol-related offense, and juries often failed to convict. Under the state of New York's Mullan-Gage Act, a short-lived local version of the Volstead Act, the first 4,000 arrests led to just six convictions and not one jail sentence.

This period lasted until the Eighteenth Amendment was repealed with ratification of the Twenty-First Amendment, on December 5, 1933. This ill-judged and ill-fated law, which condemned a large proportion of otherwise innocent Americans to hypocrisy and crime, made it an offence to manufacture, import or sell intoxicating liquors. For the Bahamas, it was truly an undisguised blessing. The term "Bootlegging" between 1920 and 1933 became a rich Bahamian Industry, in the swashbuckling tradition of privateering, wrecking and blockade running. The Bahamas was ideally suited for this illicit trade, because its nearest land was less than fifty miles from the American coast, was a neutral base for smuggling liquor into the thirsty United States. For the Bahamas no restrictive laws were ever passed or even proposed. Therefore, the Bahamas was ideally suited to become an important center for the trans-shipment of contraband, as it had been during the Civil War.

Rum-running, also known as 'bootlegging,' is the illegal business of shipping or smuggling boatloads of alcoholic beverages where such transportation is forbidden by law. Smuggling was widespread and extensive usually done to circumvent US taxation or prohibition laws within a US that banned these types of activities during the Volstead Act era. The term *rum-running* is more commonly applied to smuggling over water; *bootlegging* is applied to smuggling over land. It is believed that the term "bootlegging" originated during the Civil War, when soldiers would sneak liquor into army camps by concealing pint bottles within their boots or beneath their trouser legs. The term "rum-running" most likely originated at the start of Prohibition or Volstead Act in the United States (1920–1933), when ships from Bimini, Nassau and other Bahamian Islands transported cheap Caribbean rum into Florida and other coastal states.

With the start of Prohibition, Captain Bill McCoy one of the greatest rum-runners began bringing rum from Bimini and the rest of the Bahamas into South Florida through Government Cut. In the days of rum running, it was common for captains to add water to the bottles to stretch their profits, or to re-label it as better goods. Any cheap sparkling wine became French champagne or Italian Spumante; unbranded liquor became top-of-the-line name brands. McCoy became famous for never watering his booze, and selling only top brands. This is one of several reputed origins of the term *'The Real McCoy.'* The Coast Guard soon caught up with him, so he began to bring the illegal goods to just outside of the U.S. territorial waters and let smaller boats and other captains such as Habana Joe take the risk of bringing it into US mainland.

McCoy is credited with the idea of bringing large boats just to the edge of the three-mile limit of U.S. jurisdiction, and there selling his wares to what were called 'contact boats', local fishermen and small boat captains. These high-speed boats were often luxury yachts and speedboats fitted with powerful aircraft engines, machine guns, and armor plating. The small, quick boats could more easily outrun Coast Guard ships and could dock in any small river or eddy and transfer their cargo to a waiting truck. They were also known to load float planes and flying boats. Soon others were following suit; the three-mile limit became known as "the Rum Line" and the ships waiting were called "Rum Row". The Rum Line was extended to a 12-mile limit by an act of the United States Congress on April 21, 1924, which made it harder for the smaller and less seaworthy craft to make the trip. For 13 long years the FBI and the US Coast Guard fought a rough and tumble war to stem the flow of illegal liquor from Canada, Mexico, Cuba and the Bahamas. According to an official Coast Guard history, "Enormous profits were to be made, with stories of 700 per cent or more for the more popular Scotch, Cognac or Caribbean Rum. Probably the only reliable clues to the extent of the trade were the statistics on liquor passing through Nassau en route to the US: 50,000 quarts in 1917 to 10,000,000 in 1922." Perhaps an even better measure of the demand for alcohol was the fact that American doctors earned $40 million in 1928 by writing whiskey prescriptions. And the legal exception for sacramental wine was equally abused. It was said that some ships carried $200,000 in contraband in a single run.

At first the Bahamas lacked the vital infrastructure and necessary organization for this sort of illegal trade, and it was also not known if the Bahamian authorities would encourage or support this dubious export trade. Exports for 1920 and 1921 did not exceed by much the previous 10 years average of £30,000. It was not until the end of 1921 that it became obvious that the Bahamas would not actively support this US Law. More than twenty large liquor companies sprang up in Nassau almost overnight and fast motor-boats began the illegal operations of sneaking rum into the United States from Grand Bahama and Bimini. There were also faster boats or chartered schooners which took rum into the longer and more hazardous journey up to 'Rum Row' off New York and Philadelphia. There were also chartered planes used as well taking off from Bimini and illegally landing in secluded lakes deep into the Florida Everglades. Just off the US coast were a fleet of Coast Guard ships some seventy five feet in length and capable of over 14 knots lying in wait for these rum-running ships from the Bahamas. At sundown, it was a thrilling sight to see fifty or sixty of them in Bimini harbour, line up bow to stern, engines running, waiting for the opportunity to slip pass the ever-watchful eyes of the US Coast Guard ships.

The smugglers developed a highly effective and efficient modi operandi when it came to smuggling rum into the United States. On deserted beaches and inlets along the sparsely populated Florida east coast the receivers, by pre-arrangement, would be ready waiting for the distinctive roaring sound of the smugglers engines. A signal from a flashlight would indicate whether it was safe to offload their products. If the Coast Guard vessels or Revenue Officers were noticed or in the vicinity, the craft would quickly take off and move to a second or even third pre-arranged location. With the stern of the vessel brought as near to the shore as possible, the persons onshore would form a human chain and pass along the sacks of rum into a waiting van and speed was important so this all had to be done in less than twenty minutes or they risked being caught. During the daylight hours, small sea-planes would operate. After passing the turquoise blue waters of the Gulf Stream and the Florida east coast, they would land in some deserted stretch of water in the lonely Everglades. Their cargoes were small, twelve to fifteen sacks. But for each trip the pilot and plane were paid $500, and some of them made as many as five trips per day.

Gangsters in the 1920's and early 1930's that made a living of selling and distributing alcohol were generally known as bootleggers. Bootlegging refers to the illegal sale, transportation, or manufacturing of alcohol during the prohibition.

Usually, these power boats transported about 300 sacks of whisky or gin, containing six quarts each. The cost at Bimini or other nearby places was $12 to $14 per sack. Smuggled ashore in Florida the same sack brought $100 to $120. Each boat had a two man crew, a captain who received $1,000 a trip, and a mate who was paid $500. Often times, two round trips would be made between dusk and dawn. English and Scottish liquor manufacturers who had become accustomed to small orders from the Bahamas were soon shipping vast quantities. The steamers which brought it, were simply too large for Nassau Harbour so they had to anchor off the bar or nearby anchorages, and the cargo had to be taken ashore in smaller boats. Warehouses were built all along the waterfront as in the blockade running days, to accommodate the flood of cases and barrels of liquor. Re-exports of liquor skyrocketed in 1922 to over £1,612,12, an increase of tenfold over the figures for 1921. The total for 1923 was £1,591,538 and the average for the ten years between 1922 and 1932 was well over half a million pounds. The number of ships leaving Bahamian ports rose from 486 of 81,129 tons displacement in 1919, to 1,681 of 718,110 tons in 1922. In that year, 714 cleared from Nassau, 567 from Grand Bahama and 306 from Bimini and all available ships were hired for the transportation of rum into the United States. The Bahamas Government was one of the greatest benefiters of this Volstead Act by levying heavy taxes on these rum imports. The Customs Act of 1919 had laid comparatively heavy duties upon imported liquor and, with the great increase in the rum trade so did the revenue from these taxes to the Bahamas Treasury. Brandy paid 24 shillings per proof gallon, rum 8 shillings and whisky 12 shillings to 24 shillings for every dozen "reputed quarts." Customs receipts sky-rocketed from £103,492 in 1919 to £313,949 in 1921 and £640,798 in 1923, and this was only a small portion of the wealth that flooded into Nassau.

The headquarters of the bootleggers were the *Lucerne Hotel*, a three story building located on Frederick Street, and the well-named *Bucket of Blood* which was located on George Street and was later burned down in a fire in 1942. These hotels accommodated a steady stream of American visitors who played dice at $50 a throw, drank unlimited amount of booze and arranged their deals. The *Lucerne*, managed by a middle-aged lady from New England whom the rum-runners referred to affectionately as 'Mother', was the venue for all of the activities and parties held by the Bootleggers. Many of these persons were considered dangerous back home in the United States, and even criminal. Under the same roof slept members of rival gangs who, if they met in the United States, would greet each other with bullets. But the Commandant of Police made his inspection tour of the premises every evening, advising everyone to keep their weapons out of sight, and that there would be no gun play in Nassau, and so said, so done as there were never any problems from them.

This was a boom period for the Bahamas as revenue earned from this illicit trade helped financed a raise for the civil servants, the government debt was paid off, wages for black labourers rose to $6 a day, two new hotels were built, the harbour was deepened to a depth of over 20 feet and Prince George Wharf was built and other wharves lengthened. The electricity, water supply and sewerage systems were modernized and new cars were imported into the Capital in droves to take advantage of the newly built roads. Ten-year contracts were signed and subsidies paid for a year-round steamer service from New York and winter service from Miami. If the Out Islands, as always lagged behind, Nassau began to take on for the first time the appearance of a modern city, while losing little of its 'old colonial charm.' The boom period during this time was so great that then Governor Bede Clifford even suggested that a statue of Prohibition's enforcer, Senator Andrew Volstead be placed on the side of Christopher Columbus or Queen Victoria as a thank you gift to him for what he did for the Bahamas. In fact, in March, 1920, the *London Times* reported that Prohibition boom had changed the Bahamas Government from a debt ridden government to a surplus driven government and provided labour for many unemployed Bahamians who under normal circumstances would be broke and penniless and circulated more money into the local economy than they had seen in many years.

The American Consul in Nassau was instructed by his Government to do everything possible to suppress the trade, however, he could only report, month after month that the trade was as vibrant as ever and every time he looked around there was some new development happening around the city of Nassau. From every imported case and barrel of liquor, the Bahamas Government extracted a tax. At one time this amounted to twenty-four shillings a case, but because of fears that such a high tax would discourage the rum-runners to go elsewhere, it was reduced to twelve shillings. One hundred thousand pounds in revenue seemed to be the best that the colony could hope for during the ten years preceding Prohibition. Often, the revenue was considerably less than this. The year ending 31st March, 1920, showed an almost unprecedented upturn. The revenue exceeded expenditure by £95,000, an amount that was greater than the original total estimate of receipts. This surplus was more than enough to wipe out the public debt of £69,000. Two years later, the revenue rose to £471,000 and in another year to £853,000. Of this latest figure, £716,000 represented import duty on liquor. At that time, the Treasury surplus, despite unprecedented expenditure, had climbed to £265,000. From 1926 to 1930, Government revenue topped the million pounds mark each year and did not show a significant decline until 1931. A year after the repeal of the Prohibition Amendment, they dropped significantly to £276,000.

Actually, here in the Bahamas only a select few Bahamian families really benefited a great deal from this trade and very rarely did the profits trickled down to the average Bahamian in a significant way. However, some did benefit because an ordinary labourers, who otherwise prior to this trade were lucky enough to earn a dollar a day, were paid six times as much for handling liquor. On the other hand, if they worked at loading the American-bound vessels their gratuities often exceeded their pay. Women as well as men were employed to work on the docks, and many private individuals leased out their cellars and made some money from the trade. By February 1921, Governor Harry Cordeaux reported that 31 permanent or temporary bonded warehouses were needed to store the 13,700 barrels and 37,400 cases imported so far.

The Bahamian revenue earned from liquor imports and exports soared from £81,049 in 1919, to £1,065,899 in 1923. Even with the reduction in duties, the increased vigilance of US agents, and Bahamian customs evasion, this revenue did not fall below £500,000 a year before 1930. Some gauge of the profits to be made by the fortunate few can be illustrated by the figures supplied by F. Van de Water in his book *'The Real McCoy'* first published in 1931. A schooner-load of 5,700 cases of Scotch whisky cost $170,000 duty paid in Nassau. Delivered to the ships stationed off New York or Boston, it was worth $342,000. Landed in the States, its value had doubled again to $684,000, and by the time the actual drinker received the alcohol it might have cost $2,000,000. William McCoy of Seneca, New York, estimated that in four years he shipped 175,000 cases of liquor out of Nassau. On one voyage alone he cleared a profit of $130,000. But it must be noted that these persons who profited most from this illicit trade never even sailed one ship nor sold to any person in the United States a pint of booze. They did not have to go so far;

buyers flooded their offices, took the liquor direct to the chartered ships and sailed away.

A rare 1980, Bootlegging Era-21 Cent Stamp celebrating the Bootlegging Era in the Bahamas.

The strict foreign capital laws attracted the merchant class as well as some of the most prominent Bahamians including the Bethells, Christies, Collins, Kellys, Sands and Symonettes. Prohibition brought an almost quantum leap in the number of Bahamian born white Bay Street merchants. They all made money from this trade and a few even became millionaires in a very short time. It must be noted also that these families were the dominant persons in the House of Assembly and the Colonial Legislature. It would have been short-sighted indeed if an assembly of any composition had legislated against such windfall, one of the least happy aspects of the Prohibition boom was that it produced an even deeper divide between the 'haves' and the 'have-nots.' The Tariff Amendment Act (No. 2) of 1920 allowed an 80% drawback on liquor re-exported from the colony, provided proof could be shown by the merchant that the liquor had been landed outside the Bahamas and would not be mixed with other spirits. Furthermore, the Tariff Act of 1923 decreed a 50% discount on whisky produced within the British Empire.

Falsification of returns and manifest became a commonplace on Bahamian business practice. By a convenient myth, most of the liquor re-exported from the Bahamas was sent to the small French island of Miquelon off the coast of Newfoundland. Bahamian exports to Miquelon, none in 1920, were £25,000 in 1921 and £1,208,718 in 1922. This figure represented 66.2% of the total Bahamian exports for that year. In fact, in 1917, before the United States Prohibition era, 38,000 gallons were imported into the Bahamas. By 1922, the quantity had increased thirty-five times over and stood at 1,340,000 gallons. There were these above named regular liquor merchants in Nassau who imported and exported, advertised their products, bottled and communicated with the buyers in coded telegrams. A larger number invested their money and received their dividends in secret, and an even larger number, make an indirect connection with the trade, without too much torture to their consciences. Needless to say, the official figures for liquor re-exported only represented a small proportion of the trade. An unknown quantity not only left the colony but also entered it, as contraband, and was never assessed at the bond warehouses.

From the beginning of this trade, there was a close correlation between the rich liquor merchants and the business of real estate in the Bahamas. During the 1920s, the Bahamas enjoyed a significant boom in land investment that was really but an extension of the almost insane speculation in Florida land during the early 1900s. Pan American Airways started a daily flight, taking 2 ½ hours, from Miami in 1929, and rich American visitors began to buy cheap land and build homes they could reach in a few hours from anywhere in the States. It was a significant coincidence that one of the chief pioneers of aviation in the Bahamas made his first fortune in real estate. In New Providence during the 1920s, the Eastern Road, the Grove, Prospect Ridge and Cable Beach (once the site of J.S. Johnson's pineapple farm) became dotted with the stucco palaces of American derived riches. A new hotel, the Rod and Gun Club, and modern houses were built at Bimini, and many small Cays were bought and sold and bought again by optimistic speculators. In all, it has been estimated that approximately four to five million dollars were invested in Bahamian land and building during the ten years that followed the passing of the Eighteenth Amendment.

As with most Bahamian industries at the time, just as quickly had this boom period in the Bahamas began, so too did it end. Initially, the bootleggers had considered it great sport to play hide and seek with the slower and much more cumbersome large Coast Guard ships because they could easily outrun and out-maneuver them. But soon these fleets of Coast Guard ships were improved to include smaller and faster boats which could match speeds with the bootleggers. Also, a Coast Guard vessel was positioned to watch each and every ship anchored at 'Rum Row', and shore patrols were kept informed of every single activity by wireless telegraph. As many as twenty-one vessels patrolled the Miami-Fort Lauderdale area. The fast runners from the northwestern Bahamas faced a virtual blockade. As a result, thirsty Americans were compelled to depend more and more on their own moonshine whisky and bath-tub gin, until this act was repealed. Furthermore, the world-wide slump better known as the *Great Depression of 1929* which began in October, 1929, brought new investment into the Bahamas to a virtual standstill, but while Prohibition was still in force, there was always a steady, if declining, inflow of liquor money. Only upon the repeal of Prohibition by the Twenty-First Amendment in the first year of Franklin D. Roosevelt's first term as President did the source dry up. "Unclassified re-exports" for 1935 had fallen to a measly total of £121,000.

During the Great Depression, President Roosevelt and the American people decided to put an end to the "noble experiment" of prohibition. In 1919, those who fought for prohibition really believed it would help with the problems of poverty, crime, and other moral vices. However, crime only increased during the 1920s, and by 1930 many organizations sprung up to campaign for the repeal of prohibition. During Franklin D. Roosevelt's campaign of 1932, he ran on a platform that included repealing prohibition. The American people, especially the women who had once as a group advocated prohibition, now saw its repeal as a chance to lower crime and even help the struggling economy. The 21st Amendment was fully ratified on December 5, 1933 and prohibition ended. This "noble experiment" gave the United States one of the most colourful periods of history, where bootleggers like Al Capone ran their speakeasies, drank their bath-tub rum, and gained legendary status during this "dry" time in America.

CHAPTER SEVEN

THE SPONGING INDUSTRY DURING THE GREAT BAHAMIAN HURRICANES OF 1899 AND 1932

In the Bahamas in the 1800s, the sea itself was by no means unproductive, yet little of its abundance could be exported with ease. The exceptions were turtle shells, ambergris, and an occasional pearl. On land, the sisal industry developed in the late 1880's and 1890's also became an important industry in the Bahamas. Unfortunately, the acquisition of the Philippine Islands by the United States led to the decline of the Bahamian sisal industry. This privileged access to the American market by the Philippines meant that the Bahamas was unable to compete on an equal footing and was therefore left at a distinct disadvantage. The large Bahamian estates, many of them badly located on unsuitable and nutrient lacking soils with an insufficient labour force, fell into bankruptcy and the mills closed. Produced uneconomically on smallholdings and beaten crudely by hand in salt water, the quality and price of the Bahamian Fibre declined even further. The government ordinances supervising the production and grading the sisal became a dead letter and the Bahamian product became far inferior to those grown in vast quantities in the Philippines, India and East Africa. By the 1920s, the sisal industry in the Bahamas was dead. Worldwide, by the late 1930's it came to an end with the introduction of synthetic

Sketches of the various stages within the Sponging Industry (from the harvesting of the sponges to the shipping of the sponges) here in the Bahamas (Courtesy of the Department of Archives Nassau, Bahamas).

nylon which was much cheaper to produce and more versatile than the natural sisal plant. This opened the door to the more lucrative sponge trade.

Sponge kralls on west side of Andros

Sponge Kraals on the west side of Andros (Courtesy of the Bahamas Department of Archives, Nassau, Bahamas).

Many Bahamian men accustomed to making their living on boats or on land turned their attention from sisal production more fully to marine resource extraction, in particular the sea sponge industry. In the late 1800s and early 1900s, farming, fishing, sponging, sisal production and wrecking and salvaging were the five main ways most Bahamians supported their families. Throughout the 17th and 18th centuries, products from the sea such as, conch shells, turtle shells, and turtle meat had been exported from the Bahamas but on a much lesser scale, however, it was sponging that was the first industry which was profitable enough to employ thousands of men for nearly a century.

From 1841 to 1910 exports grew exponentially, reaching a peak of 1.5 million metric tons. The sponging industry began as early as 1841 when a Frenchman named M. Gustave Renouard was shipwrecked here in the Bahamas. He exported parcels of prized Bahamian sponges to Paris, where the varieties from *'wool'* to *'velvet'* found in the Bahamas were highly favoured over sponges from the Mediterranean(prior to this time, sponges were imported from the Mediterranean). The export trade was greatly expanded by Mr. Edward Brown,

Renouard's son-in-law, and the Great Bahama Bank was opened up to full scale development. This large extensive area offshore from the island of Andros was called *'The Mud'* and was about 140 miles long and 10 to 40 miles wide and was one of the greatest sponge beds in the world. The seabed was shallow and the water very clear enabling the sponge fishermen to easily harvest the sponges from the seabed with little effort or diving equipment as compared to other areas of the world. This trade eventually encompassed, Jamaica, Honduras, Nicaragua, and Mexico, however, the Bahamas, Cuba, and Florida were always the largest producers.

Workers at a sponge warehouse in Nassau preparing sponges for export (Courtesy of the Department of Archives, Nassau, Bahamas).

Before the Second World War, well over 47 million pounds of live sponges were harvested annually from our waters and employed thousands of people and hundreds of ships here in the Bahamas. Although marine sponges have been a highly sought after product since ancient times, industrialization created a growing worldwide demand for them in cleaning, ceramics, shoe-finishing, and printing industries in addition to household, bathing, and medical uses, which generated a lucrative international trade. As Bahamian sponges became highly favored on the world market, further beds were opened on the Little Bahama Bank, off southern Eleuthera and in Acklins. A Sponge Exchange was opened in Nassau and many Greeks familiar with the trade emigrated from Greece, bringing with them their families, language, religion and customs, which are still proudly maintained in the Bahamas today. In fact, the Vouvalis Company brought in the first Greek sponge experts in 1887. Vouvalis established his sponge warehouse on West Bay Street between the now Mayfair Hotel and the now defunct Ocean Spray Restaurant and Hotel. He then sent Aristide Daminanos and his brother George here to manage his business. The Damianos brothers would eventually set up their own business at the top of Fredrick Street steps. In the 1920s Christodoulos Esfakis established an operation on Market Street and many other Greeks sponge merchants opened similar operations in or near the Downtown area. James Mosko was brought in to rebuild the Vouvalis operation after the *Nassau Hurricane of 1926* devastated his sponge warehouse and his son would eventually establish Mosko's Construction Company. Over time the Greeks were more or less assimilated, and the second, third and fourth generations still now form a close-knit community of more than 300 professionals and business owners scattered throughout the Bahamas.

In 1901, at the peak of the Bahamian sponge industry, there were 265 schooners of up to 43 tons burden, 322 sloops of up to 16 tons and 2,808 open boats engaged in sponging. It was 5,967 men and boys, or roughly one-third of the available labour force, were employed in this trade. The sponge fishermen were all Bahamians; it was illegal for non-Bahamians to engage directly in harvesting the sponge. Before a vessel went out on a sponge fishing trip, the 'outfitter' as he was called, furnished the consumable goods and services to the sponge fishermen. This was done entirely on a credit basis and he was not reimbursed until the catch was marketed at the end of the voyage. The goods were booked at cost, plus a considerable margin of profit. These 'personal advances' to members of the crew, often including food for their families, were recovered at high rates of interest, making it almost impossible for the sponge fishermen to make any economic profit. Often he was left in debt seldom breaking even. It was very rare for a fisherman to even make three hundred dollars a year. The outfitters, however, felt justified in their high rates, as they themselves took considerable risks. Their vessels were not insured and there were risks of bad weather such as, hurricanes in the summer and gales in the winter, which affected the size of the catch, mismanagement and unscrupulous behavior on the part of the crew, theft from kraals, and damage to the catch during transit to Nassau.

Workers clipping sponges in preparation for export at the sponge exchange warehouse in Nassau, Bahamas (Courtesy of the Department of Archives, Nassau, Bahamas).

The sponging trips usually lasted from five to eight weeks. Each sponging schooner or sloop carried about five dinghies which were used for gathering the sponge. The value of the catch was almost wholly dependent upon the skill of the fishermen and the fickle luck of the Bahamian weather. At the sponge beds, the water was very clear and shallow only between eight to twenty four feet deep making it very easy to harvest the sponges. Once the sponges were harvested they would be placed in large storage and cleaning containments called 'kraals' filled with salt water which allowed the animal matter to die because the sponge is really the skeleton of a soft coral. The sponge kraal was an enclosed pen, fenced in by sticks of wood or mangrove to allow a free circulation of the ebb and tidal flow of the sea water. Here, the sponges were soaked and washed for four to six days by the action of the sea water. The sponge vessels visited the kraal once a week to land the sponge load. The sponges were then taken out and beaten with sticks until the decayed outer coverings had been entirely removed. After the sponges were beaten and gelatinous tissue removed, they were scraped to remove excess coral, sand or rock. After the dead animal was washed out and they would then be clipped, graded and strung in the boat rigging to dry.

They then took the sponges to Nassau where the sponges were sold by auction to the Greeks merchants who were agents for houses in New York, London and Paris. Once at the exchange, men and women, usually women sat on boxes clipping the sponges using sheep-shearing shears. During the clipping of the sponges the women often smoked their clay tobacco pipes and sang spirituals and other religious hymns to keep themselves occupied. The roots were cut off, and the sponges trimmed, retaining the symmetry of the sponge as much as possible. Once trimmed, and the pieces of rock removed, the sponges were thrown into large native straw baskets. A full basket was removed and handed over to the 'sorters' who trimmed the sponges further if necessary, and examined them for elasticity, size and texture. They were then placed in pens, packaged and prepared for shipping.

Until the disastrous visitation of a microscopic fungus which devastated up to about 90 percent of all the West Atlantic sponges and all the Bahamian 'velvet' variety in November and December of 1938, sponge continued to be the major item in the Bahamian economy. In December 1938, spongers instead of pulling up intact sponges, hooks came to the surface with only slivers and strings and the rest of the sponge skeleton at the bottom of the seafloor had disintegrated due to this deadly fungus. Within two months from the time it was first observed, the disease (fatal only to sponge) had reached epidemic proportions and had wiped out ninety-nine percent of the sponge; as a result, thousands of Bahamians lost their livelihood because of this disaster. The sponge disease appeared in Florida about three months after it had struck the beds in the Bahamas. It was believed to have been transmitted to the Florida sponge beds by means of the ocean currents. In addition to the fungus which destroyed the sponge beds, hurricanes, the introduction of synthetic sponges and over sponging also led to a great decline in the trade. Sea sponge is a very slow growing sea animal and whenever the sponges were harvested; the entire sponge was removed from the sea bottom thereby not allowing re-growth by the sponge. Furthermore, the sponges in the area of the Mud was a finite resource so gradually, the sponges in the late 1920's and early 1930's were already starting to see a drastic decline in the industry even before the fungus attacked the sponges. As a result of this decline, the demand for sponge at this time was high, and so consequently the price, due to the scarcity of it. Up to 1925 it must have seemed that sponge-fishing would endure forever and get better and better. At that time, the total annual income earned by sponge fishermen soared to over £200,000, and the local song, *'Sponger Money Never Done,'* commemorated both the durability and prosperity of the sponge trade.

Workers at the Sponge Exchange in Downtown Nassau (Courtesy of the

Department of Archives, Nassau, Bahamas).

The series of severe hurricanes(hurricanes of 1866, 1899, 1926, 1928, 1929, 1932 and 1933), which began in 1866, did much damage to the sponge beds and schooners, but apart from this, there developed unmistakable evidence of over sponging. The deadly 1899 Hurricane, the three hurricanes in 1926(plus a tropical storm), the 1929 Hurricane and a series of other hurricanes in the late 1920's and 1930's devastated the sponge beds. In addition, these hurricanes especially, the three powerful hurricanes in 1926, one in 1929, one in 1932 and a series of other powerful hurricanes in the 1930's (1933 had four hurricanes and one tropical storm which hit the Bahamas) destroyed the sponging infrastructures such as, the warehouses and the sponging schooners and sloops. For example, H. & F. Pritchard were among the most important Bahamian sponge merchants, and in 1899 this powerful hurricane struck the Bahamas and totally destroyed both their ships and the sponges. Another hurricane struck the Bahamas in 1883 totally wiping out the sponge beds in Eleuthera. After the three hurricanes of 1926, the sponge industry was crippled and sponge cultivation diminished considerably in spite of efforts on the part of sponge businessmen Mr. H.C. Christie, father of the late Sir Harold Christie, to encourage artificial sponge cultivation.

Although sponge planting produced encouraging results, output still diminished considerably, largely due to over-sponging of the beds, and the practice of hooking the younger, and not-quite matured sponges. This abuse led to the Agricultural and Marine Products Board Sponge Amendment Rules of 1937 which forbade the fishing of sponge under a certain size and imposed a closed season. In 1929, a powerful and deadly hurricane known as *'The Great Bahamas Hurricane of 1929'* devastated the sponging infrastructures in Nassau and wiped out many of the sponging schooners on some of the Family Islands, especially on the islands of Andros, Eleuthera and Abaco, further crippling the industry. In fact, from 1926 to 1940 at least two storms a year devastated the Bahamas and the sponge beds (except for 1930 when there was none and 1931 when there was only one). So these storms changed the economy of the Bahamas and it can be argued that hurricanes played a minor if not a major role in the decline of the sponging industry.

Sponge fishermen on the west side of Andros inside of a sponge kraal containment beating the sponges to get rid of the decayed animal matter contained inside of the sponge. The purpose of the kraal was to allow the tidal flow of the sea water to wash away this decayed animal matter (Courtesy of the Department of Archives, Nassau, Bahamas).

The optimism of Bahamian sponge fishermen about the sustained growth of sponging was reflected in the local song, "Sponger Money Never Done." A popular version sung by the late great Bahamian folklore artist George Symonette. He was a black musician hired by Alexander Maillis and was originally part of Leonard White's Chocolate Dandies Orchestra, a superb athlete, musician and pharmacist; he became renowned for his piano playing and singing skills. George Symonette made this song famous on an album called *'George Symonette, Bahamian Troubadour: "Calypso" and the Native Bahamian Rhythms.'* On this album, it featured the popular songs called *'Delia Gone,' 'Sponger Money' and 'Peas N Rice.'* His other popular Bahamian songs were, *'Don't touch me tomato,' 'Nassau*

Samba (when you come to little Nassau),' 'No Lazy Man (Did you see Uncle Lou when he fall in the well),' 'Jones Oh Jones,' and '*See how it flies (Run ma mama come see da crow).'* If you mention any of these popular Bahamian folk songs by George Symonette, most older Bahamians will not only immediately recognize them but will perhaps give you a few words from each of them or if you are lucky enough, they may even sing you a chorus. However his most popular song was *"Sponger Money Never Done"* based on life and money made in the sponging industry during its' heyday. A song of the era and was perhaps one of George Symonette's all time favorite songs. As the song goes, in those days it seemed as if the sponger money would really never done. His unique style no doubt helped earn him the much deserved title as *"King of Goombay."* George was a star attraction in Nassau where he delighted both locals and tourists with his easy going personality and sharp wit. George Symonette was not only tall in stature, measuring at nearly six and a half feet, but is said to have been like a tower over the music scene in the Bahamas during his reign as the King of Goombay.

The late great George Symonette in the front of his piano.

A pharmacist by profession, George worked at the Bahamas General Hospital, the now Princess Margaret Hospital for a time before opening his own drug store in the Kemp Road area of Nassau. George was an avid sportsman, a fine gentleman, and a talented pianist all in one. He enjoyed playing to the extent that his passion for performing could no longer remain on the back burner. His beginnings in music were no doubt influenced by the music of the church. His father, the late Reverend Alfred Carrington Symonette of Acklins, Bahamas, no doubt was pleased with his son being the organist at the St. James Baptist Church off Kemp Road. While the guitar and assorted percussion instruments were the instruments of choice for most calypsonians, George entertained from behind the piano. He was one of the original performers in the region to capture the native sound of the Bahamas which continues to play on stereos all over the world today.

SPONGER MONEY NEVER DONE

Go gal go, go gal go, gal ya gat sponger money,
sponger money never done ya gat sponger money,
sponger money is a lotta fun ya gat sponger money,
sing gal sing, sing gal sing ya gat sponger money,

Laugh gal laugh, laugh gal laugh ya gat sponger money
Ya gat Bay Street money, Bay Street money is a lot of fun
ya gat Bay Street money, Bay Street money is a lot of fun
ya gat Bay Street money
sing gal sing, sing gal sing ya gat sponger money,

Laugh gal laugh, laugh gal laugh ya gat sponger money
Ya gat straw work money, straw work money is a lot of fun
ya gat straw work money, straw work money is a lot of fun
ya gat straw work money
sing gal sing, sing gal sing ya gat sponger money,

Laugh gal laugh, laugh gal laugh ya gat sponger money
Ya gat tomato money, tomato money is a lot of fun
ya gat tomato money, tomato money is a lot of fun

ya gat Tomato money
sing gal sing, sing gal sing ya gat sponger money,

Laugh gal laugh, laugh gal laugh ya gat sponger money
Ya gat tourist money, tourist money is a lot of fun
ya gat tourist money, tourist money is a lot of fun
ya gat tourist money
sing gal sing, sing gal sing ya gat sponger money,

Laugh gal laugh, laugh gal laugh ya gat sponger money
sailor money never done ya gat sailor money, sailor
money is a lot of fun ya gat sailor money,
sing gal sing, sing gal sing ya gat sponger money,

Go gal go, go gal go, gal ya gat sponger money,
sponger money never done ya gat sponger money,
sponger money is a lot of fun ya gat sponger money,
sponger money never done ya gat sponger money,
sponger money is a lot of fun ya gat sponger money,

Another song written about the Bahamas sponge trade was the very popular song called '*The John B Sails*' which was sung by most of the popular local Bahamian folk Artists like, Blind Blake, Joseph Spence and George Symonette and popular international Artists like the Beach Boys, Jerry Butler, The Kingston Trio and Johnny Cash. This song was written in 1900 a year after the Great Bahamas Hurricane of 1899 and during the peak of the sponging era, hence the need for sloops to travel around Nassau. "The John B. Sails" is a folk song that first appeared internationally in a 1917 American novel, *Pieces of Eight*, written by Richard Le Gallienne. The "secret" narrator of the story describes it as "one of the quaint Nassau ditties," the first verse and chorus of which are:

Come on the sloop *John B.*
My grandfather and me,
Round Nassau town we did roam;
Drinking all night, ve got in a fight,
Ve feel so break-up, ve vant to go home.

(Chorus)
So h'ist up the *John B.* sails,
See how the mainsail set,
Send for the captain—shore, let us go home,
Let me go home, let me go home,
I feel so break-up, I vant to go home.

There are many versions of this song and below is another version:

SLOOP JOHN B

We come on the Sloop John B., my grandfather and me.
Around Nassau town we did roam.
Drinking all night, got into a fight,
Well I feel so break up, I want to go home.

So hoist up the John B's sails, see how the main sail sets,
Call for the captain ashore, and let me go home.
Let me go home, I want to go home,
Well I feel so break up, I want to go home.

The first mate, he got drunk, broke up the people's trunk,
The constable had to come and take him away.
Sheriff John Stone, why don't you leave me alone?
Well I feel so break up, I want to go home.

So hoist up the John B's sails, see how the main sail sets,
Call for the captain ashore, and let me go home.
Let me go home, I want to go home,
Well I feel so break up, I want to go home.

The poor cook he caught the fits, threw away all my grits,
Then he took and ate up all of my corn.
Let me go home, I want to go home,
This is the worst trip I've ever been on.

So hoist up the John B's sails, see how the main sail sets,
Call for the captain ashore, and let me go home.

Let me go home, I want to go home,
Well I feel so break up, I want to go home.

"Sloop John B" was the seventh track on The Beach Boys' popular *Pet Sounds* album and was also a single which was released in 1966 on Capitol Records. It was originally a traditional West Indies folk song, 'The John B. Sails,' taken from a collection by Carl Sandburg in 1927. Alan Lomax made a field recording of the song in Nassau in, 1935, under the title "Histe Up the John B. Sail." This recording appeared on the album *'Bahamas 1935: Chanteys And Anthems From Andros And Cat Island.'* The song was adapted by The Weavers member Lee Hays and they recorded it as "The Wreck of the John B." The Kingston Trio's 1958 made a recording of the song, also under the title "The Wreck of the John B.," was the direct influence on the Beach Boys' version. Popular Country artist Johnny Cash recorded the song in 1959 as "I Want To Go Home." Jimmie Rodgers recorded the song in 1960 as "The Wreck of John B.", which reached #64 on the Billboard pop chart. The Beach Boys version of "Sloop John B." was ranked #271 on Rolling Stone's list of *'The 500 Greatest Songs of All Time.'* The Beach Boys' version of the song, titled *"Sloop John B"*, influenced by the Kingston Trio's 1958 version, but with modified minor chord changes by Al Jardine and slightly altered lyrics by Brian Wilson, entered the Billboard Hot 100 chart on April 2, and peaked at #3 on May 7, remaining on the chart, in total, for 11 weeks. It also charted highly throughout the world, remaining as one of the Beach Boys' most popular recordings. The *John B.* was a real old Bahamian sponger boat - presumably a sloop and not a schooner - whose crew were in the habit of getting notoriously merry or drunk whenever they made port after a sponging trip. It was wrecked and sunk at Governor's Harbour in Eleuthera, in about 1900 just a year after the Great Bahamas Hurricane of 1899 devastated the islands of the Bahamas during the sponge trade.

When the first signs of disease appeared in 1938, the industry and sponge population were already severely stressed from devastating hurricanes, over-sponging and only a few reserve populations remained. This disease ultimately reduced the remaining commercial sponge populations by up to 99%. Over sponging, the introduction of synthetic sponges, hurricanes and sponge disease caused a drastic decline in the sponging industry in the 1930s. By the 1940s, the economic situation in the Bahamas was again so desperate that the British (the Bahamas was still a colony of England at the time) and Bahamian officials began in earnest to develop export and subsistence fisheries to support the local population. In 1935, the Bahamas export in sponges ranked third in quantity but seventh in value. Sponge output had been diminishing for a little while due to over-sponging of the beds. For example, the total weight of the sponge exported in 1940 was 70,848lbs, and the total value was 13,986($41,958) as compared to 164,000($492,000) in 1917. This shows the tremendous decline in the total sponge exports brought about by over sponging and the disease of 1938. The low output was also attributed to a poorer quality of sponge being fished from the beds. Probably with diminishing output, the sponge fishermen were not conscientious of the quality of the sponges they removed.

A Sponge Yard in Downtown Nassau, which shows sponges laid out in lots, sized and graded in preparation for an upcoming auction. If you look real close you will see the sponge vessels in the background.

The sponging industry received a devastating blow from the Great Bahamas Hurricane of 1899. As a result of the Great Bahamas Hurricane of 1899, a fleet of approximately 336 vessels were destroyed, with twice that amount being badly damaged. If this hurricane did not hit the Bahamas, the vessels would have been used to harvest the sponges. It was estimated that during the Great Bahamas Hurricane of 1899, at least eighty nine percent of the sponging vessels throughout the Bahamas were destroyed. The entire sponging industry fleet in 1899 represented an actual loss value of well over £15,707 to shipping alone. In addition to the losses of the sponging vessels and the schooners which were owned by the sponge brokers and merchants, they also had to absorb the loss of outfitting the fishermen and schooners, including stores and advances to the crewmen and their families during the lying up period. After this storm was over, well over 334 persons died and over 3,000 were left homeless or a similar amount of men that were left unemployed as a result of the destroyed sponging vessels at Andros and Exuma. Many remained unemployed for well over a year after the storm, further exacerbating

Numerous sponging schooners in Nassau Harbour (Courtesy of the Department of Archives Nassau, Bahamas).

the economic hardships that these residents throughout the Bahamas faced. In addition, these men had families to support so this storm affected them in a negative way as well and many women became instant widows and had to fend for themselves after their husbands were killed. This sponger money was vital because it circulated throughout the country and kept the industry and the Bahamian economy going and helped sustained the majority of Bahamian families. As a result, many persons especially on the Family Islands found it very difficult to make ends meet and many Bahamians went to bed hungry with little or no food for many months to follow.

Today in the Bahamas, the sponge industry has almost come to a complete halt with the more commercially viable industries of Tourism, Agriculture, Sports and Commercial fishing, and Banking and Finance providing sustainable economic growth for the Bahamian Economy. However, it is important to note that today sponging is still harvested and exported from the Bahamas but on a much lesser scale than during its heyday, such as in Mangrove Cay and Red Bays, Andros. Some of it is sold locally in the tourism market mainly for souvenir sales and the rest is exported. Aside from its cultural fascination, the history of the Bahamas sponge industry has important lessons for the future of other valuable marine resources like conch, lobster and grouper. That is that these resources are not limitless and requires careful management or we risk losing them just like we did with the sponging industry. The era of sponge fishing lasted less than a century, but it left its mark on the culture and economy of the Bahamas and the ecology of the reefs that will never ever be forgotten.

CHAPTER EIGHT

THE GREAT BAHAMAS HURRICANE OF 1899 IMPACT ON THE ISLANDS OF THE BAHAMAS.

METEOROLOGICAL TRACK OF THE GREAT BAHAMAS HURRICANE OF 1899

One of the most remarkable storms to ever hit the Caribbean was the Great Bahamas Hurricane of 1899(San Ciriaco Hurricane), which cut a swath of destruction from the West Indies to the coast of France in the late summer of 1899. This powerful and very destructive hurricane, with maximum sustained winds of about 150 mph, was responsible for many deaths and much destruction during its lifetime. This storm has the distinction of being the eleventh most deadly storm in the annals of the North Atlantic hurricanes. The 1899 North Atlantic hurricane season ran through the summer and the first half of fall in 1899. The season was an average one, with 9 tropical storms, of which 5 became hurricanes and only two became major hurricanes. The most notable storm was Hurricane San Ciriaco (or the 1899 Puerto Rico Hurricane), or locally known as the Great Andros Island Hurricane of 1899 or the Great Bahamas Hurricane of 1899 in the Bahamas, which caused more than 3,800 fatalities. Hurricane San Ciriaco also lasted almost a month. The hurricane was tied with

Hurricane Ginger for the longest lasting hurricane on record in the North Atlantic hurricane basin.

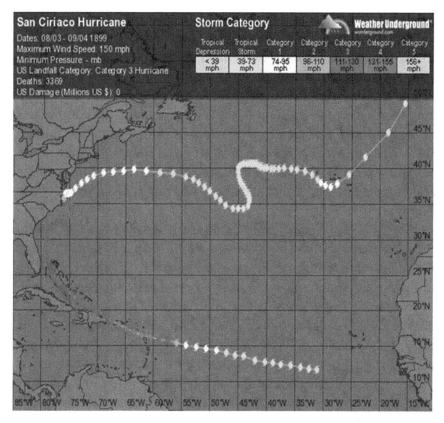

This map shows the track of the Great Bahamas Hurricane of 1899 (also called the San Ciriaco Hurricane) as it moved through the Bahamas (Information courtesy of Weather Underground).

Hurricane Ginger was the second-longest lasting North Atlantic hurricane on record. The eighth tropical cyclone and fifth hurricane of the 1971 North Atlantic hurricane season, Ginger spent 27.25 days as a tropical cyclone, lasting from September 6 to October 3. The storm formed northeast of the Bahamas, and for the first nine days of its duration tracked generally eastward or northeastward while gradually strengthening to peak winds of 110 mph. On September 14, Ginger slowed down considerably and took a general westward track, passing near Bermuda on September 23. There, the hurricane produced gusty winds and high waves, but no major damage was reported. This storm was significant for another reason and that was, while over the western Atlantic Ocean, Ginger became the last target of Project Stormfury, which sought to weaken hurricanes by depositing silver iodide crystals into tropical cyclone rainbands. Ginger ultimately struck North Carolina on September 30 as a minimal hurricane, lashing the coastline with gusty winds that caused power outages across the region. Heavy rainfall flooded towns and left severe crop damage, with 3 million bushels of corn and 1 million bushels of soybean lost. Damage in the state was estimated at $10 million (1971 USD or $54.2 million had it occurred today). Further north, moderate precipitation and winds spread through the Mid-Atlantic States, although no significant damage was reported outside of North Carolina.

The *1899 San Ciriaco Hurricane*, also known as the *1899 Puerto Rico Hurricane* or the *Great Andros Island Hurricane of 1899*, was the longest-lived North Atlantic and the eleventh deadliest Hurricane in the North Atlantic basin. It was an extremely intense and long-lived Atlantic Cape Verde-type hurricane which crossed the island of Puerto Rico over the two day period August 8 to August 9, 1899, causing 20 million(1899 USD)of dollars in damage. Many deaths occurred as a result, due to flooding and the hardest hit was the coastal city of Ponce, where five hundred people were killed. This deadly hurricane then crossed over the Turks and Caicos and then over the Bahamas where it killed well over 270 people on the island of Andros and 64 people on the island of Exuma. The cyclone kept tropical storm strength or higher for 28 days, which makes it the longest duration North Atlantic hurricane on record and the second-longest anywhere in the world. *Hurricane John* (also known as *Typhoon John*, international designation: *9420*, Joint Typhoon Warning Center (JTWC) designation: *10E*) formed during the 1994 Pacific hurricane season and became both the longest-lasting and the farthest-traveling tropical cyclone ever observed. John formed during the strong El Niño of 1991 to 1994 and peaked as a Category 5 hurricane on the Saffir-Simpson Hurricane Scale, the highest categorization for hurricanes. Over the course of its existence, it followed a 7,165 miles path from the eastern Pacific to the western Pacific and back to the central Pacific, lasting 31 days in total. Because it existed in both the eastern and western Pacific, John was one of a small number of rare tropical cyclones to be designated as both a hurricane and a typhoon during its existence. Despite lasting for a full month and breaking a few records, John was a non-issue storm and barely affected land at all, bringing only minimal effects to the Hawaiian Islands and a United States Military base on Johnson Atoll.

This is a famous water colour painting called *'After the 1899 Hurricane,'* painted by world renowned water colour artist Winslow Homer in 1899 while he was in the Bahamas. The scene shows a man lying on a sandy beach in the Bahamas surrounded by rough seas and pieces of his dinghy boat destroyed by the Great Bahamas Hurricane of 1899. Winslow Homer is considered one of the foremost painters in the 19th century America and a pre-eminent figure in American Art.

This Great Bahamas Hurricane of 1899 formed somewhere near the Cape Verde islands but the exact origin of this hurricane is still unknown because of the lack of satellite data to determine its origin. However, it was first observed on August 3, to the west-southwest of the Cape Verde Islands. That day, a British steamship *Grangense* reported tropical storm force winds and a barometric pressure of 995 mbar as it passed directly through it just 1,880 miles east of

Guadeloupe. At noon that day, located at latitude 11°51' north and longitude 35°51' west, Captain Spedding noted in his log book that the weather began to change for the worse: *"Clouds increased, and by 4pm the wind was blowing out of the north-northwest, with Beaufort Wind Scale force being increased to fresh gale, accompanied by heavy rain."* An hour later, the ship's barometer reached its lowest reading of 29.38 inches as the winds calmed and the rain ended temporarily but it returned with even greater force after the lull. The storm was over by 10pm, and the sky began to clear for good. Captain Spedding continued on his voyage, observing that in his many years of travel between Europe and the Amazon, this was the farthest east he had ever encountered such a storm. For a few days, its exact path was unknown due to lack of observations, although it is estimated that the storm continued to move on a west-northwestward track and it became a hurricane on August 5.

On August 7, after stations in the Lesser Antilles reported a change in wind from the northeast to the northwest, the United States Weather Bureau posted warnings and ordered hurricane signal flags to be flown at Roseau in Dominica, Basseterre in St. Kitts, San Juan in Puerto Rico and Santo Domingo in the Dominican Republic. Information on the hurricane was also sent to other locations throughout the Caribbean including the Bahamas. Estimates of storm-related fatalities range from 3,400 to 3,700, with millions of dollars in crop damage in Puerto Rico. The Bahamas reported millions of dollars in damage to the sponging industry and over well over 334 deaths, many of them sponge fishermen from the islands of Andros and Exuma. North Carolina had considerable tobacco and corn damage from the longevity of the strong winds and torrential rain. Overall, the island of Puerto Rico was swamped by 28 days of heavy rain, contributing to the overall disaster. As it approached the northern Lesser Antilles, passing directly over the islands of Guadeloupe and Montserrat, the hurricane began to be tracked continuously by ship and land observations. It was during this time that, it quickly intensified into a powerful storm, and a station on Montserrat reported a pressure of 930 mbar. The latter of these two islands reported that *"All the churches, estates, and villages, were destroyed, and nearly 100 persons drowned,"* a correspondent for the New York Times observed. *"In addition, many were injured and rendered homeless, and terrible distress exists amongst the sufferers."* This suggested sustained winds of 150 mph, making it a strong Category 4 Hurricane of the Saffir-Simpson Hurricane Scale. Thankfully, this was the strongest intensity of the hurricane.

Late on August 7, the hurricane moved through the northern Lesser Antilles, passing directly over the island of Guadeloupe and a short distance to the south of St. Kitts; in the latter island, a station reported winds of 120 mph. On the island of Guadeloupe, the hurricane made landfall near Point-à-Pitre at approximately 11:00am and lasted until about 4:30pm. The damage was extensive and widespread along the coast as well as in the interior of the island. A correspondent noted, *"Many houses had their roofs blown off and were flooded, and some of them were demolished, but no fatalities were reported. Twenty three flat boats and fishing boats were sunk in the Harbour, in addition to schooners, two small steamboats, and a steamship, 'Hirondale,' which were wrecked at other places. 'The Aleyou' had her stern damaged. The French cruiser 'Cecille,' which was in the harbour, did not suffer at all."* Antigua endured severe damage, but there was no report of life lost. On Nevis, the destruction was general, and at least twenty-one people were known to have died as a result of the hurricane. With its continuing west-northwest track, the hurricane skirted just south of the Virgin Islands. The island that suffered most in this group was St. Croix. One eyewitness noted: *"Nearly every estate has been wrecked, the large buildings in the towns have been unroofed, stock has been killed, and a minimum of eleven deaths have occurred among the labourers."*

It then continued on a west-northwestward track and the hurricane weakened slightly before making landfall on August 8 along the southeastern coast of Puerto Rico. This island was trying to recover from the turmoil following the end of the Spanish-American War, and many communities were ill-prepared to cope with a natural disaster of this magnitude. The city of Guayama recorded a pressure of 940 mbar, suggesting a landfall intensity of 140 mph. On August 8, the feast day of Saint Ciriaco, it crossed the island of Puerto Rico in an east-southeast to west-northwest direction, causing maximum sustained wind speeds between 110 and 140 mph. The most devastating effect of San Ciriaco on the island of Puerto Rico was the destruction of the farmlands, especially in the mountains where the coffee plantations were located. San Ciriaco aggravated the social and economic situation of Puerto Rico at the time and had serious repercussions in the years that followed. After it passed Puerto Rico, it grazed the northern section of the Dominican Republic as a Category 3 hurricane, but passed north enough to not cause major damage. It then passed through the Bahamas, retaining its strength as it moved slowly northward.

Captain Lobb, the Bahamas Inspector of the Lighthouses made the following observations from the log of the Imperial Lighthouse Ship *Richmond* who experienced this hurricane living in the Bahamas and at a lighthouse station: *"On August 11th at 8am, wind NE, force 6 (equal to 31 miles an hour) barometer 30.00 inches; no shift of wind, but increasing in force until 10pm. ENE, barometer 29.58 inches, midnight barometer 29.46 inches; 1am 12th, wind ESE barometer 29.33 inches; 3am lowest barometer 29.32 inches; force of wind, 11 to 12 (equal to 75 to 90 miles an hour) full force of hurricane. Wind ESE until 6am shifted to the SE and at 2pm began to abate, barometer 29.68 inches; wind SE by S; midnight S barometer 29.83 inches."*

After slowly drifting northeastward, the hurricane then made a northwestward track, hitting the Outer Banks of North Carolina near Diamond City as a Category 3 storm of 140mph on August 17. As it then passed over the Outer Banks of North Carolina, entire islands were flooded and fishing villages were destroyed. Some villages never recovered and were forced to relocate further inland. It drifted northeast over the state, re-emerging into the Atlantic on the 19th. Ships were damaged and destroyed all along the Atlantic seaboard from Florida to Massachusetts. For several weeks after the storm, ships came into ports all along the East Coast with reports of encounters with this powerful tempest. Some survivors of ill-fated vessels who were lucky just to be alive told stories of the difficult time of trying to stay alive on the high seas. Others told accounts of how they had to abandon ships that had lost their rigging and their crew and were floating aimlessly on the high seas. It continued eastward, where it became extratropical on August 22. The extratropical cyclone then took a southeast track where, on August 26, it became a tropical storm again. Like most of the rest of its lifetime, it drifted, first to the northwest then to the east. It strengthened as it moved eastward, and on September 3, as it was moving through the Azores, it again became a Category 1 hurricane. The intensification didn't last long, and the hurricane became extratropical for the final time on the 4th. It dissipated that day while racing across the northeastern Atlantic.

One of the most tragic episodes of the hurricane was the ordeal of the men aboard the Norwegian bark *Drot*, which encountered the hurricane well out in the Atlantic between Cape Hatteras and Florida. The crew bravely fought the howling winds and raging seas, but eventually nature prevailed. A gigantic wave hit the ship, washing the captain and seven of his crewmen overboard. Despite their best efforts, the ship was being thrashed to pieces by the waves. The men finally decided to save themselves before the ship was totally lost. A raft was pieced together from planks ripped from the *Drot's* deck, upon which the mate and the seven remaining seamen took to the sea. In the rough seas and raging storm, their makeshift raft broke into two pieces. On one part rode the mate and one of the men. Being overcome with fear, the mate jumped overboard and committed suicide. The remaining man did not give up so easily and continued riding out the storm. His confidence paid off, as he was picked up off Carolina coast by the *Titania*, a German steamship, and subsequently landed in Philadelphia. The six men on the other portion of the raft had their own particular hell to deal with. One man lost his mind and jumped into the raging sea where he drowned. As time passed and the storm continued unabated, two of his companions followed his example, taking their own lives by plunging into the sea. The three remaining men were Maurice Anderson, Goodmund Thomason and a German whose name was not recorded. They drifted on the storm-tossed waters of the Atlantic, without water to quench their thirsts, or food to prevent starvation. Realizing that they would die of thirst or starvation, the three men agreed to draw lots-the loser would be killed and consumed by the other two. The German lost the wager and was immediately killed by Thomason and Anderson, who quenched their thirst by drinking the blood from his veins.

This gruesome act of murder and cannibalism was too much for Anderson's conscience to deal with. The thought of the brutal deed wreaked havoc on his mind, and he soon went insane. In the fit of madness, he attacked Thomason, biting huge chunks of flesh from his chest and face before he could be subdued. On August 31, 1899, after two weeks of terror on the high seas, the raft containing the pitiful men was picked up by the British steamer *Woodruff* drifting 250 miles off the South Carolina coast. They were taken into port at Charleston, where they were given to local authorities. Word of their story soon leaked out, and press reports noted: "Anderson is a raving maniac, and his companion is shockingly mutilated from bites of the crazed man." Both men were hospitalized and then turned over to the Norwegian Consul in Charleston, who took them back to Norway to answer for their crimes. Wrecked ships littered the coastline of the Atlantic seaboard from Florida north to New England. In North Carolina alone on the US East Coast, over fifty ships were wrecked along the coast between Cape Fear and Currituck. These wrecks were distributed on the beaches facing the ocean, as well as in the sounds where the smaller vessels that plied these local waters fared badly from the effects of the storm.

After making landfall in the vicinity of Cape Lookout, the slow-moving storm made a sharp right turn and passed back out to sea off the vicinity of Ocracoke. After leaving the Outer Banks, the San Ciriaco Hurricane continued to be a menacing storm for mariners in the Atlantic. The long-lived storm was tracked by the U.S. Weather Bureau across the Atlantic, past the Azores and on to France. A report in October 1900 edition of the *Monthly Weather Review* noted: "On September 9, it was central of the coast of Provence, France, gales prevailed in this region until September 12, on which date the storm apparently had united with an area of low barometer covering southeastern Europe."

In all, this remarkable and deadly storm existed for about thirty-six days, making it the longest-lived tropical cyclone ever observed in the North Atlantic Basin. Along a dangerous stretch of coast of the Caribbean and the Eastern Seaboard renowned for its turbulent weather, few storms have ever equaled the San Ciriaco Hurricane. Hurricane San Ciriaco set many records on its path. Killing nearly 3,500 people in Puerto Rico, it was the deadliest hurricane to hit the island and the strongest at the time, until 30 years later when the island was hit by the Hurricane San Felipe Segundo, a Category 5 hurricane, in 1928. It also killed over 334 persons in the Bahamas, the deadliest hurricane since the Great Bahamas Hurricane of 1866. The next hurricane to have that significant amount of death toll in the Bahamas was the Great Nassau Hurricane of 1926. It was also the tenth deadliest North Atlantic Hurricane ever recorded.

With an Accumulated Cyclone Energy (ACE) of 73.57, it has the highest ACE of any North Atlantic hurricane in history. In 2004, Hurricane Ivan became the second North Atlantic hurricane to surpass an ACE value of 70, but did not surpass the San Ciriaco Hurricane. ACE is a measure used by the National Oceanic and Atmospheric Administration (NOAA) to express the activity of individual tropical cyclones and entire tropical cyclone seasons, particularly the North Atlantic hurricane season. It uses an approximation of the energy used by a tropical system over its lifetime and is calculated every six-hour period. The ACE of a season is the sum of the ACEs for each storm and takes into account the number, strength, and duration of all the tropical storms in the season. The highest ever ACE estimated for a single storm in the Atlantic is 73.6, for Hurricane San Ciriaco in 1899. This single storm had an ACE higher than many whole Atlantic storm seasons. Other Atlantic storms with high ACEs include Hurricane Ivan in 2004, with an ACE of 70.4, Hurricane Donna in 1960, with an ACE of 64.6, Hurricane Isabel in 2003 with an ACE of 63.28, and the Great Charleston Hurricane of 1893 with an ACE of 63.5. San Ciriaco is also the longest lasting North Atlantic hurricane in recorded history, lasting for 28 days (31 including subtropical time).

DAMAGES

NASSAU

A special session was held by the House of Assembly and the members voted to support a measure authorizing expenditure to provide hurricane relief throughout the islands of the Bahamas. Several vessels were dispatch by the authority of the Colonial Secretary to dispatch relief supplies and to render assistance to the respective Out Islands. The schooner *E.B.A. Taylor* was dispatched to the Exuma

Cays and Long Island. *The Attic* was dispatched to the Berry Islands, Williams Cay and Bimini. The sloop *Eastern Star* was dispatched to Behring Point and Cargill Creek. The *Albertine* was dispatched to Abaco, the schooner *Glynn* for Eleuthera and *Sappho* for the island of Andros. In all of the cases, the boat captains were expected to take relief supplies to the respective islands and to make a complete report of the damages sustained and report it back to the Colonial Secretary and the Legislature. Collections were taken by many of the churches in Nassau, to send to needy residents throughout the Bahamas left devastated by the storm.

When morning arrived, the daylight revealed the severity of the damages that had occurred from this powerful storm during the night. Among the first serious losses observed was the destruction of a new building recently erected by Mr. G.B. Adderley to the west of the Sponge Exchange, which was completely leveled to the ground. It had been constructed of a wooden frame and enclosed with corrugated iron. Its close proximity to the water side left it exposed and the building was blown over from the foundation. The covering of the J.S. Johnson Company's wharf fell in and portion of the wharf to the east was carried away. Numerous sheds in front of the stores on Bay Street and other streets were blown down and business signs removed. Several house properties in the city sustained comparatively little damage as compared to the suburbs. In the suburbs the humble dwellings of the poor sustained considerable damage. Small houses throughout the suburbs were totally devastated and many houses and out houses were blown down. The British Colonial Hotel was not in the least shaken by the effects of the storm. Within the hotel however, the temporary cloth frames that were set in the windows allowed rain water to access the building, which inflicted damage to the new plastering. The building otherwise was left intact. The walls of the building in the course of erection at the Hotel Royal Victoria fell to some extent. Boundary walls and fences of most houses and businesses were blown down in every direction both in the city and outskirts. At the Casino on Hog Island the roof of the dancing pavilion was blown away.

The prison roof was damaged at one corner and a long length of the boundary wall was blown down. The wind anemometers at

Government House and the Verandah Wharf were damaged but could be repaired. Several fences and walls were blown down in the Government House grounds and a few slates were blown off the roof. A piece of fence at the Eastern Burial Ground was blown down. The gate and signal hut at Fort Fincastle were slightly damaged. At Hog Island some shingles on the Keeper's dwelling were blown off. At the Quarantine Station at Athol Island, the Wharf was entirely blown away and displaced about ½ mile to the west by the Sea Gardens. The hospital kitchen roof was partly blown off. The Hospital (main) leaders were blown away and walls cracked. The Hospital (convalescent) leaders around the building were blown away. One of the strange turn of events after the storm was the loss of a steamboat *Minnie* at Hog Island but was refloated just before the hurricane. It was then anchored in Nassau Harbour but during the hurricane it was blown out of the harbour. Eventually the engine was found near Silver Cay, a piece of board with her name on it was found in the Berry Islands, and the remainder of the hull with the propeller still attached at Water Cay, Grand Bahama.

In St. Mary's Church, the recently erected chapel was badly damaged by water and all of the books and other miscellaneous items were destroyed or badly damaged. The clock in the tower of St. Matthew's Church stopped working when water from the storm affected its machinery and the windows of the church sustained minor damage. The southern district was in some portions flooded when the flood waters reached the floors of a number of dwelling houses. The flood waters on the main roads were reported to have been at least two feet deep in some places. One of the most devastating losses to many people in the 'Over-the-Hill' areas was the loss of fruit bearing trees and vegetables. After the storm it was said that the ground was literally covered with young fruits and vegetables. The beautiful foliage around the Library grounds was destroyed and the trees on the avenues and in private and government grounds were blown down. It was done to such an extent that it made the city and country look desolated. There was a fire which broke out at the Colonial Hotel after the hurricane but thankfully it was quickly extinguished by a group of workmen using buckets of water. During the hurricane between 1am to 2am a house the property of Mrs. Adelaide Burns blew down and almost crushed her to death but she was rescued by Mr. Erskine Mason. When he heard her screams he immediately came and moved the house of her chest with the assistance of another man. She was taken to the hospital for treatment of her injuries.

The following damages were sustained to several multi-family homes around Nassau, on Shirley Street-3 multi-family homes destroyed, Mackey Street-2, Kemp Road-2, Fowler Street-1, Christie Street-1, Armstrong Street-2, Dowdeswell Street-1, Delancy Town-12, Grant's Town-12 and Bain Town-8. The homes destroyed were all built of wood and were already very frail and dilapidated. After the storm, many of the homes in Adelaide were blown down and many of the residents (twelve families in all) were forced to live in the church. At Gambier there was a church and part of a house blown down. A house belonging to Mr. Henry Mostyn at Orange Hill near Gambier was destroyed and three persons on the inside were badly hurt. The orchard of Mr. David Patton in Bain Town and that of Mr. Robert Forcecr in Grant's Town, suffered severely because many trees were uprooted and thousands of fruits were lost.

Shipping in Nassau also suffered severely. Many lives were lost and many people were reported missing. A number of schooners and sailboats were seen lining the southern shore of Hog Island some of which had been anchored off *"Burnside's"* and getting ashore on the soft bottom sustained no damage. A few sloops were damaged on the Hog Island side of the harbour and several boats sunk at their moorings. A sloop was driven against the rocks near the Lighthouse, the schooner *Thrasher* drifted as far as the Bar and her masts were cut away when she held on. The crew of this vessel remained on board and the ship *Richmond* captain by Mr. S.A. Dillet had to rescue the nine member crew. The steamboats *Minnie* and *Non-Pareil* owned by Mr. Ernest were blown away never to be seen again. The old tug *Nassau* was blown away from its anchorage in Nassau Harbour and destroyed. It was reported that the settlement of Gambier was totally devastated and the local Baptist Church was blown down. The sisal factory at Old Fort was totally destroyed and all of the other sisal plantations were also destroyed.

As the schooner *Rapid* drifted down the harbour it came in contact with the J.S. Johnson Company's Factory Wharf when the crew took the opportunity of getting ashore. One of the crew Robert Edden, who was the first to leave the vessel but he was injured by a beam when he fell in the water. The rest of the crew managed to extricate him but his injury was so severe that he had to be taken to the New Providence Asylum for treatment but eventually succumbed to his injuries. The schooner *Waterloo* owned by the Estate of W.R. Pyfrom was driven out of the Harbour and four of her crew went missing and were never found. They were, Alfred Evans of Nicholl's Town, Andros, Alex Smith, Jason Rahming of Long Island, and Herbert Gibson of Grand Bahama. Captain Dillon of the ship *Cocoa* while using a searchlight from his ship reported seeing many dead bodies floating past his ship in Nassau Harbour. The schooner *Southern Queen* and sloop *Guide* were blown out to sea from the south end of New Providence with 18 men onboard. The schooner *Waterloo* sunk on the western end of New Providence.

After this storm and the massive death toll incurred as a result, the British Government, decided to put into law a Hurricane Warning Act to establish special hurricane signal flags which would be prominently displayed from the signal staffs on Forts Charlotte and Fincastle. Before this hurricane, signal flags were hoisted at the various forts but only randomly based on the location and strength of the hurricane. The new regulation required that signals be hoisted when the barometer fell below a certain point. In addition to this, it was required that there should be some means by which mariners should become acquainted with any information that was acquired by means of telegraph so as to decrease the loss of life and property both at sea and land. Because of this hurricane, all British Imperial Lighthouse Service light stations were issued a set of signal flags, which were kept ready once there was an approaching storm to warn incoming or outgoing ships and residents of an approaching hurricane. For centuries before the introduction of radios, sharing of information between ships, from shore to shore and from sea to shore posed communications problems. The only way for mariners to pass a message from one ship to another or from ship to land was by visual signals. For many years preceding the invention of the telegraph(and during its invention), some type of semaphore signaling from high places, towers or forts were used to send messages between distant points.

To this day, we still signal ships at sea with flags flown from shore-based towers and from other ships displaying storm warning flags. On Hog Island (now called Paradise Island), there was a lighthouse and to the right of this lighthouse was a flagpole which displayed the Union Jack of Great Britain. If there was a hurricane travelling in the vicinity of the Bahamas that flag would be removed and be replaced with a specialty hurricane flag. This flag consisted of a red coloured flag with a black square in the middle. Similarly, if there were any gale conditions being experienced, the gale flag would be used (two red triangle flags indicated gale warnings with winds between 34 to 47 knots). These flags were only taken down after the dangers associated with the hurricane or the gale conditions had dissipated. There were also hurricane flags placed on Fort Charlotte and Fort Fincastle to warn residents of an impending storm. Similar events would also take place on the Family Island lighthouses if they had knowledge of an approaching hurricane. These signal flags also gave residents on Nassau and the Family Islands a small grace period to prepare for a storm. In this day and age of satellite communications, radios, televisions, computers and instant information everywhere, these flags are rarely used.

The use of the barometer was used in the Bahamas as early as 1854 but came into widespread use after this storm. Sponging was the number one industry in the Bahamas during this hurricane. Most if not all Bahamian fishermen going out at sea on fishing or sponging trips would take with them a barometer. If they noticed a steep drop in atmospheric pressure indicated on the barometer, they would immediately turn the boat around and head back to shore because it meant that a hurricane or some other form of severe weather was approaching that part of the Bahamas. The following rules for its use were explained by an unnamed observer, an inhabitant of Harbour Island:

1. *In the hurricane months if the barometer falls with a N or NE wind, it should awake attention, and if it falls below*

29.90 inches, it is almost certainly a gale approaching, even though it might be perhaps a 100 miles off.

2. *During the approach, the barometer falls from noon until morning and then rises to noon again; every day falling lower than the previous day.*

3. *From sunrise to noon, any rise less than 0.05 inches is unimportant, but the smallest fall during that period, certainly indicates bad weather.*

4. *On the contrary, from noon to morning, its fall is not conclusive of bad weather, but its rise certainly indicates improved weather.*

5. *Though the weather is ever so threatening at sunset, the rise of 0.05 inches or upward assures you that there will be no gale before morning.*

6. *Though the weather be ever so fair in the morning, the fall of 0.05 inches before noon, betokens a gale before night (provided it's already below 29.90 inches).*

A normal barometer reading in the Bahamas is 30.00 inches. An area of depression which is generally attended by winds varying from moderate to hurricane force causes a fall in the barometer at a rate varying with the rapidity of the approach of the storm. As the storm recedes and the depression fills the barometer and rises to normal. The distance away from the center can only be estimated.

Fall of Barometer per hour from:	Distance in Miles from the Storm Center:
0.02 to 0.06 ins.	250 to 150 miles.
0.06 to 0.08 ins.	150 to 100 miles.
0.08 to 0.12 ins.	100 to 80 miles.
0.12 to 0.15 ins	80 to 50 miles.

The following may serve as a slight guide but too much reliance should not be placed on it. In these latitudes storms travel at varying rates of progression ranging from 5 to 20 miles per hour generally decreasing as the storm track turns northward and recurves, increasing again as it reaches the North Atlantic. The storm area is usually small, the region of violent winds seldom extending more than 150 miles from the center. The barometer falls rapidly as one progresses from the circumference toward the center. There are two periods of high barometer readings each day, one occurring about 10am, the other at 10pm and two corresponding periods of low barometer reading at 4am and 4pm.

These rules and guidelines were strictly adhered to by most of the residents and fishermen on the various Family Islands to give them some kind of indicator of an approaching weather system. These rules or laws governing the barometer usage remained in place until 26th May of 1936 when ZNS Radio began broadcasting as a hurricane warning station.

INAGUA

Three vessels were lost and the schooner *Vivid* was stranded at Lantern Head and the boats that were hauled up on the bay were badly damaged. A Turks Island schooner was lost at Little Inagua and a Crooked Island craft was damaged on the south side of Inagua. The rain fell on this island from 3pm on the 10th to 2am on the 11th and the lowest barometer reading was 28.28 inches with a southerly wind.

LONG CAY

The canal of the salt pond was seriously damaged. Between 50,000 to 60,000 bushels of salt or about one-third of the year's crop, were destroyed. The damages sustained to the homes on this island were slight in nature.

CAT ISLAND

Very light damage was reported on this island. The schooner *Leader* in coming to Nassau rescued a small child east of the island. Captain Burns attention was attracted by the loud cries of a boy on the shore. He immediately stopped the vessel and sent a boat on shore in the direction from which the voice was heard. A boy named David Mackey of Cat Island was discovered to be on the island, totally naked and was there for several days. He was one of the crew of the schooner *Choir* who with four others had clung to the booby hatch of the schooner when it capsized. All but Mackey were washed off the hatch, Captain Russell, Elijah Whymns, and two others were reported missing.

RAGGED ISLAND

From this island, it was reported that the public school house was blown down, but none of the private dwellings were seriously impacted.

LONG ISLAND

Deadman's Cay did not report any losses in life or damage to buildings but the plantain and banana plantations were completely destroyed.

RUM CAY

The hurricane occurred on the 10th at 12noon and did not abate until 5pm on the 11th but very little damage was done to the properties on this island. About 10 bushels of salt that was not beached was lost. This was mainly due to the sea breaking in over the Eastern Canal. The schooners *Signal* and *Professor* which were in the harbour were beached. The sloop *Annie D* which runs the mail service between Rum Cay and Watling's Island was blown ashore and considerably damaged. The *Signal* was not damaged so it was re-launched on the 17th. The keel of the *Professor* was broken but it was quickly repaired.

EXUMA

This island suffered tremendously, as all of the boats and means of transportation were destroyed in this hurricane. Many of the plantations on this island were destroyed by salt and rain water, the salt water at some settlements rose several feet above the land. The following boats were reported missing: *Choir, Phoebe, Solent* (crew onboard), *Savage* (crew reported to be lost), Sloop *Experience* (3 of the crew saved), *Terror* badly damaged. However, the schooner *Phoebe* would later be found out to be sunk between Normon's Cay and Ship Channel Cays. *The Sea Breeze* sunk and the Schooners *Emma, Charlotte, and Minerva* were dismasted. The schooners *Emmeline, Choir* and *Phoebe* were blown out to sea from Pigeon Cay, Exuma with all hands on board. The schooner *Lizzie Wall* and sloop *Lillian* were lost at Exuma. The mail schooner *Hattie Darling* was wrecked at Pipe Creek, Exuma. The sloops *Linnet* and *Syren* went out on the Sunday and Monday shortly after the storm and rescued many persons from different Cays. Several dead bodies were discovered on the shore and were immediately buried. It was reported that 46 lives were lost from the vessels in the neighbourhood of Exuma and many native Exuma women were left widows with no means of support. Of the many lives lost, quite a number of children were among the dead, including a few children eight years of age.

Mr.E.H. McKinney went to Exuma, mainly to Highbourne Cay, Gray's, Black Point and along the shore as far as George Town, shortly after the hurricane to take relief supplies, determine the needs of the people of Exuma. He then reported this information to the Central Government in Nassau. False keels of three vessels and other small pieces of wrecks were found up on the rocks at Highbourne Cay. At Shroud's Cay two houses were blown down and one small kitchen was destroyed. The schooner *Savage* was destroyed at Hall's Pond with Captain Ernest Rolle being the sole survivor, as he was forced to swim on a spar from Compass Cay to Belle Island a distance of about 4 miles. He was rescued by the sloop *Linnet* and taken to Black Point. Captain Rolle received several cuts which were in the process of healing at the time of the rescue. The schooner *Annie* was also lost at this Cay.

At Compass Cay which was not inhabited at the time, the sloop *Terror* went up on the rocks and was destroyed, while the sail boat and a schooner went ashore. At Stanyard Cay, Gray's Settlement-forty-five people lived here and several of their houses and out buildings were destroyed and those that remained received slight damages. The Baptist Chapel was also destroyed. In many instances the roofs of buildings blew away to sea. At Barritarri, the roof of the Baptist

Chapel and a few small buildings were destroyed. At Rolleville, the roof of the Baptist Chapel was destroyed and several small boats were lost. Corn seed was freely distributed to all of the needy residents of Exuma after the storm. The number of vessels lost or damaged along the Exuma Range of Cays: Lost-11 and Damaged-9. In addition to the above, about 25 small boats were lost or damaged. The number of buildings destroyed in the storm numbered 97 and 131 were damaged and these do not include 14 kitchens and barns and houses reported to have been destroyed at Stuart's Manor and Alexandria. As far as it can be ascertained, the number of lives lost from Exuma and its Cays amounted to over 64 persons, several persons were left widows with no support. Of the number of lives lost in Exuma, several were young children from eight years of age.

SAN SALVADOR

On this island, two Episcopal churches and several private dwellings were totally destroyed. Other than that very little damage was reported to homes on this island.

ELEUTHERA

The sloop *Lilly* was totally destroyed at the Current but all of her crew and her cargo were saved. The schooner *Ghost* was lost at East End and Captain Bethel and one other person was reported missing. During the storm Mr. Albury has lost his smack *Wm. Elder*, which was forced out of the harbour at Nassau and totally wrecked on North Cay. His smack *Royal* lost a mast in the same port, and is otherwise undamaged. The boat *Harrison* of Bluff was reported missing. The *Siren* was totally wrecked on the east end of Eleuthera.

ABACO

Damages sustained on this island was said to be widespread and quite devastating. At Hole-in-the-Wall the lowest reading of the barometer during the time of the storm was heaviest at 4pm on the 12th with a reading of 29.21 inches. The smack *Dazzle*, owned by Henry Albury of Cherokee Sound, was lost on the 12ᵗʰ in the hurricane at Crab Cay in the Berry Islands with three of her crew drowned.

ANDROS

In the settlement of Red Bays, two churches were destroyed and most of the homes were washed away by the storm. The center of the hurricane passed over Red Bays as the wind there was reported to have been from the NE with a period of calm and then it blew from the SW. One house was left standing in this settlement after this storm. In Red Bays many sponging vessels were blown ashore and the causalities were said to be astronomical. At Nicholls Town there were only seven houses left standing in this settlement and an Episcopal Church at Staniard Creek was blown down. Several houses at Coakley Town were blown down and several vessels sunk and stranded. Several schooners *Forest Belle, Alert, Vigilant, Eager, Lealy Lees* (Thos Evans, master, and Robert Murphy, mate drowned); Sloops *Complete, Snowbird, Nonsuch* (all of the crew but one missing) *Douglass, Stinging Bee, Challenge* were all lost near Andros. Many schooners were driven ashore and were either badly damaged or totally destroyed in the storm. Among them were *Traffic* (six men missing), *Admired, Alcia, Victoria, Equal, Naomi, May Queen, Beaureguard, Experience, Eunice, Hattie Don, Seahorse, Rosebud,* and others, about 30 in all. In addition to the many persons who succumbed to the storm at sea, the following persons were drowned at Lowe Sound and Red Bays-Simon Demerritt, Mary Brown, Christopher Miller, Gladys McQueen, George Miller and David Miller.

In the northern part of Andros, many of the settlements were devastated and many loss of lives occurred and the agricultural products were completely wiped out. About 114 persons lost their lives in this location on land and many houses were blown down and it mostly occurred to that part of Andros lying north of the Northern Bight. The Resident Justice went to Nicholl's Town and surrounding settlements and provided hurricane aid to all persons in need, particularly the widows and those who lost their main support. All of the crops including, oranges, grapefruit and coconuts were totally destroyed and the fields of corn, peas and potatoes and other plants were also destroyed and it was speculated that it would take many months for them to recover. Mr. E.H. McKinney was dispatched to Andros by the Government at the request of the Hurricane Relief Committee for the purpose of giving assistance to the Resident Justice, also to assist people in starting to repair the damage done to their houses. Also, to direct and supervise the Government's rebuilding efforts with regards to all public works.

The Central Relief Committee dispatched two expeditions to Andros with 50 barrels of relief aid under the care of Mr. K. G. Malcolm. His instructions were to proceed as rapidly as possible to Staniard Creek and to make connection with Mr. Forsyth, the Resident Justice at that place. Failing to find Mr. Forsyth there he was told to find out his whereabouts and join him and place himself under the jurisdiction of the acting Resident Justice. At Mangrove Cay the roof of the resident Justice's Office was very much damaged. The Government flagstaff was blown down and smashed; and the jail yard wall was broken in several places. All of the settlements between Nicholls Town and Fresh Creek suffered significant damage both on land and at sea. But the most significant damages sustained were at Nicholls Town and Mastic Point. Three Government buildings were badly damaged, the Jail roof was blown down, part of the schoolhouse was lifted and the teacher's residence was completely destroyed. The number of houses blown down at Nicholl's Town was 58. There were about 23 schooners which were lost in the Pine Barrens at Red Bays. Of the 104 houses in Staniard Creek, 48 were more or less damaged and 42 were completely destroyed. The Rev. F.W. Gostick, Superintendent of the Wesley Missions, Mr. K.G. Malone, Mr. E.Y. V Sutton went to North Andros shortly after the hurricane to take relief supplies, determine the needs of the people of North Andros and then report back this information to the Central Government in Nassau.

THE BERRY ISLANDS

The Episcopal Church at Bullock's Harbour was blown down. The schooner *Lena Gray* belonging to Mr. Thomas Sweeting was lost. The Ven. Archdeacon Churton, who in company with the Rev. S. Floyd was on a visit to the Berry Islands and Bimini in the schooner

Wayne Neely

Leander. Not having returned before the hurricane, the Rev. Audley J. Browne left in search of them in the schooner *Ready.* Fortunately, they were found safe on the Berry Islands and were towed back to Nassau. Another boat captain Robert Ranger was lost in the Berry Islands. There were at least twelve boats driven ashore and wrecked on the coast of Berry Islands in this storm.

BIMINI

Damage to the island was widespread and quite devastating. In one settlement, two houses destroyed, five houses blown off their pins and carried some distance away. Twelve houses were more or less badly damaged or destroyed. Clement Pinder's house had his gable ends blown down and the kitchen destroyed. Thomas Kemp's new house was blown off its pins. Adriana Saunders house was blown down and badly damaged and his tenant Joseph W. Saunders furniture and clothing were badly damaged by the sea water. Mrs. Jesse Roberts's kitchen was destroyed. The Government Office north gable end was blown in and many of the books, forms, papers were more or less destroyed or damaged. Joseph H. Kelly, kitchen was badly damaged. All of Edward Wilkinson out buildings were destroyed and his residence and kitchen were badly damaged. John Charles Kelly's house was blown away and the roof badly damaged. George Bethel house was blown down and his kitchen was destroyed. St. Mary's Methodist Church belfry was blown away and the church badly damaged. The Mission House was badly damaged and the kitchen destroyed. The belfry of the Wesleyan Church was blown away and the building sustained significant damage. Sarah Cash house was blown off the pins. James Symonette's kitchen was destroyed and the house badly damaged. Mr. W.J. Saunders, furniture and clothing were damaged and John Wright house sustained some damage. George S. Sherry, kitchen and other out buildings were damaged, Mr. W.A. Butler house was destroyed, and Mr. Prince Alfred Rolle house was blown down. Mr. Henry Rolle Jr. new house was blown 10 feet from its pins. Mr. James Pinder roof was badly damaged, and Mr. Daniel Smith house was badly damaged and the kitchen destroyed. Rev. James A. Hanna who

152

was a Baptist minister had his house very badly damaged and his outbuildings totally destroyed. Mr. Alex Pinder house was damaged and his roof partially damaged, and Mr. Alex Deveaux house was damaged and the outbuildings badly destroyed. Mrs. Elinor Forbes kitchen was blown away and the house was blown off its pins. One vessel the *Glide* was washed ashore but not badly damaged. The soil was completely rendered unusable because it was contaminated with salt water.

This hurricane commenced on Friday morning, and the barometer fell from 30.20 inches at 8:06am on the 13th August and continued to fall. Every family on Bimini received more or less significant losses especially those on the high ridge. Many of those residents lost everything including their furniture, bedding and clothing. All of the crops were also lost, so many residents simply starved for many days until outside help arrived to bring in much needed hurricane relief aid. The lowest barometer reading at the peak of the storm was 28.00 at which time the winds were blowing from the SW to W.

GRAND BAHAMA

There was considerable damage reported on this island, as most of the homes and all of the crops were lost. At Eight Mile Rock, there were 22 houses blown down along with a Church and a Chapel. At West End, there were 6 houses which were blown down. At Rhode Rock, one schooner was lost. At Holmes Rock, one house was blown down. At Brandy Point, 11 houses were blown down. At Barnett's Point, 17 houses were blown down and others damaged. At Free Town, 4 houses were blown down and many others badly damaged and at Water Key, 4 houses were blown down. Not only the crops of peas, sugarcane and a variety of fruits were totally lost but many of the farmers were rendered homeless. No less than sixty two houses from Smith Point East, to Settlement Point West were destroyed and among them were St. Stephen's Church and the Mission House. St. John's Baptist Chapel was badly damaged and the roof blown off. All of the streets and bridges were wiped away. Eight Mile Rock school room and West End Church were only slightly damaged. Smith's Point, Russell Town, and Grant's

Town residents suffered greatly when an ESE wind destroyed their homes. At Smith's Point, six homes were destroyed, four houses at Russell's Town, and five at Grant's Town. Mr. Joseph E. Adderley, the Resident Justice reported that the entire island looked as if it had been ravaged by fire.

CHAPTER NINE

THE GREAT ABACO HURRICANE OF 1932'S IMPACT ON THE ISLANDS OF THE BAHAMAS.

METEOROLOGICAL TRACK OF THE GREAT ABACO HURRICANE OF 1932

In the midst of the Great Depression a furious hurricane lashed the islands of the Bahamas with devastating force. Its record-setting winds of over 160 mph and over twenty feet storm surge, which led to the deaths of more than 18 persons on the island of Abaco. Abaco is one of the largest islands in the Bahamas and is most frequently affected by storms so frequently, mainly because of its large size and geographical location. On average, it gets hit or brushed by a hurricane once every 1.77 years but gets a direct hit once every 3.68 years and is ranked as the fourth(out of a total of 155 cities or islands) on the list of storms affecting cities and islands within this region. The Great Abaco Hurricane of 1932 became the first known and well documented Category 5 hurricane on record to hit the islands of the Bahamas. The 1932 North Atlantic was an extremely busy and devastating one for the Caribbean and the Americas. There were many notable and quite destructive hurricanes this year. An early season storm formed during the month of May and skimmed Hispaniola causing minimal damage. Then a powerful hurricane

Wayne Neely

struck the coast of Galveston, Texas finally testing the true worth of a seawall built after the deadly Great Galveston Hurricane of 1900. A Category 1 hurricane hit Alabama and a late season Category 4 hurricane hit Cuba and devastated that island leaving over 3,000 persons dead. However, the most notable hurricane for the Bahamas was the Great Abaco Hurricane of 1932. This storm was a powerful hurricane which struck the Bahamas with peak winds in excess of 160 miles per hour and a barometric pressure of 931hPa. The island which sustained the most significant damage and greatest death toll was Abaco.

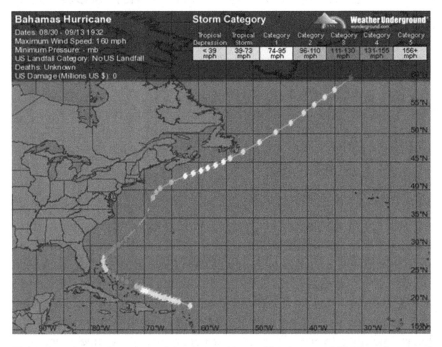

This map shows the track of the Great Abaco Hurricane of 1932 as it moved through the Bahamas (Information courtesy Of Weather Underground).

The Great Abaco Hurricane of 1932 was first noticed just to the north of the US Virgin Islands as a minor tropical storm on August 30th. It then moved on a west-northwest track, passing just to the north of the Greater Antilles. It strengthened into a hurricane just as passed near the Turks and Caicos Islands, and began a period of rapid intensification shortly after that. The storm passed just to the

156

east of the main islands and Nassau while continuing to strengthen. A gradual turn to the northwest and north began soon, and the storm peaked at Category 5 status with estimated sustained winds of around 160 mph at this time. Maintaining its strength, the storm passed over the island of Abaco on September 5th and gradually began to curve northeast away from the mainland United States. It continued northeast while weakening in intensity, delivering large sea swells to the northeastern United States and winds of 56 mph to Nantucket as the storm bypassed New England. The storm became extratropical around September 9th and eventually passed near Iceland and Jan Mayen Island. It dissipated on September 13th.

This photo shows a few persons walking on the beach and in the background it shows some homes damaged and some building rubbles on the far right and left (Courtesy of the Albert Lowe Museum, Abaco–Used with permission).

In the 1930's, the hurricane preparedness technology and tools for tracking hurricanes we use today were in their infancy, if it had even been conceived in the first place. As such, hurricane preparedness for the 1932 Bahamas Hurricane was lacking, to say the least. While we did have some tools available for tracking hurricanes in the 1930's, they lacked a certain degree of sophistication. While we could detect a hurricane in its earlier stages, it was very difficult to predict with any degree of accuracy where it might strike or how strong it might be. As such, people were only able to put up hurricane shutters and barricade hurricane windows and doors at the last second, and hope for the best. Furthermore, this was in a period where mass communications was still in its infancy. Even if we could have, theoretically, been able to predict the exact details of a hurricane, it would have been next to impossible to issue warnings in a timely manner. As such, hurricane preparations were predictably slim or virtually non-existent at all.

The death toll in Abaco after the Great Abaco Hurricane of 1932 was great. This photo shows a man pouring carbolic acid over one of the decaying corpses (Courtesy of the Albert Lowe Museum-Used with permission).

In total, the Great Abaco Hurricane of 1932 claimed eighteen lives, all taking place on Abaco, though at least three hundred others suffered minor and major injuries either directly or indirectly as a result of the hurricane. Affected areas included the Bahamas, the United States, Iceland, Newfoundland and the Jan Mayen Islands, with the Bahamas being the hardest hit. Two brick churches were destroyed on Green Turtle Cay, near the island of Abaco, with some of the stone bricks being carried up to a half a mile away. Several vessels were caught in the storm off the Coast of Abaco Island. Fortunately, in spite of some minor hurricane damages, the majority of the ships survived the ordeal. Sadly, the 1932 Bahamas Hurricane occurred well before any sort of national hurricane relief program had been put into place, and while hurricane protection was still a developing concept, hurricane shutters and hurricane windows being relatively new inventions. There was little in the way of government relief for those who had suffered. However, many charitable contributions from many persons and organizations were collected for the Abaco residents affected by the storm. Overall, many residents on most of the Out Islands had to fend for themselves in order to recover.

While the hurricane destroyed many stone churches on the mainland of Abaco and on Green Turtle Cay, today, nearly eighty years later, it is nearly impossible to tell that such a fierce storm once struck the Bahamas. Simply put, as quickly as the hurricane was able to destroy property on land and ships at sea, most of the areas hit recovered and rebuilt just as quickly. This can perhaps be credited to the fact that the hurricane moved quickly over Abaco.

The death toll was not too high, however it was reported that only 18 people were killed in the Bahamas, along with an additional 300 injured. The entire death toll occurred in the Bahamas, notably on and around Abaco Island; total damage estimates in dollars, however, were not released but it was considered to be in the millions of dollars. The storm was very destructive on Abaco Island, where the reported barometric pressure was unofficially below 27.50 inches (931 mbar). On Green Turtle Cay, near Abaco Island, two brick churches were destroyed by the storm and winds were estimated by one resident to have exceeded 200 mph. Some of the stone blocks from the churches were reportedly carried a half mile away. Newspaper reports and photos helped to establish estimated prevailing winds on Green Turtle Cay possibly exceeded 150 mph during the hurricane. After the storm passed Abaco on September

6th and 7th, several vessels caught in the storm recorded winds of Force 12 (Beaufort Wind Scale) and low barometric pressures; the *S.S. Yankee Arrow* recorded a pressure of 27.65 inches (936 mbar) on the 7th, while the nearby *S.S. Deer Lodge* reported a lower pressure of 27.58 inches (934 mbar). Although storm warnings were posted for the Florida and eastern United States coastline, the storm's recurvature prevented a landfall, leaving the main effects as heavy coastal swells and high winds. At the storm's closest pass to the country near New England, Nantucket where the highest winds peaked at 56 mph, as the storm remained offshore, although it still packed hurricane-force winds. The storm then passed Newfoundland where it morphed into an extratropical storm and passed near Iceland and Jan Maven Island where they reported barometric pressures of 29.00 inches or lower.

This photo shows a few persons walking among the rubbles of their homes in Abaco (Courtesy of the Albert Lowe Museum, Abaco –Used with Permission').

DAMAGES

NASSAU

Two conflicting weather reports were received from Washington and Miami in regard to the track of the storm. Washington reported the storm on Monday morning to be some 90 miles east-southeast of Nassau, while our weather indications were that it was well to the northeast of us. Consequently, Monday was an anxious day for most residents and it was not until the report was received at 10 o' clock that night that the population as a whole was assured that all of the danger from the storm had past. This proves conclusively the supreme value of the Out Island weather reports. "It was not until we were in possession of news that the Bight, Cat Island, was feeling the effects of the storm, reporting winds from the northwest, and subsequently, a report of the wind direction from Governor's Harbour confirming this, that some of our experienced citizens felt reasonably sure that the storm would pass to the north of us," reported one resident.

On Sunday at 6 o'clock the three blasts on the sirens situated over New Providence, caused considerable alarm. When it was realized that the storm would not pass over New Providence before Monday, many persons went to their evening church services. During Sunday night, gusts of wind reached speeds of 40-45 mph, but the mean speed was 30 mph. All of the tomato crops on this island were destroyed.

ANDROS

A report from the Commissioner at Fresh Creek reported that the hurricane passed over this part of the island from 4pm on Sunday to 3pm on Monday. No deaths or damages were reported.

WATLINGS ISLAND

No damage was reported on this island with the exception of a blown down radio station, which was quickly repaired and put back in service.

ELEUTHERA

At Governor's Harbour during the storm sustained winds were measured at 75 miles per hour from the northwest and then later from the southwest with the peak of the winds occurring between noon and midnight on Monday. Damages were reported to the roads and to the tomato crops on the island. A large portion of the stone part of the Government Wharf was demolished and the foreshore near the Wharf was washed away. There was significant damage reported to the island crops and other plants.

This aerial photo shows total devastation in this Abaco Settlement where some homes were totally destroyed, some shifted and others left unscathed (Courtesy of the Albert Lowe Museum, Green Turtle Cay, Abaco –Used with permission).

GRAND BAHAMA

The hurricane passed over this island on the 5th and 6th September, destroying a few houses and wrecking several vessels. Many of the crops were destroyed. The Commissioner who was stationed at Sweeting's Cay during the storm, reported that several houses were blown down and that there was a shortage of food from there to Eight Mile Rock. At Water Cay the sloop *Regulator* and the schooners *Relief* and *Increase* were totally destroyed and considerable damage was done to many of the other remaining boats. The water was said to have risen to a height of 9 feet in Hawksbill Creek on the north side. At West End, there was considerable damage to the citrus crop. The Government also dispatched supplies to the districts which suffered significant damages. They were put in the care of Mr. J.L. Lightbourn, the Auditor and he was also responsible to see that the residents of Moore's Island got relief supplies as they also suffered significant damages as well. At Moore's Island the water rose to a height of 5 feet in some places, causing several houses to float off their foundations. Entire roofs were blown off four houses and many others were well shaken up. The fields were badly damaged and several people were slightly injured.

CAT ISLAND

At Cat Island many telephone lines were blown down but were quickly repaired.

ABACO

There was complete devastation reported on this island. At Green Turtle Cay it was reported that twelve houses out of a total of eighty were left standing and all of the coconut and fruit bearing trees were blown down. At Green Turtle Cay, initially the winds blew from the north and then it increased with incredible ferocity until mid-day during the height of the storm. This was followed by that ominous and practically complete calm as the center passed over, to be followed immediately by strong winds from the south. Over 70 residents found shelter in an old quarry, and at the height of the storm they were completely surprised when a horse fell in the midst of them. The heroes of the day were Mr. Murray Atwell and Dr. W. Kendrick, Plymouth Brother, who organized the people in seeking shelter and probably were indirectly the means of saving many lives. The courage of Mrs. Atwell was superb, for at the height of the storm she went to find food for the little children. Dr. Kendrick has had some medical experience and was able to render valuable first aid assistance. His house during the storm was converted into a temporary hospital giving shelter to one hundred injured persons. There were twenty five persons who suffered broken limbs but were thankfully tended to by Dr. Kendrick at his home. Dr. Kendrick, apart from his medical assistance to the residents of Abaco, organized a united church service after the storm to pray for the storm victims and those who were killed. By the stroke of luck, Dr. Kendrick's electric generator was not destroyed so he was still able to supply light. Mr. E. H. McKinney was in charge of food and building supplies and was also hard at work organizing parties to distribute the hurricane relief aid. The distributions of supplies were put in charge of committees which were appointed by Mr. E.H. McKinney to distribute the goods and clear away the wreckage.

This aerial photo shows total devastation in this Abaco Settlement where some homes were totally destroyed (Courtesy of the Albert Lowe Museum, Green Turtle Cay, Abaco –Used with permission).

The swiftness and savage fury of the wind and waves were realized by the fact that four churches, the Government Wharf and the hotel were demolished almost immediately when the storm reached its peak. The wind blew there at an unofficial estimated speed of 200 miles per hour and the terror of those few minutes were added to by a very loud thunderstorm. One hundred dwelling houses were practically or totally destroyed, and only twelve houses were left standing, along with a few coconut trees. One of the most gruesome sights was the burial ground, where all of the tombstones were blown down and dead bodies were scattered everywhere. Six victims were interred by the local Burial Society. Mr. Arthur Holland, a pilot of a seaplane was sent out by the Government on a fact finding mission to Abaco following the storm and his report came as a great shock to everyone because of the great devastation on Abaco. After hearing of this great devastation on Abaco, the Acting Colonial Secretary, after consultation, ordered that the *Lady Cordeaux* make a special trip to Abaco with hurricane relief supplies, including food supplies, building materials, blankets and additional tanks of water. When the *Lady Cordeaux* arrived at Hope Town, Cherokee Sound and Marsh Harbour building operations were already in progress; and at the latter place four sides to a house were already to be seen being built back up again. Among those who boarded the *Lady Cordeaux* at the stricken settlements for the return trip to Nassau were, Mr. and Mrs. F. T. Buel and Mrs. Buel, who were taken on at Green Turtle Cay, Miss Roslyn Roberts, Great Guana Cay, Mr. J. S. Hall, Marsh Harbour, and Mr. R. H. Stratton, Mr. and Mrs. R. C. Johnson, Mrs. C. T. Malone and the Misses Madge and Dorothea Malone, the Rev. Walter Crowe, who were taken on at Hope Town.

Eventually, His Excellency the Adhaminstrator and the Hon. Mrs. Bede Clifford with Dr. H.A. Quackenbush would also take a tour and they left in a seaplane piloted by Captain Arthur Holland to take a survey of the devastated settlements of Abaco. Bluff Point was the first settlement visited by them and they were stunned to see that the settlement was completely demolished, forcing Mrs. Bede to remark *"There is nothing left"* of the settlement. Many of these residents required urgent medical attention and were quickly attended to by Dr. Quackenbush because their wounds were already showing signs of infection. Broken collar bones had to be set and nail wounds to feet were just some of the injuries he attended to while he was there. Among the injured were Zachary Swain, Napoleon Davis and Lina Swaine, who because of the nature of their injuries were required to seek medical assistance at the Public Hospital in Nassau. Looking at the damage at Bluff Point, it would appear that the damage was caused by the storm surge. Every inhabitant in this settlement was left homeless.

This photo shows the roof of the house on the right completely gone (Courtesy of the Albert Lowe Museum, Green Turtle Cay, Abaco –Used with permission).

After visiting Green Turtle Cay, His Excellency remarked *"Green Turtle Cay is a sight. They must have had a terrific blow."* He noted that the Anglican Church, a solid stone building was reduced to a heap of rubbles. Three persons were so badly hurt that they had to be brought up to Nassau to seek medical attention at the hospital. One man was reported missing but many believed that he was simply buried beneath the rubbles. In this settlement, a mother with six children lost her eldest and youngest in the storm. One witness Dr. Kendricks told His Excellency of how he saw one Government building being blown about 100 yards by the wind and landed on its roof. However, in each settlement, His Excellency marveled at the brave and heroic attitude of the people and the way in which they had already started replanting seeds in their farms and rebuilding their houses. Amazingly, His Excellency noticed that in all of the settlements, the wooden houses seemed to have withstood the fury of the storm better than the stone buildings which had all collapsed. This was especially noticeable in Hope Town. Three cases of typhoid fever had broken out in Hope Town and Green Turtle Cay after the storm. His Excellency stressed to the people the urgent need to boil all drinking water. He was also of the opinion that it would have been better if the people had stayed in one single sheltered spot before the worst of the storm and not remained in the individual houses. The wisdom of doing this was proven by the group of persons who sought shelter in the quarry at Green Turtle Cay. Those who stayed in their houses were caught like rats in a trap he said.

The members of the Government, Major Hugh M. Bell Director of Publicity, Mr. E.H. McKinney, of the Customs Department, were in charge of the distribution of food and building supplies, Miss Webster of the Bahamas General Hospital staff, were responsible for bringing all the necessary medical supplies and accompanied by an orderly from the Hospital, press representatives, and about a dozen persons who had relatives in various settlements in Abaco all took the trip to Abaco on the *Lady Cordeaux*. When the team of Government officials travelled to Abaco to render assistance to the people, different works were assigned to different members of the party. Major Lewis was placed in charge of the distribution of clothes which were donated to the centers at Government House and at Moseley's Book Store. He was instructed to get in touch with the Commissioner or some responsible person and give the clothes to them for distribution to the needy persons in the community. The women on the trip were separated into three groups and each was dispatched to three different hurricane ravaged settlements. Mrs. Kinneard and Mrs. Brice went to Great Guana Cay, to help the sick people there. Mrs. Millar and Mrs. Mallon went to Bluff Point and

Mrs. Symonette, Mrs. Robertson and Miss Pritchard went to Green Turtle Cay. They took with them milk for the babies, soup for the invalids, but their main objective was to try and help the people with sanitary conditions, take care of the sick and if necessary, open soup kitchens. Furthermore, a large quantity of provisions and clothing were sent by private individuals and relatives of Abaconians to the distressed people of Abaco. The Hon. Charles Dundas as Chairman of the Agriculture and Marine Products Board issued instructions to see that all available seeds at this office be sent to the hurricane stricken residents of Abaco.

A Relief Fund in aid of the hurricane victims in Abaco was opened at the Royal Bank of Canada on Bay Street at the request of the Central Government and many persons contributed to this relief fund. Many churches throughout Nassau held special services to raise funds and made special offerings in the regular services to help the victims of the storm. Furthermore, the Government House was opened to the general public as a collection center for relief aid for Abaco, where persons could bring food, clothing and building supplies to ship to Abaco. Various other places also offered this drop off service including, Moseley's Book Store. A benefit show was held at the Nassau Theatre Club where they showed Edward G. Robinson's *'Two Seconds'* and the entire proceeds from this show was sent to the victims of the storm in Abaco. A special meeting of the Daughters of the Empire was held and a special collection was made to give to the residents of Abaco and they also held a special luncheon with all of the proceeds benefitting the victims in Abaco. A polo match was organized to be played at Fort Charlotte and all of the proceeds from this game were donated to the residents of Abaco. A very enjoyable and well attended concert was held shortly after the storm at the Victoria Hall in aid of the Hurricane Relief Fund. In attendance at the event was the Governor General and other high ranking officials in Government. The Grand Central Café held a special luncheon and dinner and all of the proceeds went to the Abaco victims. His Excellency the Governor and the Hon. Mrs. Bede Clifford were represented at the dinner. A special dance was held at the Bahama Country Club and all proceeds were sent directly to the Commissioners at Hope Town and Green Turtle Cay. They were then responsible for distributing it in small sums to the needy persons. Furthermore, some Miami, Florida residents hired the boat *Ena K.* to bring twenty-one packets of clothing for the hurricane sufferers at Abaco.

The hurricane devastated Bluff Point, which caused persons to move to Moore's Island. Some of settlers of Bluff Point, Abaco moved to Murphy Town and the Great Abaco Hurricane of 1932 legacy is preserved in common family names on the island, such as, Davis, Swain, Curry, Dawkins and Knowles who all moved there shortly after the hurricane. In the settlement of Green Turtle Cay, it was reported to be in a state of complete and utter ruins. Sheets were seen hanging high up on trees as distress signals and a Red Ensign was seen floating upside-down on a flagstaff after the storm. The entire population, numbering about 250, was clustered together in large groups and the general atmosphere was one of complete bewilderment. Six persons had been badly injured and almost everyone had minor injuries. There was no food of any kind in the settlement and as a last resort water was obtained from a few small puddles. Every boat had been destroyed and it was not possible, therefore, to catch any fish. The seas had swept right over the settlement destroying every building and all vegetation. At least six persons had been killed and 26 badly injured. Very little food or water could be obtained after the storm.

Dr. W. A. Kendrick, who acted in a medical capacity around the settlements of Abaco, worked untiringly night and day among the injured. Disinfectants were very badly needed to be applied to many of the wounds which occurred as a result of the injuries sustained during and after the storm. Almost every house had been swept away. At Water Cay, shipping suffered significantly as one schooner, one sloop and several small crafts were lost. Six houses and all the crops were destroyed at Sales Cay. All of the citrus crops were destroyed but otherwise there wasn't any other damage reported in this settlement. A report by Mr. J.H. Saunders from Old Place, Abaco, said that 60 families there were left homeless and the following houses were blown down in the various settlements-Blackwood-40, Cornish Town-50, Cedar Harbour-10, Riding Rocks-7, Cherokee Sound-24, and Cooper's Town-40. He also reported a total of 7 deaths, 3 in addition to the 4 reported by Mr. Salter. The pier, 1,400 feet long by 7 feet wide, was swept away. Individuals collected lumber from their ruined houses and took the nails out which were not rusted and re-used again. If a house was 18x24 it was rebuilt to 10x12 or 12x16 as there was not sufficient lumber to rebuild it to the same specifications as before.

This photo shows many homes in the foreground reduced to rubbles in Abaco after the storm (Courtesy of the Albert Lowe Museum, Green Turtle Cay, Abaco –Used with permission).

At Great Guana Cay, only four of thirty five houses were left standing. Fifteen persons had been injured and one man named James Sands was killed. Mrs. Teresa Sands housed 42 persons during the hurricane, which lasted from midnight on Sunday to 9pm on Tuesday. The only houses which remained standing were, Richard Sands, Melvin Roberts, Thomas Sands, Lawrence Cash, Stanley Weatherford and Wilfred Albury. The seas swept over this settlement and had taken its toll on the people and the town. In addition, boats of all kind, including the mail boat *Priscilla* were blown ashore and destroyed. All of the livestock of all kinds and crops were destroyed and the wells were contaminated with seawater and many persons faced starvation after the storm. At Marsh Harbour, extensive damage had been done and all the crops were destroyed. Thousands of fruit trees of many varieties were totally destroyed, torn up by the roots, included in this total were 3000 banana trees. The hurricane destroyed the Marsh Harbour Post Office and the school building so school had to be held in the Methodist Church for quite some time after the storm until a new school could be rebuilt. The house of Mr. Goodwin Roberts, M.B.E., was badly damaged. According to Mr. Silas Cash, twelve houses were badly damaged and the water rose over the settlement to a height of over 8 feet. He also said that the storm surge in this settlement was worse than the ones which occurred in the hurricanes of 1926. There were fortunately no deaths or injuries in this settlement.

Unfortunately, Hope Town met the same fate. The wireless station was completely destroyed and the Methodist Church among other buildings including, the gaol and post office were also completely demolished. All eighty three homes in Hope Town, except Dr. Dolly's house were all completely destroyed. One resident, Captain Holland reported that during the storm, the wind lifted a house out of the settlement, across the harbour, and smashed it on the rocks near the lighthouse, a distance of about a quarter of a mile. Ninety persons had to seek shelter in Mrs. Kelly Sand's house during the storm. Again, there was no loss of lives. Cooper's Town was wiped out but Cherokee Sound sustained very little damage. Elbow Cay was said to have had a terrific wind velocity estimated by some at 150 miles per hour. It seems as if during the peak winds it was situated directly over the settlement of Elbow Cay. The settlement of Dundas Town began after this disastrous hurricane destroyed Cornish Town, Big Grape Tree, and Old Place. A tin washtub travelled in the hurricane from Hope Town to the eastern end of Marsh Harbour-a distance of seven and a half miles. The strong hurricane winds deprived the roosters of their crowing apparatus. Not a crow was heard in the settlements since the hurricane and strangely enough the dogs were also very quiet as well. Commander R. Langdon-Jones, D.S.O., Inspector of Lighthouses, heard from Mr. J. O'Brien, who went to Abaco on the

Lady Cordeaux reported that the Imperial Lighthouse at Hole-in-the-Wall was undamaged by the hurricane. The lighthouse at Elbow Cay, according to a message received from the *Patricia K.* received only minor damages.

Mr. and Mrs. Frederick T. Buel, with Mrs. Townsend Buel, Mr. Buel's mother, returned to Nassau from Green Turtle Cay, Abaco on the *Lady Cordeaux* after the storm. The Buels went through a dramatic and unforgettable experience during the storm. Spanish Cay, 30 miles northwest of Green Turtle Cay was before the hurricane a picturesque island of about 300 acres, covered with beautiful shrubs and with an abundance of coconut trees. The Buels bought this Cay quite a while before the storm and built a very charming little home on one of the prettiest spots. Several weeks before the storm they left Nassau, where they had been staying all summer, for Spanish Cay in the motorboat *Tramp.* They had scarcely arrived and moved into their new island home when the hurricane swept down upon them completely demolishing the house and its contents. Fortunately, the *Tramp* rode out the storm with success and the Buels left as soon as they safely could for Green Turtle Cay. On the way they stopped at Cooper's Town, where they rendered valuable first aid to a young coloured boy who suffered a compound fracture of the left leg. After putting the leg in splints they carried the boy with them to Green Turtle Cay where he was put on board the *Lady Cordeaux* and brought to Nassau. The Abaco boy undoubtedly owed his life to the prompt action of these American visitors.

The following weather observations were made by Mr. David Salter, a resident of Abaco. Marsh Harbour-The height of the storm was at 9am on Monday. The wind blew from the northeast until 3pm when it shifted to the southwest and blew until nightfall. The lowest barometer reading was 27.00 inches and the calm lasted for 15 minutes. Several schools, a teacher's residence and thirteen houses were totally destroyed and most of the remainder of the houses were badly damaged. Fortunately, there were no deaths reported in this settlement but several boats were damaged. The crops and fruit orchards were totally wiped out and two Government Wharves were demolished. Hope Town-The height of the storm was at 10am on Monday. The wind blew from the northeast then shifted to southeast where it blew the hardest when it was in this direction. The lowest barometer reading was 27.20 inches. In this settlement there were 83 houses totally destroyed, 63 badly damaged and 40 slightly damaged. Mr. Russell, Sr., had his house blown down and Mrs. Carey had her dining room destroyed. Two boats were destroyed but fortunately there were no deaths reported but two persons were badly injured. Food supplies were very low and no medical supplies were available as they were destroyed when the doctor's residence and office were damaged. Little drinking water was available in this settlement as all of the wells were contaminated by salt water. All of the public buildings and the radio station were destroyed. The Commissioner's Residency and the office were slightly damaged. Both of the Anglican and Methodist churches were destroyed. At Man O' War Cay-11 houses were completely demolished and 13 badly damaged.

This photo shows some houses in the background badly damaged and one completely destroyed in Abaco (Courtesy of the Albert Lowe Museum, Green Turtle Cay, Abaco –Used with permission).

At Green Turtle Cay-The height of the storm was at noon on Monday. The wind blew from the northeast and then shifted to the southeast and then to the south. Captain Roberts turned his house into a hospital and many people were taken there for treatment during and after the storm. All of the houses, churches, schools, and Government buildings were totally destroyed in this settlement. Six persons were killed and they were, George Lewis, Thomas Roberts, Mrs. Irvin Lowe, Miss Insley Sawyer, Louise Lowe and Bert Lowe. There were 25 persons badly injured, including limb injuries, head wounds and bruises of all description were also reported. After the storm most residents lacked food or good drinking water and they were in desperate need of medical supplies. The *M/V Priscilla* reported some damage to the structure of the boat. At Bluff Point-The height of the storm was at 2pm on Monday. The wind blew from the north to northwest. The settlement was totally destroyed with all of the boats, churches, school room, burial ground were all washed away. Most of the damages sustained were caused by the storm surge. After the storm, no food or water was available in this settlement. Five persons were badly injured when they were sheltering in a house on a wet mat and the hurricane blew the roof off their house and this was when they sustained some injuries. At Great Guana Cay, only four houses were left standing, but the all sustained some form of damage, and all of the boats were lost. At Cooper's Town, 4 persons were killed and only 6 houses were left standing.

CHAPTER TEN
DAMAGES SUSTAINED TO SHIPS AFTER THE GREAT BAHAMAS HURRICANE OF 1899

In 1899, the majority of Bahamian men were engaged or gainfully employed in the sea sponging industry here in the Bahamas. To collect the sponges required these men to go out at sea to selected areas of the Bahamas by boat, where the sponges were quite prevalent and easy to harvest from the sea floor. One of the more popular areas was 'the Mud' on the western coast of Andros. As a result of this, many of the boats that were lost occurred in this general area (the Mud). The Great Bahamas Hurricane of 1899 was such a deadly hurricane that hundreds of homes were left without fathers and many Bahamian women throughout the country became instant widows. This storm impacted the sponge industry for many years because of the significant number of ships lost during the storm. The ships were indeed very costly and it took quite awhile and a tremendous amount of money to replace them. Most of the information obtained in this chapter came from the Nassau Guardian, Family Island Commissioner's Reports, the Governor's Dispatches (CO-23), Shipping Reports to the Governor of the Bahamas by Mr. Nigel B. Burnside who at the time was the Acting Registrar of Shipping and other sources. In total, the lost to ship owners amounted to well over £15707. The different lists below are by no means complete because of the significant number of ships lost and persons who drowned in this storm are too numerous to mention. Therefore, I am including excerpts from the various reports.

LOST TO SHIPPING

Ship's Name:	Type of Vessel:	Owner:	Type of Damage/Comments:
Mary	Schooner	J.S. Johnson	Totally Destroyed. Boat Captain Mr. Forbes drowned.
Neptune	Schooner	Unknown	Blown over the Bar.
Post Boy	Smack	Unknown	Totally Destroyed.
Minnie	Yacht	Mr. Ernest Bethel from Saratoga, Florida	Totally Destroyed.
Non Pareil	Yacht	Mr. Ernest Bethel from Saratoga, Florida	Totally Destroyed.
R.J.C.	Schooner	Unknown	Slightly Damaged and lost rudder.
Clarita	Sloop	Owner from Exuma	Totally Destroyed when it sunk between Silver Cay and North Cay and Captain and crew missing and presumed dead.
Wonderful	Sloop	Unknown	Slightly Damaged.
Sprite	Sloop	Unknown	Lost spar and badly damaged.
Glide	Schooner	Unknown	Damaged at Silver Cay.
Trent	Schooner	Unknown	Capsized east of Nassau.
Sparkle	Schooner	Unknown	Badly Damaged.
Challenge	Schooner	Unknown	Damaged.
Ralph	Schooner	Unknown	Dismasted.
Frolic	Schooner	Unknown	Dismasted.
Priscilla Maud	Schooner	Unknown	Sunk.
Royal	Smack	Unknown	Sunk.
Sun	Schooner	Unknown	Damaged.
Thrasher	Schooner	Unknown	Dismasted.
Invincible	Schooner	Unknown	Came ashore on Hog Island but sustained only slight damage and was refloated.
Julia Howard	Schooner	Unknown	Slightly Damaged.
Greyhound	Schooner	Unknown	Slightly Damaged.
Gem	Schooner	Unknown	Mainmast blown away.
Old Sal	Smack	Unknown	Very badly damaged.
Daisy	Schooner	Unknown	Damaged.
WM Elder	Smack	Unknown	Washed up on North Cay and was totally destroyed and one crew member lost.
Income	Sloop	Unknown	Sunk and damaged.
Muriel	Pilot Boat	Unknown	Sunk.
Monstrat Viam	Pilot Boat	Unknown	Sunk at Bar.
Ghost	Yacht	Unknown	Sunk but was refloated.
Idler	Yacht	Unknown	Sunk.
Southern Queen	Schooner	Unknown	Sunk on Southern Side of New Providence.
Guide	Sloop	Unknown	Sunk on Southern Side of New Providence.
Elder	Smack	Unknown	Drifted out to sea but the crew saved.
Lena Gray	Schooner	Unknown	Lost at Berry Islands.
Lizzie Wall	Schooner	Unknown	Lost at Exuma
Lillian	Sloop	Unknown	Lost at Exuma
Hattie Darling	Schooner	Government Mailboat	Lost at Pipe Creek, Exuma
Experience	Schooner	Thomas Russell	Lost at Andros
Hero	Schooner	Rev. D. Wilshere	Lost in the creek at the East end of Nassau.
Gold River	Schooner	James Wemyss	Badly Damaged and lost at Staniard Creek, Andros.
Gypsy Queen	Schooner	John Brown	Badly damaged and lost at

Lost to Shipping.

			Exuma.
Hattie Don	Schooner	G.B. Adderley	Badly damaged and lost at Red Bays.
Handsome	Sloop	H.C. Albury	Badly Damaged.
Handsome	Sloop	J.P. Nixon	Badly damaged at Farmers Cay, Exuma.
I-See All	Sloop	Manuel La Fleur	Lost at Conch Sound.
Lady Lees,	Schooner	G.B. Adderley	Came ashore and badly damaged and 5 persons died.
Prudence	Schooner	W.P. Sands	Badly damaged.
Phoebe	Schooner	G.B. Adderley	15 persons died in Pigeon Cay, Exuma .
Queen of Clippers	Schooner	W.H. Deveaux	Lost at Port Howe, San Salvador.
Remembrance	Sloop	Estate, W.R. Pyfrom	Damaged at Red Bays.
Sea Horse	Schooner	O.F. Pritchard	Came ashore and 8 persons died on this boat.
Soud	Sloop	R.N. Musgrove	Lost at Staniard Creek and 2 persons died on this boat.
Southern Queen	Schooner	P. Bullard	Lost at Nassau and 11 persons died on this boat.
Savage	Schooner	G.B. Adderley	Came ashore and 12 persons died on this boat.
Try Me	Sloop	L.E. Forsyth	Slightly damaged.
Waterloo	Schooner	Estate, W.R. Pyfrom	Totally lost with 4 persons on this boat.
Dolphin	Schooner	Estate, W.R. Pyfrom	Lost at Conch when it sunk.
Height	Schooner	John Edgecombe	Slightly damaged.
Income	Schooner	Edward Wilchombe	Dismasted at Grand Bahama.
Linnet	Sloop	W.H. Curry & Sons	Lost at Exuma
Let Her Be	Sloop	Cupid Brown	Badly damaged at Moore's Island, Abaco.
Magic Light	Schooner	J. Pinder	Lost at Red Bays with 3 persons on board.

Lost to Shipping.

The list below shows the Names of the persons, who perished in the Great Bahamas Hurricane of 1899 on the 11th and 12th August, 1899.

Deaths occurring on the sponging vessels and the names of the persons and vessels lost during the Great Bahamas Hurricane of 1899

Ship's Name:	Type of Vessel:	Number of Persons who Perished:	Names of the persons who Perished:
Solent	Schooner	9	Wm Nixon Fred K Smith Thos Sands T. Dawkin Jos Miller Samuel Miller Robert Wilson Hezekiah Tynes Daniel Miller
Catherine Ella	Sloop	1	Fred McKenzie
Ghost	Schooner	4	Daniel Bethel Luke Humes Two others names not known
Traffic	Schooner	6	Albert Kemp Esau Miller James Miller W. Black Horatio Summons Israel Aunett
Annie	Schooner	6	Hamilton Forbes George Mackey Thomas Sweeting Alexander Franks Samuel Adderley Simeon Thurston
Lilla	Sloop	2	T. Roach James Burke Roach
Sea Horse	Schooner	8	Captain Glinton, his son and six others drowned.
Claretta	Sloop	Unknown	Names unknown.
Terror	Sloop	8	Granville Wilson Nathaniel Humes Percival Wilson Naaman Sumner Daniel Knowles Thos Adderley Joshua Rolle Michael Knowles
Empress	Schooner	3	Robert Russell Nathaniel Bode Michael Rolle
Remembrance	Sloop	8	Matthias Woodside Solomon Woodside Cubit Woodside Jack Colebrook John White James Nottage Wm Flower Joe Ormond Woodside
Savage	Schooner	12	James Clarke Alfred Edin Jeremiah Pattern James Rolle Tobias Rolle Theophilus Rolle Gabriel McPhee Buddie McPhee Mitchell Rolle 3 others unnamed
Magic Light	Schooner	3	James Moxey Daniel Kemp Newton Jones

Lost to Shipping.

Eager	Schooner	1		Charles Martin
Snow Bird	Sloop	4		Charles Saunders
				John Bennett
				Robert George Miller
				Joseph Johnson
Magnolia	Sloop	1		Unknown
Complete	Sloop	11		Edward Johnson
				Sylvester Mackey
				Ramon Dorsett
				Uriah Bain
				Alfred Davis
				James Davis
				Wm. Johnson
				W. Pratt
				Benjamin Johnson
				Henry Evans
Soud	Sloop	2		Jeremiah Storr
				W. Rodgers
Waterloo	Schooner	4		Alfred Evans
				Alexander Smith
				James Rahming
				Herbert Gibson
Uno	Schooner	3		James Ball
				Virginius Gordon
				Horatio Rolle
Sea Horse	Schooner	8		W. Glinton
				Horatio Lightbourn
				George Thompson
				Joshua Thompson
				Henry Edgecombe
				Samuel Glinton
				W. McBride
				Hezekiah Pinder
Julia	Schooner	8		Jeremiah Ferguson
				W. Adderley
				Wilfred Sands
				Melville Moxey
				Theodore Bain
				Alex Williams
				Thos Johnson
				Henry Douglas
Unknown	Schooner	6		Joseph Rolle
				Castilio Butler
				John Fox
				James Coakley
				Smith
				Coakley Johnson
Challenge	Sloop	9		Joseph Hamilton
				Jas Taylor
				Joseph Williams
				Frederick Deveaux
				Herbert Edgecombe
				Achilles Rolle
				Joseph Johnson
				Robert Bennett
				1 Unknown
Western Queen	Sloop	10		Joseph Eulin
				Jacob McKey
				Joseph Bootle
				Joseph Western
				George Eulin,
				Daniel Taylor
				Thos Minnis
				Zodoc Armbrister
				George Weech
				Andrew Francis

Lost to Shipping.

Southern Queen	Schooner	11	Jas Adderley Norman Adderley Alex Bain Joseph Finn Arthur Pratt Felix Gibson J.F. Miller Sylvanus Hepburn Jas Rolle Jonathan Reckley Simeon Rolle
Guide	Sloop	7	Nathl. Wright H. Wallace Alphia Wallace Richard Thompson Simon Simons Adolphus Adderley Anthony McKinney
Dazzle	Schooner	3	Menin Albury Harthy Pinder Daniel Pinder
Mary	Schooner	4	Robert Forbes Tim Higgs Hezekiah Stubbs Joseph Rolle
Douglass	Sloop	7	Prince Woodside Tim Marshall W.H. Mackey Nathaniel Marshal Arthur Oliver Smith Sirus Butler W. Marshall
Will o' the Wisp	Schooner	6	Caiaphas McKenzie Wilson Rolle Leslie Rolle Henry Humes Isaac Curtis Nathl. Taylor
Equal	Schooner	1	W. Bain
Bowkin	Schooner	6	George Bain Ezekiel Nesbit Richard Farrington Three names unknown
Stinging Bee	Sloop	12	Benjamin Oliver 11 names unknown
Alert	Schooner	10	Sidney Delancy Alix Lightbourn Hezekiah Reckley John Moxey Alex Miller Saml Bowe Alfred Ferguson Jonathan Williams Thos Gould Neptune Storr
Proceed	Schooner	8	Wm Rolle Stephen Romer Daniel Forbes Nathan Forbes Samuel Rolle John Rolle Andrew Forbes P. Rolle
Choir	Schooner	6	Chas Russell Absalom Dorsett W. Haley

Lost to Shipping.

			Elijah Humes
			Jos Miller
			Alfred Frances
Jane	Schooner		J.T. Mckey Jr.
Experience	Sloop	6	Hezekiah Farrington
			Alfred Brown
			Theo Munroe
			Jos Sims
			Jos Allen Winder
			Herman Boyd
Nonsuch	Sloop	12	Jas Rattray
			Ruben Sweeting
			Jas Mackey
			Jeremiah Strachan
			W. Rodgers
			Bruce Boyd
			Jas Bowleg
			Isaac Evans
			Wilfred McKenzie
			Three names unknown
Phoebe	Schooner	15	Isaac Bethel
			Liberty Sturrup
			Thaddeus Bethel
			Isaac(Sardens) Hart
			William Sturrup Jr.
			Enoch Bethel
			Chas Clark
			Mark Marshall
			Jas Wallace
			Michael Bethel Jr.
			Five names unknown
Lady Shea	Schooner	5	Robert(John) Murphy
			Daniel(Pompey) Whyley
			Abraham Rolle
			Edward Dean
			Thos Evans
Florence	Schooner	1	Israel McQueen
Alpine	Schooner	2	Samuel Demerritt
			Christopher Brown

Lost to Shipping.

The Colonial Secretary Mr. J.S. Churchill on the 15th November, 1899, published the list of persons who died in this storm from the island of Andros. This list of names of the persons who died in this storm was provided to him by Mr. Lennox E. Forsyth the Resident Justice for the entire island of Andros but was stationed at Mangrove Cay, Andros.

Below are some of the names of the men who drowned at Red Bays:

Dan Russell	Wm Glinton & Son	John Bunch	Robert Murphy
Charles Saunders	Sydney Delancy	Charles Martin	Thomas Evans
Abraham Rolle	James Ball	Thaddeus Johnson	William Dorsett
Uriah Bain	Henry Evans	Solomon Woodside	William Fowler
Bartheus Woodside	James Nottage	John Colebrooke	Jonathan White
Cubit Woodside	Levi Marshal	Cyrus Butler	Charles O' Brien
James Anderson	James Moxie	Darrell Kemp	

Names of men who drowned at Red Bays.

Below are the names of the persons who drowned at Andros during the Great Bahamas Hurricane of 1899:

Name:	Where They Drowned:	Name:	Where They Drowned:
Ambrister, Zadoc	Joulter Cays	Bain, Bartholomew	Joulter Cays
Bain, Joseph	Red Bays	Bain, Daniel	Joulter Cays
Bain, Uriah	Red Bays	Bennett, John	Red Bays
Bennett, Robert	Joulter Cays	Bode, Nathaniel	Red Bays
Bootle, Joseph	Joulter Cays	Boyd, Bruce	Joulter Cays
Bowleg, Jos-Alex	Joulter Cays	Bunch, John	Unknown
Bain, George	Joulter Cays	Colebrooke, John	William Cays
Davis, James	Red Bays	Davis, Alfred	Red Bays
Duncombe	Unknown	Deveaux, Fred	Joulter Cays
Dorset, Ramon	Red Bays	Duncombe, Claudius	Joulter Cays
Evans, Henry	Red Bays	Evans, Thomas	Red Bays
Edgecombe, Henry	Red Bays	Edgecombe, Sylvanus	Joulter Cays
Edgecombe, Herbert	Joulter Cays	Forbes, Hamilton	Fresh Creek
Franks, Alexander	Fresh Creek	Fowler, William	Williams Cay
Ferguson, Esau	Unknown	Francis, Andrew	Joulter Cays
Farrington, Richard	Joulter Cays	Glinton, Samuel	Red Bays
Glinton, William	Red Bays	Gordon, Virginia	Red Bays
Hepburn, George	Joulter Cays	Hanna, Theophilus	Joulter Cays
Hamilton, Joseph	Joulter Cays	Johnson, James	Red Bays
Johnson, Joseph	Red Bays	Johnson, Joseph	Joulter Cays
Johnson, Edward	Red Bays	Johnson	Unknown
Lightbourn, Horatio	Red Bays	Mockey, G	Fresh Creek
Miller, Robert Geo	Red Bays	Mackey, Henry	Red Bays
Mickey, James	Joulter Cays	McKenzie, Wilfred	Joulter Cays
McQueen, Israel	Unknown	McKay, Jacob	Joulter Cays
McBride, William	Red Bays	Moxey, James	Unknown
Martin, Charles	Joulter Cays	Thomas, Minuis	Joulter Cays
Miller, Solomon	William Cays	Murphy Robi	Red Bays
Nottage, James	William Cays	Nesbitt, Nicholas	Joulter Cays
Oliver, Samuel	Fresh Creek	Oliver, Samuel	Joulter Cays
Oliver, Benjamin	Joulter Cays	Oliver, Cornelius	Joulter Cays
Pinder, Hezekiah	Red Bays	Rolle, Horatio	Red Bays
Rolle, Michael	Red Bays	Russell, Robert	Red Bays
Rattray, Joseph	Joulter Cays	Rolle, Archillus	Joulter Cays
Rolle, Graham	Red Bays	Rodgers, William	Joulter Cays
Simmons, Edgar	Unknown	Saunders Charles	Unknown
Simmons, Horatio	Unknown	Simms, Theophilus	Joulter Cays
Sweeting, Reuben	Joulter Cays	Sweeting, Thomas	Fresh Creek
Saunders, Charles	Red Bays	Strachan, Jeremiah	Joulter Cayss
Thurston, Simeon	Fresh Creek	James, Taylor	Joulter Cays
Thompson, George	Red Bays	Thompson, Joshua	Red Bays
Ulin, Joseph	Joulter Cays	Ulin, George	Joulter Cays
Wemyss, Henry	Red Bays	Williams	Joulter Cays
Woodside, Mathis	Williams Cay	Woodside, Jno. Sol	Williams Cay
Williams, Joseph	Joulter Cays	Woodside, Cubit	Williams Cay
White, John	Williams Cay	Wylly, John	Williams Cay
Daniel, Wylly	Red Bays	Wylly, John	Joulter Cays

The names of the persons who died at Andros.

In addition to above, there were 4 persons lost whose names are unknown. List of persons drowned by the overflow of the land in the hurricane. They are, Mary Brown, Simon Demeritt, Samuel Demeritt, Gladis McQueen, David Miller, George Miller, and Christopher Miller.

CHAPTER ELEVEN
TERRENCE KEOGH'S TWO ACCOUNTS OF THE GREAT ABACO HURRICANE OF 1932

While I was writing my second book called *'The Major Hurricanes to Affect the Bahamas'* this Terrence Keogh's account of *'The Great Abaco Hurricane of 1932'* was brought to my attention by Patricia Beardsley Roker. It is such a compelling account of this great hurricane that I decided to include it in this book. I hope that you find it just as fascinating as I did when I first read it. This account describes the great impact this hurricane had on the island of Abaco as experienced by Terrence Keogh. (Copyright © 1933 by Harper's Magazine. All rights reserved. Reproduced from the May issue by special permission.):

On the morning of Wednesday, August 31, 1932, I noticed that the signal station at Nassau was flying advisory storm warnings, indicating that the center of the storm was expected to pass close by. I had arranged to take passage on the following day for Abaco Island, in the diesel mail boat Priscilla. At ten o'clock the following morning-Saturday, September 3rd the Priscilla came to anchor at Green Turtle Cay. At the time the people made their living by sponging, fishing, and growing fruits on a small scale. The day of my arrival, which was Saturday, September 3rd, I spent almost entirely with Basil Lowe, a fine fellow who used to be in the shark-fishing business.

We sat round all day and talked the business over from one end to the other in great detail, as I was thinking of going into it.

The weather in the meantime was beautiful with not the slightest sign of an approaching hurricane. As a matter of fact, I had forgotten all about it, and I guess everybody else had too. I spent that night in the Court House, where the resident Commissioner had kindly arranged for me to sleep while I was in Green Turtle Cay. The next morning, Sunday, September 4th, I did not get up till very late. During the afternoon I took a long walk along the sandy shore of the Cay with three boys of the town. One of them was Basil Lowe's son, a fine strapping young fellow of sixteen. Little did I think that the following day I should be picking up his dead body with the dead body of his baby brother clutched tightly in his arms. The fateful day of Monday, September 5th dawned with the hurricane obviously only a few hours off. At daylight, when I turned out, it was blowing a heavy gale of wind with a steady downpour of rain.

By ten o' clock that morning it was blowing such a violent gale and the rain was pouring in such a deluge that it was really impossible to do anything more outside. With four or five other men I went to a store kept by Mr. Willis Bethel and there sat talking and waiting to see what was going to happen. Mr. Bethel had a barometer, and when I looked at it I am sure that my heart missed several beats. I have spent practically my entire life at sea, which means constantly watching barometers in all parts of the world and under all kinds of weather conditions; but I had certainly never seen anything like this before. It then read 28.82 inches, which in itself is disconcerting enough in this part of the world, but what was worse, I could actually see it going down all the time. I tried to time it but found that my watch had stopped and was full of water. When the barometer reached 28.00 inches I thought it would surely stop, but instead it started going faster. The last time I can remember noticing it, it read 27.50 inches. I had never before even heard of a barometer being this low.

The wind had by now reached what I judged to be hurricane force, and seemed to be getting worse every moment. The squalls came sweeping over at shorter intervals and would strike with terrific blast of wind and driving stream of water like a fire hose. Shingles, fence palings, and almost every other kind of article imaginable were by this time flying through the air. It was beginning to look serious. The building which I was in would obviously not hold together for much longer, and Mr. Bethel decided to abandon it altogether and take refuge in his dwelling with his family. I abandoned it too, with the idea of going back to the Court House, which I considered the most substantial building in the settlement. But when I got outside I realized just how hard it was blowing. To stand upright was almost impossible, but I managed to get down the main street by crouching over and pulling myself along the sides of buildings, fences, or anything that happened to be within reach. The buildings were still standing all right although there were plenty of boards and pieces of lumber flying about.

Right in the center of the town there was a store kept by a woman named Mrs. Roberts, and I stopped in there on my way by as I noticed the door on the lee side was open. Inside the store at the time I found Mrs. Roberts, her daughter, one old man almost sixty years old, and a little girl of about five or six. They all appeared very frightened and were naturally anxious to have news of what was happening on the outside and how other people were making out. The water got so deep on the floor that I ripped up a plank in the lowest part to let it run out underneath. I was in the store, I should say, at a guess, for about fifteen minutes before the whole strength of the hurricane struck. It came with one terrific blast of wind and water, like a judgment of the Lord, sweeping everything before it. The building creaked in every joint and the sides bulged like rubber balloons. The women immediately became hysterical and after a few moments threw themselves upon their knees and prayed. Never before in my life have I felt so utterly helpless and insignificant. There was literally nothing that anybody could do.

Any estimate that I make of the velocity of the wind is only the wildest guess. I do know that the weather observatory at Hope Town, twenty-five miles away, registered a velocity of one hundred and sixty miles an hour before the place blew down. This was several hours before the real hurricane struck. When the onslaught struck, my first impulse was to run outside as it was perfectly obvious that the building was not going to stand it. I went to the door and stood there looking out, trying all the time to remain cool and keep my senses, which was nearly impossible with the hurricane howling outside and the women hysterically screaming inside.

Never have I seen such frightful destruction. The crash of the buildings being smashed to pieces could be heard even above the roaring of the wind and rain. Directly across the street there stood a big three-storey stone house in which fourteen people were gathered to ride out the storm. As I stood there watching, the first few blasts ripped all the shingle off the roof and sent them off to leeward like a shower of leaves. An instant later the entire building collapsed, some of the heavy stones being carried off with the wind, but most of them crashing down among the wreckage of floors and partitions that remained. I had not seen anybody leave the house and thought that they had surely been killed. If they had not been killed they were probably trapped in the wreckage, but even so, I was perfectly powerless to give them any help. To leave the shelter of the house and go out in the storm now seemed like sure death. There were roofs, whole sides of houses, boats, and all kinds of wreckage hurling through the air and crashing right and left into other buildings.

It is really impossible for me to describe the frightful havoc, as anything I say is inadequate. At about this time a man suddenly appeared, apparently from nowhere, crawling up to the house on his hands and knees as best he could, his head streaming with blood. I dragged him in the door and tried to find out where he had come from, but he did not seem to know himself. He said that he had been in two different houses that had gone down, and had been struck on the head by something. He had quite a bad cut just over his ear which I bound up as well as I could with a handkerchief. After this he just sat on the floor moaning and praying. His nerve was completely gone, but I could not make out if he was just scared or if he had been really hurt. He certainly did not improve the morale of the women, who by this time were screaming and carrying on in the most frightful way. The next people to come in for shelter were a young fellow about my age with his wife and a little boy who had been in the big stone house that I had seen demolished. They had had an awful time. As the building was collapsing the man had thrown his wife, with the baby in her arms, out clear of the wreckage, and then jumped after himself. They seemed to think that the other people had been killed instantly. Since then they had been buffeted about the storm, desperately fighting to get in under some kind of shelter. How that fellow managed to drag his wife and child over piles of wreckage, and protect them from fury of the hurricane will always be a mystery to me. They were cut and bruised and completely exhausted. Their nerves were also completely gone and they immediately joined the others in weeping and praying.

During all this time the hurricane had been raging unabated-getting worse if this were possible. I had been watching the building which we were in very closely, and had just about decided that it was time to leave, as it would most certainly not hold together much longer. The sides were bulging out and the roof seemed about to lift off any minute. The fastenings had started in all joints and the ends of the rafters had come away from the plates about six inches. I broke up the prayer meeting and suggested that we all go out and fight our way to the nearest house that was standing, and which could be reached by crawling over the ruins of two other houses. As I was talking there came one terrific squall of wind accompanied by a ripping and tearing noise, and then the whole building simply took off from its foundation like an airplane. All hands were sent sprawling on the floor and the things on the shelves came piling down on us. It was an awful moment. The whole building, with us in it, was flying through the air, and it seemed to me then as though it would never come to earth. It finally landed with a splintering crash that broke in the floor in several places.

This was enough for me. I decided to leave without any further loss of time and try to find shelter in some other house that would have more regard for laws of gravitation. I sang out to the others that I was going, and I tried to persuade Mrs. Roberts and her daughter to come with me. However, by this time they were in such a state of combined hysterics and devotion that they had not even got up off the floor. I started out the door, which was on the lee side of the building, and immediately was picked up, off my feet by a puff of wind, blown bodily in the air across the street, and crashed through a picket fence on the other side, which for some reason was still there. I was then blown and bumped over a pile of wreckage that had once been a house, until I finally got a firm grip with both hands on an old piece of floor joist. I hung on to this for dear life, trying to collect my thoughts, while the deluge poured down on my back, and the wind roared by with such force that it sometimes took all my strength to keep from being torn away. It was hard for me to see anything in the driving rain; in fact. It was altogether impossible even to open my eyes if I was facing it.

The howling of the hurricane and the general noise and confusion of the destruction going on around me, combined with the constant danger of having my brains knocked out by something flying in mid-air, made it very difficult even to think. From the position I was in I could see only two houses left standing. The rest of the town was simply a tangled mass of wreckage and ruins. As there was certainly no point in remaining where I was, lying flat on my stomach, completely exposed to the weather and everything else, I began to make my way towards the nearest house, which I should say, was about two hundred yards off. Getting there was an awful job. I did it on my hands and knees, sometimes crawling and sometimes literally dragging myself along against the wind. In the particularly heavy squalls I had to stop all progress and stretch flat on the ground, hanging on to whatever was near with all my strength to keep from being blown away. I had one very close call. The whole gable end of a house suddenly appeared from nowhere, driving through the air and coming right at me. I did not have time to do anything but throw myself flat on my stomach, and when I looked up again it had passed clear over me and was disappearing to leeward, gaining altitude all the time.

I finally managed to work my way round to the leeward side of the house that I was heading for, and went in through an open door. Everything inside was crazy. There were five or six men and women and two little children, all in a state of hysterics. The house was shaking and vibrating so that you could hardly stand up, and the water was pouring down through the ceiling in perfect deluge. As soon as I got inside one of the men told me that he was afraid the house would collapse at any moment, and that they were all about to leave it. Before he had finished talking there was a noise like an explosion, and the roof and part of the second storey were torn off. Next the windward wall blew in and the ceiling above started to come down on top of us. All hands piled pell mell through the door, out into the hurricane. As I went I grabbed one of the children, a little girl about six or seven, who had apparently got separated from her family. The confusion and chaos outside had by this time reached a point impossible to describe. I had no idea what the others intended doing, but I immediately started struggling along, with the child under my arm, toward a house that was still standing nearby.

The rest of the people, or rather those of them that I could see, struck out in the opposite direction. They looked like ants as they crawled along the ground, desperately clutching at pieces of wreckage and cowering behind ruins of buildings. It was a fearful moment, and I will confess that I was having difficulty in thinking clearly myself. The child simply clung to me, with her two arms around my waist, whimpering and crying. I looked back once and saw the remains of the house we had just left being smashed to matchwood by the fury of the wind. The next moment a whole dinghy boat came flying out of space through the air and landed with a terrific crash a few feet from us. My face was cut and bleeding badly in several places from the sand and gravel driven horizontally before the wind, and I was having great difficulty in protecting the child from it. After going a little way I noticed a flight of stone steps built up from the ground and leading apparently to nowhere, but just rising up into space. There was a section of a roof wedged in behind them, and several other pieces of wreckage lying strewn about which gave evidence that a house had once stood there. I got round to leeward of the steps and crouched behind them to rest for a few moments before continuing on my way. The first thing I noticed was a pair of legs protruding from under the roof. I pulled on them and dragged out the body of a rather old man, cold and quite dead.

After I had finally reached the house for which I was aiming I had quite a job to get in, as all the windows and doors were boarded up and nailed shut. The door on the lee side was fastened from within, and it was only after I had started to batter it down with a piece of rafter that the people realized there was somebody trying to get in. This house was a large two-story stone building that had formerly been used as a store. It had been unoccupied for some time, but when the hurricane struck, several families took refuge there; several families took refuge there, as it was a most substantial building. When I arrived there were about fifty people all told inside, men, women, and children. Never before have I seen a more frightened, helpless, and thoroughly miserable gathering of human beings. The windows being all boarded up, it was as black as night inside. The water was pouring down in streams from the floor above, and everybody was soaked to the hide. The women and children lay huddled together on the floor, their teeth chattering with the cold, praying hysterically to the Lord for mercy. The roaring and howling of the hurricane outside made it almost impossible to think, and to talk it was necessary to shout at the top of your lungs.

Although the storm was now at its very height, the house showed no signs of giving way. I was afraid that if anything struck it, it would come down very quickly and, therefore, started at once to plan a course of action in case we should have to leave it. I stood at the door on the lee side and from there could see only one house standing-and that had half the roof gone. This house, I was told, belonged to Dr. Kendricks, the local doctor, and was obviously the place to go next if we had to move. The darkness came quickly and with it, to my great relief, came a decided change for the better in the weather. The wind in the space of a few moments went right down to nothing but a strong breeze and the rain stopped altogether. The general opinion of the rest of the men seemed to be that this was the end of the hurricane, but I did not think so. I was afraid that it was just a temporary calm while the center passed over us. As soon as it moderated, all hands went to work at something.

The most important need was something to eat for the women and children, as the majority of them had had nothing the entire day. Three men went to the remains of Mrs. Roberts' store to search around for some food and for some lanterns and oil. Two other men went to work on the building, battering up windows on the top floor which had blown open, reinforcing doors, and a hundred other much needed repairs. I tried to get them to nail up the doors and windows on the south side, which so far had been to leeward, in case the wind came from that direction, but they did not think this was necessary. I would have done it myself but we had only one piece of iron for a hammer, practically no nails, and only what lumber we could rip off partitions inside. Their failure to do it nearly cost the lives of everybody in the building an hour or so later.

In the meantime, I went to Dr. Kendricks' house to see how many were there, and also to try to find out what the barometer was doing. I found Dr. Kendricks' house in much the same condition as the one I had just left. There were about one hundred people crowded into it, many of them quite badly hurt. The women and children lay huddled together in the darkness crying and praying. I tried to raise their spirits and comfort them but there was practically nothing that I could do. Never before in my life have I been so totally unable to cope with a situation. Nobody had any idea of how many people had been killed, and the darkness and confusion of the night it was certainly impossible to find out. Dr. Kendricks appeared to be the only man who was really keeping his head. He went about his work of giving first aid to the injured in the calm, businesslike manner, although he had himself suffered as much loss of property as anybody. I found Mrs. Roberts here, unconscious, with a fractured skull. Dr. Kendricks had brought her in himself. Kendricks' barometer stood at 27.60 inches and showed no signs of rising. This convinced me that the hurricane was really only half over, and that the calm which now prevailed would soon be broken by the wind coming howling from out of the south.

I had no sooner got back inside the stone house than the wind came again, this time from the southward, in violent squalls, accompanied by the usual downpour of driving rain. There were several more people in the building now, who had taken advantage of the lull to crawl from under the ruins of their homes to this shelter. By this time the known deaths amounted to seven, with about two hundred still unaccounted for. I now began to feel a pain in my right side which was caused, I found out a week later, by one of my ribs being broken. This had probably happened when I was blown through the picket fence but had not noticed it till now.

The hurricane was now raging outside with the same violence and destruction but from the opposite direction. Right away we found ourselves in a very bad position, because the windows and doors on the south side of the building had not been boarded up. On account of the shift of the wind this was now the windward side. The very first squalls had smashed the sash right out the window frames and torn the doors off their hinges. The water was pouring in and there was a steady barrage of sand, rocks and small pieces of wreckage. All hands had to move to the leeward side, which meant almost sure death if the building collapsed. It would not have been possible to get out as all these doors and windows were fastened on the outside. I was afraid that the wind, by getting inside the building, would lift the roof off or blow the walls right out. Already the wooden partitions inside were beginning to buckle badly. Something had to be done and done quickly. I went outside with two men to help me, and after an awful battle, lasting nearly an hour; we managed to get the openings boarded up to a great extent. It was surprising thing to me how a lot of these men appeared to lose their nerve. Many of them just simply gave up and joined the women in prayer, rather than make any effort to help themselves.

The moaning of the injured, together with the weeping and screaming of the women, made a most frightful experience that could be heard even above the storm. One old man started singing hymns at the top of his lungs and was immediately joined by everyone else. This would have been very nice except that he chose for his opening number "We will meet in the sweet By and By." It was the last straw for me, and I could not help suggesting that he sing something a little more cheerful. It was about midnight when I noticed that the wind had started to moderate slightly. The rain continued just as hard but the squalls were considerably lighter than they had been. Somebody came up from Dr. Kendricks' house with the welcome news that the barometer had started rising rapidly. This was very reassuring and convinced me that the worst of the hurricane was now over. For the remainder of the night the weather continued to improve steadily until by daylight the wind had moderated to strong gale, and the rain, though still pouring down, was nothing like what it had been. As soon as the danger was obviously past the people all began to brighten up. Somebody during the lull had managed to get a kerosene stove out of Mrs. Roberts' store, so I turned to and made strong tea for all hands. We had also a couple of boxes of soda biscuits. After this the women and children lay down on the floor and through sheer exhaustion were soon fast asleep. I had dried out my pipe and tobacco over the stove.

After drinking six cups of boiled black tea, munching a couple of handfuls of biscuits, and smoking three pipes of strong tobacco, I was once again ready for anything. I really thought that dawn would never come. People kept coming in with reports from different parts of the town, and the list of the dead and injured was mounting steadily. The most serious thing for the immediate present was the condition of the people who were still living but trapped under the ruins of their houses unable to get out. This was the first job to be tackled. Every man who was physically able turned to, but, nevertheless, it was a slow, hard job to get these poor people out, as the gale of wind and pouring rain made it very difficult to work.

With the first signs of daylight I started for Basil Lowe's house to see how he and his family had come through. Nothing appeared to be left standing, and the streets were piled so high with wreckage that it was impossible to follow them. Where Basil Lowe's house had stood the day before was a litter of smashed timbers. In the middle of the mess I came across the body of his eldest son, a fine boy of sixteen, lying face downward on the ground, cold and stone dead. I rolled him over and found that his neck had been broken. With a death grip, he still held in his arms the body of his baby brother, also cold and dead. I carried them both out to an open space and laid them on the ground side by side, then covered them with loose boards, weighted down with stones, so that they would not blow away. As I was doing this Basil himself appeared. It was the most harrowing moment of my life and there was little that I could say to him at the time. He had had a frightful experience during the hurricane and was in a dazed condition. When his house collapsed he, his wife, six children, and his mother-in-law all had to run for their lives. His wife had fallen through the floor and was unconscious, which meant that he had to carry her in his arms after dragging her out. He had seen his two children killed, by the gable end of the building, as they ran through the door. In some way or other he had managed to get the rest of them into a near-by- house, but had only been there a short while before this also collapsed.

I returned to the stone house, in which there were now about one hundred additional people who had come in from different parts of the town, all in the same state of exhaustion and hysteric. It was now so full that it was almost impossible to get in through the door. By this time everybody in the settlement had been accounted for, and the death toll amounted to eighteen, with twenty five badly injured. We held a kind of council of war to talk over our position and see what was to be done next. Obviously the dead had to be buried, but this was practically impossible until the weather cleared up. It was still blowing too hard to walk round without holding on to something, and the rain was pouring down in a steady torrent. Luckily there had been quite a quantity of food salvaged from the ruins of the various stores. Some people had managed-how, the Lord only knows-to unearth some clothing, blankets, and quilts that were still fairly dry, and these were immediately distributed amongst the women and children. The women got busy brewing gallons of strong tea and baking Johnny cakes. Somebody collected several dead chickens from among the ruins, and we soon had steaming hot soup, which I thought at the time, was the best thing I ever tasted.

Very discouraging reports came back of how people in other communities had feared in the storm. Their houses were all built in one district at the eastern end of the town, and had all been destroyed with the very first blasts of the hurricane. The people had run out and, not knowing where to turn, had very sensibly taken to the open country. At the very height of the storm, men, women, and children, about eighty of them altogether, had desperately crawled, dragged, and fought their way up the side of a high hill, and had taken refuge in a stone quarry at the top. The quarry was a huge round pit about three hundred feet in diameter and sixty feet deep, which afforded shelter from the wind but not from the cold and wet. They had all huddled together at the bottom on the windward side, while the hurricane went thundering by overhead. The poor coloured people in the quarry, nearly blue with the cold, had been in this godforsaken hole, completely exposed to the weather with nothing to eat, for over twenty four hours. I had brought a few tins of beef along with me, which I quickly divided up among the women, and then dispatched somebody back to town for more. They were all so terrified and exhausted that I had difficulty in persuading anybody to venture up out of the pit. I noticed a dead horse lying at the bottom of the quarry and was wondering how in the world it had got there. They told me that they had no idea where it had come from, but at the height of the storm it had suddenly appeared flying through the air, and had dropped about sixty feet to where it now lay.

One Negro preacher said that he had thought it was the dove coming down upon the Apostles, but could not exactly see the smile. He apparently considered it as some kind of omen and immediately launched out into a long sermon, much to the edification of his audience, about the Ark full of animals landing on "Mount Arral" after forty days of flood. He managed to work into it something about the waters of the Red Sea being opened, then rambled on about Saint Simon fishing in the Lake of Galilee; in fact he used every part of the Scripture that had anything to do with water. I thought it was most appropriate as both he and his congregation looked more than half drowned. I spent the afternoon in the quarry, trying to keep out of the rain by crouching under a shelf of rock, getting colder, wetter, and more miserable every minute. Toward evening the wind seemed to moderate considerably, and I returned to the town in search of a more comfortable place. There was not much comfort to be found. But at least the hurricane was over.

A HURRICANE-TERRENCE KEOGH'S DESCRIPTION

Interviewed for a second time in New York by a representative of the *New York Herald Tribune*, Mr. Terrence Keogh gives the following entertaining description of his adventures in the Bahamas and during the Great Abaco Hurricane of 1932. This account was taken from the Nassau Guardian, December 31, 1932. Below is the excerpt of his account of the storm:

Terrence Keogh, one of the last of a long line of Irish adventurers and filibusters, was in New York recently for the first time in four years, visiting his aunt, Mrs. Nicholas Biddle, at 530 East Sixty-Sixth Street. Although he never has led a revolution, as did his great-great uncle, Robert Emmet who was hanged for it with the gallant Lord Edward Fitzgerald and others of his United Irishmen in 1803 and although he never has been in the public eye as anything more than a minor member of scientific expeditions, he has his legend. A trip to the Bahamas, alone in an open boat that ended in a hurricane and the salvaging of an island community has recently added to it.

From Cowes, where he goes after the trans-Atlantic races he delights in, to the dives of Shanghai that knew him when he passed years with the Roosevelt Lines, the exploits of the son of the "lame judge," the late Martin J. Keogh, Justice of the New York Supreme Court, have created excitements. Last winter he was in America again, and by spring he was in America again, and by spring he was finding a family life dull. To escape it he sold all his worldly possessions and brought a one volume edition of Shakespeare, a large supply of provisions and the Snug, a twenty-foot sloop which he modestly describes as "rather a small boat." On May 14 he set off alone in it from Woods Hole, on Cape Cod, for Kingston, Jamaica.

Finds Weather Unreliable

Sitting in Mrs. Biddle's pleasant dining room over coffee and a glass, after an excellent luncheon, he seemed an inconspicuous, ruddy sort of person until he began to tell his story. He had made the Southern trip often enough and expected fair weather after the first day or so. He was disappointed.

"I had vile weather all the way down," he said; "southerly that meant tacking constantly and six bad storms. It was cold the first day or so, but after I crossed the Gulf Stream it was all right."

He described how he treated the storms, which he called "little dangerous in a boat as small as that." He would take all sail off, lash the tiller, put out a sea anchor and retired to his cabin with his pipe and Shakespeare until the wind had gone down enough to make sailing sensible again.

"One of them lasted for three days and nights," he said, "and one of them fooled me. Of course, the only really difficult thing in such a small boat is staying on it. Sometimes that's something of a problem. About 200 miles south of Bermuda, when I was twenty five days out of Wood's Hole, a bad blow came up. Nothing would have happened, except that the calm centre passed right over us, and therefore, the wind change. Supplies were getting lowish, so I wanted to run before

it. I went up to set the mainsail, and while I was at it I slipped, tripped on something, and went over. Fortunately, I had hold of a rope. In those circumstances you hang on pretty hard, and I was able to pull myself in."

The rest of the trip to Kingston was he said, uneventful. He ran into the worst storm he has ever seen at sea, and only saved himself from being blown onto the seashore of a small island by stripping all sail and hiking the Snug over a bar into a harbor. The storm past, he put in at Nassau for supplies, and was feted there for ten days.

Arrived at Kingston on August 18, he found himself penniless, and raised the wind by selling the Snug. Between parties in Nassau he had interested himself in the shark fisheries, and, after a "dull week at Kingston," he returned to Nassau and there went to Abaco Island, one of the larger ones in the Bahamas. On Sunday, September 4, he was ensconced in the Courthouse at Green Turtle Cay, a settlement of 500 whites on an islet off Abaco. They lived by sponge fishing, shark fishing, turtling, and he was getting to know them, and finding out more about shark fishing quietly in their midst.

"That Sunday night we had our first warning," he said. "Of course, before I left Nassau there had been storm warnings from Washington of a hurricane brewing by Turk's Island, but that was so far away no one paid it any attention. On Sunday night the whole eastern sky was pitch black. Monday morning there was a good gale and rain in squalls. At noon, I decided we were going to have real trouble, so I started for the general store to get some kerosene, so that I could lock myself in the Court House, which was a stone building, and read until it was over. By that time it was so bad you could barely walk, and shingles and bits of porches were getting kind of active. I got to the store and ten minutes later it started."

There were five others in the building with him, two men and three women, and their immediate reaction was to throw themselves face down on the floor and pray.

SEES STONE HOUSE CRUMPLE

"I looked out," he went on, "and the first thing I saw was a big stone house across the street, that I knew had fourteen people in it, go down before my eyes. It went in like a spokeless umbrella. I tried to

go out to rescue some of them, but I could barely hold on to the side of the store. You can't describe a hurricane. The wind is simply an incredible force and the rain strikes you so hard that it left my back black and blue and skinned my face as you'd skin an animal. So I went back into the store."

"That didn't do much good, since the minute I got into it it took off like an airplane and sailed for what seemed like an hour, actually about a hundred feet, to land on some rocks with the floor boards bursting like an explosion and people and provisions flying in every direction. After that I concluded there might be a healthier place, so I said goodbye."

He crawled out on his hands and knees, with his head well down, trying to find another place.

"Getting about was quite a business, but it was just possible that way." He said. "I passed two or three corpses, and any amount of wreckage. I looked up once and saw two boats flying along overhead. I reached a house, where there were a man, his wife and two children, and as soon as I got there the roof took off. The man had a broken leg, so the woman grabbed one child and I the other, and we started again, with the man crawling after. We were out fifteen minutes that time, but we finally got to a stone house which seemed to be standing up well. It had thirty people in it, all with hysterics, not one of them knowing what members of his or her family were alive."

At 9pm the wind went down slightly, but it was useless to try to do anything in the dark. Tuesday dawned, with wind and rain still strong, but the rescue work began. Every house on the island was down except the stone house in which Keogh had taken refuge. Three persons had been blown off the island. The wind had lifted the tombstones in the churchyard and deposited them on the beach. A horse had been dropped over a cliff "like a sea gull." An iron wash tub was found seven miles away on another island, and three houses had been taken across the channel to Abaco. Eighteen persons had been killed, and most of the livestock was buried in the ruins. The velocity of the wind as registered Monday morning was 160 miles an hour.

"In point of fact," he said, bringing the attention back to the quiet dining room by pausing for a moment to light the pipe that had

accompanied Shakespeare, "the island was a complete, absolute wreck. That was the worst part of it. Every one was hurt somehow I had a rib broken, but we all turned to digging out the ruins, with people finding relatives or not finding them as the case might be. There was one old man he had been in the first house I saw go down, whose wife had had her arm cut off in the falling house. He was near her; she was almost in his arms. She died six hours later, and he was there next to her for forty-eight hours. He was made when we got him out."

RESCUE WORK GETS UNDER WAY

The next day the sun came out. Provisions were getting low, and only two of the cisterns that contained the island's water supply were standing. He helped launch a motor boat, which had been carried some hundred feet inshore, and he and its owner started for Nassau to get help.

"When I got back to Green Turtle Cay," he continued, "things were still in terrible shape. If a thing like that had happened in New York it would have been about like Jehovah smiting Sodom, but there things weren't so close together. Still, typhoid and cholera had put in an appearance, and the island's doctor, Kendrick, was doing an unbelievable good job. I had sort of offered my services, so I put myself in unofficial charge of Green Turtle. We organized camps, and some of the people found a kind of shelter under the roofs that were lying about. We collected as much household goods as we could, and started to build again out of the wreckage. A good many of the timbers were still useful, and we could generally put up a smaller house. The main thing attended to was health however."

After two months of it he had done all he could and set out for Nassau again in the schooner.

"We had quite a trip," he said. "I was captain, of course. My crew consisted of two beldames, neither able to do more than cook, which they did on the deck, an epileptic, a lunatic and a leper. The last was by far the most useful man on the boat. The lunatic was an old man who thought he was an admiral. He spent most of his time forward, a bottle held to his eye like a glass."

At last he sailed for the United States, but not before making friends with Nassau's plentiful population of rum runners. He expected to land at Miami on Election Day. He did so, but was immediately utilized by a detachment of his new friends to help capture a steamer with some of their property aboard from hijackers. He succeeded, left it for a pilot boat beyond the twelve mile limit and arrived in Jacksonville in sneakers, and old yachting cap and a few odds and ends of clothing, with $2 in his pocket. Funds were supplied him and he set off for Boston by bus.

"Things always seem to happen to me," he said as he closed his tale. "A woman in the bus proceeded to have a baby several miles from nowhere, and I had to act as assistant midwife."

CHAPTER TWELVE

PERSONAL RECOLLECTIONS OF THE GREAT BAHAMAS HURRICANE OF 1899 AND THE GREAT ABACO HURRICANE OF 1932 IMPACT ON THE BAHAMAS.

Mr. H.G. Christie, after seeing the great devastation the Great Bahamas Hurricane of 1899 left on the city of Nassau and Andros, decided to put pen to paper and wrote a very riveting poem about this storm called *"Our Visitation."* It was first published in the Nassau Guardian on Wednesday, August 16, 1899.

OUR VISITATION

I heard the trumpet blast that blew,
To the winds of the frozen North,
Behold the Angel, as he flew,
To let the Storm King forth,
I saw him breathe on the Tempest's hands,
And his crystal chains fell free,
And the Storm King loosed from his frozen hands,
Was charged with the Lord's decree.

I heard the shouts from his husky lips
As he sprang from his icy home,
I saw him ride on the Ocean's hips,
And drink of her boiling foam,
And he cried "What! Ho!" for the Sunny isles,
And he smote his mighty hands,
And straight he flew ten thousand miles,
To shares of our Southern lands.

The Nimbus clustered round his head,
As he roared up to the sky,
And the Ocean whitened at his tread,
As he hurried breathless by,
And he hang his robe upon the sea,
And his mantle o'er the sun,
And he told us all what was to be,
Ere the August night was done.

And dim and dark the wild night grew,
And frantic storm came down,
And out of roaring lungs he blew,
From under his somber frown,
Now, rack and woe, to the panting ships
And the mariner, watch worn,
As the cable parts and the anchor slips,
And the masts from their steps are torn.

And woe to the dwellers on the land
And the toilers in the field,
For the blow on blow, from his chant hand,
Makes the house and the tree to yield,
The tempest spreads his arms apart,
With a foot each on land and sea,
And strong studs quake and rafters start,
As the house shakes frightfully.

I saw the Tempest as he passed,
Through the streets of our pleasant town,
I heard the snort of his nostrils blast,

As he blew the houses down,
And fence and wall and tree and all,
He met in his set career,
Was scared and torn as God had sworn,
Ere he sent His Judgment there.

From Western shore to Southern bound,
From Gambia to Adelaide,
From the North and the East, yea all around,
Fox Hill to the Eastern Parade,
The Tempest trod, with the voice of God,
And the power of a hopeless might,
But the awful shaft, that the Tempest grasped,
Was the beaming sword of Right.

And I heard the Angel as he blew,
Again the trumpet clear,
And he checked the Tempest as he drew,
New strength for a fresh career,
And I saw him bind the storm again and his fetters forge anew,
And backward over the Northern main,
The storm and his Master flew.

H.G. Christie
August 14th 1899.

Here's an account of some persons preparation for the Great Bahamas Hurricane of 1899 as reported by the Nassau Guardian, August 14, 1899.

We feel assured that our subscribers and patrons will understand that the issue of the Guardian on Saturday was prevented by the circumstances attending the hurricane, and will therefore excuse this our first departure from the regular day of publication since the hurricane of 1883. Destruction of houses, vessels, fruits and many lives feared to be lost. The weather on Thursday night indicated that a storm was approaching, yet the barometers did not cause any immediate alarm until early on Friday morning when the regulation warning signals were hoisted at the light station at Hog Island, and at the signal staffs at Forts Charlotte and Fincastle, and a little later the customary flags for a falling barometer were displayed on the Imperial Lighthouse Tender Richmond. The wind in squalls during the previous night was at times very strong and Friday morning the rain continued at short intervals with wind of considerable force from the northeast. The mercury kept falling during the day, and shortly before noon a cable was recorded from Washington stating that the wind and readings of the barometer indicated that the hurricane center was approaching Nassau. This information was soon put in circulation and special attention was given to the mooring of the vessels in the harbour, the small craft having already been removed to the eastward anchoring ground. Precautions were also taken on board the steamer Cocoa which had been alongside of R.H. Sawyer & Co.'s Wharf discharging cargo; she steamed into the stream and her heavy anchors were put down. The occupiers of houses also saw to the fastenings of their dwellings, and everybody became deeply interested in the storm which was correctly believed to be slowly moving towards us. The glass continued to fall and at sunset there was a difference of five tenths in the reading of the glass between morning and evening. After sunset the squalls came in faster and faster and the winds also increased in strength all the time, until the rain became incessant and the wind howled. The mercury went down more rapidly as the night advanced but at two o'clock on Saturday morning it became steady and showed signs on rising. During the night the wind shifted more easterly going to east and then southeast from which direction it was blowing at daylight. It continued to blow furiously during the day, and it was not until the afternoon that it began to moderate; the cyclone lasted about eight hours.

When morning arrived the light revealed the damages that had occurred from the storm in the night. Among the first serious losses observed by us was the destruction of a new building lately erected by Mr. G.B. Adderley to the west of the Sponge Exchange which was completely leveled to the ground. It had been constructed of a wooden frame and enclosed with corrugated iron, and being near the water side and very much exposed was blown over from the foundation. The covering of the J.S. Johnson Company's wharf fell in and portion of the wharf to the east was carried away, numerous sheds in front of the stores on Bay and other streets were blown down and business signs removed. House property in the city sustained as far as we are aware comparatively little injury, but in the suburbs the humble dwellings of the poor suffered considerably. Small houses here and there were to be seen in a state of complete collapse and many out buildings also down. The number of houses is estimated at forty. The Colonial Hotel was not in the least shaken by the effects of the storm. A force was engaged in watching the temporary cloth frames that are set in the windows through which the water found access to the building and which will probably inflict damage to the new plastering. The building otherwise is intact. The walls of the building in the course of erection at the Hotel Royal Victoria fell to some extent.

A group of sportsmen went on a hunting expedition to Green Cay, which is a large isolated cay located in the middle of the Tongue of the Ocean, just east of the east coast of Kemp's Bay, South Andros. They experienced the Great Bahamas Hurricane of 1899 while there. Below is their compelling account of their encounter with this storm. This account was taken from the Nassau Guardian, August 16th 1899.

THE LOSS OF THE SCHOONER JANE

The fears expressed in our last issue in regards to the safety of the schooner Jane which conveyed a shooting party comprising Messers J.A. North, David Patton, L.G. Brice, H. Lightbourn, Edmund Knowles and D.S. Mosley were we regret to state warranted, by the fact that that vessel encountered the hurricane at Green Cay and was lost on Friday last.

The schooner Attic, owned by Messers R.H. Sawyer & Co., who upon application readily consented to the schooner proceeding in search of the Jane, sailed on Sunday afternoon for that purpose. Mr. E.Y. V. Sutton and Mr. Frank Pritchard who kindly volunteered to go in her rescue the party in case their vessel was stranded, took passage in the Attic. This schooner left with a high southerly wind which was ahead. She arrived at Green Cay about 11 o' clock on Monday night and upon a fire on shore being observed it was concluded that the party was on the Cay. The light of the schooner was also discerned by those on shore who at once proceeded to meet the approaching vessel.

One of the boats saved from the Jane was immediately dispatched from the shore to the Attic, and thus information was given that the party was safe. No time was then lost in getting on board of the Attic, sail was soon set and the vessel started on her way to Nassau. She left about 1am and arrived here at 11 o'clock am yesterday.

We have gathered the following in relation to the experiences of those on board of the Jane, from one of the party which was on board of her at the time of the hurricane.

A change in the weather was noticed on the morning of Friday the 11th, but the barometer on the vessel did not show any motion of falling(this instrument it was discovered afterwards was entirely worthless). Suspecting about moonlight it might blow harder, extra anchors were put down making four in all, which it was supposed would be sufficient to hold the vessel. As the afternoon advanced it was quite evident that a hurricane was on, and in a short time the schooner started to drag her anchors and finally touched the ground. Following this her chains parted and she immediately went on the rocks. The sea at the time was very high and the vessel was riding heavily. As she gained the shore she rolled first one side and then another. All on board held together until this juncture when, unfortunately, Captain Mackies's little boy was washed overboard and was drowned. The vessel being on the rocks and liable to break up it was considered best by all hands to quit and they jumped over her side into the water they jumped over her side into the water and reached the shore safely, but with bruises. The schooner soon broke up and everything in the shape of clothing, guns and stores washed away. It was then about 4 o'clock in the afternoon. The party accompanied by Captain Mackie and crew, numbering 21 in all, proceeded to look for a small house known to be on the Cay. This spot was reached about five o'clock and refuge taken in it, the occupants being a man named Burrows, three women, two boys and an infant. The house was placed at the disposal of the distressed party who were glad enough to avail *themselves of the shelter that the place afforded. The roof had been partly removed by the hurricane so that the rain beat in upon the occupants. Burrows succeeded however in patching the main hole which afterwards made the house more comfortable. No meals had been partaken of since noon. Bread made in a crude manner was at this time served to all by Burrows and such as it was the hungry party were pleased to receive and were grateful for it. Small stores did not exist in this cabin, but the hospitality of the residents was notwithstanding truly appreciated by those in distress. But little rest was had during the night, the wind roaring and the rain falling in torrents continuously. Clothing was scarce and wet and much discomfort was experienced*

On Saturday morning the weather had not abated and the hurricane blew until evening when it became moderate and the worst was over. That morning the wreck was visited by two or three of the crew who went in search of clothing, a few pieces of which were found at distances from the scene of the disaster. The vessel was then discovered to have broken in pieces. Bread, crabs, conchs and pigeons served as food during the time the party was on the Cay. The body of Captain Mackie's little boy was found in the morning and buried during the day.

On Monday night the sight of a light was discovered and it was not long before it became known that it was on a vessel sent in search of the missing people which it need not be said brought joy to the distressed ones. Sail was made for Nassau without delay and in a few hours the vessel entered our harbour.

The wharf to which the schooner was made fast was lined by persons who took a deep interest in the safety of their friends, and a hearty welcome was accorded to the distressed sportsmen and the crew of the ill-fated vessel. The wind at Green Cay commenced NE, backed NW and finished SW.

Mr. Benjamin S. McPherson from Eight Mile Rock, reported to the Editor of the Nassau Guardian, the state of affairs of Grand Bahama after the Great Bahamas Hurricane of 1899. Below is his report on this storm as reported in the Nassau Guardian of August 23rd, 1899.

To the Editor of the Nassau Guardian.

Dear Sir:

I am no writer, neither do I trouble myself with newspaper correspondence, but at this time, I beg permission in your column to announce to the 'public' the suffering that I and my countrymen are undergoing through a severe hurricane which happened here on the 12th. Sir, I am in my fifty second year, a native of Grand Bahama. I have witnessed many hurricanes, but never seen or heard one like this. My parents before me, never witnessed such, seeing the storm has not only destroyed our crops but rendered us houseless. Over 60 houses more or less are totally destroyed or severely damaged from West End to Barnett's Point. Our Church, S. Stephen, unroofed, also the Baptist Church. My shop, which had been replenished a few days with provisions brought by the Mail is totally lost, the whole stock shop and all. Our condition, Mr. Editor, is very pitiable, no food to eat, no house to dwell in, and no Church to worship in. Believe me Sir.

Your obedient servant,
Benjamin S. McPherson
Eight Mile Rock,
Grand Bahama,
Aug. 16th 1899.

This account below was reported by the Resident Justice of Andros to the Colonial Secretary located in Nassau. This account was taken from the August 26th, 1899 issue of the Nassau Guardian.

Since our last publication the following official information has been furnished to the Government by the Resident Justice at Andros Island with reference to the late hurricane.

"August 17th-Arrived at Nicholl's Town this afternoon. What a sad and distressing sight it presented from the sea? Looked as if it had been scorched by fire. On landing I found that with a few exceptions, all the houses had been leveled by the mighty force of the

hurricane, and the poor people without food, except that of coconuts. I at once distributed some food finishing up the next morning.

Nicholl's Town is in a dreadful state, I cannot see, unless aid is rendered how the people will be able to subsist for the next two or three months, they are in a dreadful plight, no food, no home. Some of the people crawl under the roofs of their houses which lie on the ground and find shelter from the wind and rain.

August 18th-I distributed food to about 175 or more starving people at Nicholl's Town and about fifteen ship-wrecked spongers from Red Bays. Total number of barrels of provisions distributed at Nicholl's Town-12.

From information received I understand that there was very little of the storm at Williams Cays but the loss of life and damage to property at Red Bays (the ranching place of spongers) are something terrible. I intended to take in Williams Cay but after hearing there was no hurricane there I thought it advisable to change my route and proceed to Bimini via Orange Cays.

August 19th-Arrived at Orange Cays, had a search, found nothing, came onboard, proceeded for Bimini. August 20, arrived at Bimini just before dark, too late to find out anything. August 21, had a meeting this morning of the leading gentlemen of the town, they informed me that there was no immediate want at Bimini, but they would need aid very soon, owing to all of their crops being destroyed by the hurricane. The schooner President of this town turned up just as I was leaving. She scudded from Beach Cay (Biminis) up over the Banks, out over Ginger Bread Ground and eventually brought up at Bahama.

August 22nd-Arrived at 8 Mile Rock this morning had a walk of about four miles around the settlements. Destruction and distress reign supreme. Mr. Adderley, R.J., informed me that my arriving with food was a "God-send" and that the people would appreciate it very much. I landed the balance of the provisions, eleven barrels in all, and gave instructions to the Resident Justice. I might mention that this coast (Bahama) is settled for several miles, three houses here, five there and so-therefore I was able to superintend the distribution of food personally. Great destitution prevails at Bahama, many of the people are homeless. The Resident Justice alone having four families at his house. The fury of the hurricane was not so great at Bahama apparently as at Andros. Bay Street all along the settlements is completely filled with debris, cast there from the bed of the ocean. The best way of locomotion is along the sea rocks."

This account of the after effects of the storm was written by Mr. E.Y.V. Sutton who was dispatched by the Central Government in Nassau to take relief supplies to the residents of Andros and to give a complete report on the damages sustained on the island. This was taken from the Nassau Guardian Newspaper on Friday, September 02, 1899.

I left Nassau for Andros Island, on the morning of the 17th, arriving at Nicholl's Town the next day at daybreak. At this place I met Mr. W.T. Cleare, who was distributing supplies to the people. I immediately made a personal inspection of the settlement, and found that the inhabitants were in a destitute condition, many of the houses had been blown down, rendering numbers homeless, and I gathered from the people, that the small supply of provisions at the settlement had been badly damaged. The crops owing to the severity of the weather, are completely destroyed, orange, grapefruit, and coconut trees blown down and stripped of fruit and foliage. The fields of corn and potatoes, etc. have been so badly damaged that it will take months for them to recover. Potatoes are rotting in the fields. Stranded on the beach was a schooner owned by Mr. H.G. Albury. A number of homes were damaged or destroyed. Three Government buildings have suffered. The Jail roof has fallen in, part of the roof of the schoolhouse has lifted, and the teacher's residence completely destroyed.

After consultation with Mr. Cleare, who was relieving the immediate wants of the people, I decided to proceed at once to the Red Bays Settlement and call again at Nicholl's Town on my way back, which I did, and with the assistance of Mr. McGregor, the Public School Teacher, I distributed one barrel of flour, and two barrels of grits. Having been informed that the people at Conch Sound were in a very bad shape, I handed over to Mr. Gostick two barrels of flour, he having kindly undertaken to give them to the superintend for distribution of it to the people at that place. I should have gone to Conch Sound, and would have personally relieved the people, but hearing that the people at Red Bays were in a much worse condition, I thought it advisable to accept the services of Mr. Gostick, and proceed at once to Red Bay Cays, at which place I arrived on Sunday am, and landed immediately. The settlement being some distance away from the shore, I at once dispatched the Captain of my schooner to inform the people of my arrival. In the meantime, I occupied myself in searching for any dead bodies that may have been in the vicinity as I had detected a most unpleasant odour. My attention was called to a vessel which had been capsized and driven ashore some distance into the pine yard. I was informed by some who had come round from Nicholl's Town with me, that the vessel was the schooner ''Alicia,' owned by Mr. A.M. Brice of this city, and that there was a dead body on board of her. The men refused to go with me to the schooner, so in company with Mr. S.J. Johnson and Mr. O.F. Pritchard, Jr., I went to her and climbed on board and found the dead body of a man lying in the hold, in an advanced state of decomposition. Not being able to obtain any assistance, and the body being in such a bad condition, I regret to say, I was forced to leave it where it was. I then left the schooner and proceeded to make an inspection. I found that this part of the island for miles had been submerged. In proof of this I noticed parts of hawsers made fast to the higher branches of the Pine trees, and numbers of vessels were scattered throughout the Pine Yard, in a more or less damaged condition. I visited several of them, but found no more dead bodies in the vessels. The men from the settlement having by this time arrived. I made an enquiry as to the condition of the people and having fully satisfied myself that they were badly in need of food. I issued supplies to them.

Frederick McQueen having informed me that he knew where several dead bodies were lying unburied, after a considerable amount of persuasion, I induced James Uling one of the crew of my vessel, and McQueen to go with me, and Messers, Johnson and Pritchard again accompanying me. I went down to the beach and found on the Red Bay shore, three bodies and at Crab Cay one body. The first body we found had been buried but had been dug up by land crabs. We again buried it. The next body we discovered was so wedged under the roots of the mangroves that it was impossible for us to get at it, so I caused it to be freely sprinkled with carbolic acid. The third body was found a short distance away under the roots of a tree, which we buried. The fourth body was found lying on the shore, at Crab Cay, this we also buried.

I was unable to obtain the names of these people, with the exception of the body found in the 'Alicia' which was supplied to be the remains of one Elijah Pinder. The great loss of life at this place, which from information I received, I estimate to be between 100 and 150, (I enclose a list of names given me by men of the different vessels who are supposed to have been drowned) was caused by the sudden uprising of the sea, similar to a tidal wave which arose when the wind shifted to the SW after a sudden calm. The man having taken advantage of the calm to go to the small Cays to gather some of the dead bodies.

Judging from the smell, which is most noticeable, I am of the opinion that there are yet remaining unburied a number of bodies through the Creeks in the vicinity of Red Bays Settlement, but not being able to obtain any reliable information as to the state of the people at the other places that I had visited after leaving Red Bays and having done what I could for the living at this place, I decided that the living at other places had prior claim to my attention, and I was therefore unable to make a more thorough search for dead bodies.

The houses and crops at these places were also destroyed by the sea at this time and two women and one man I am informed were drowned, while swimming in the pine yard.

This sudden uprising of the sea, in my opinion was undoubtedly caused by the shifting of the wind to the SW which drove the sea with tremendous force upon a very low lying coast, and it was at this time that most of the damage was done. The houses at these settlements are very nearly all damaged or destroyed. The people are living under the roofs of the houses that have been blown down. The crops are all destroyed, and as I have already said in respect to Nicholl's Town, some time must elapse before the people can derive any benefits from their fields.

I regret to add while reporting on this settlement that everything that can possibly be removed from the vessels is being stolen. I might state as a most glaring instance, the cutting into the bottom of a new sloop so as to get at her cargo of sponge, and the chopping away of the brass rudder braces.

Having done all in my power to relieve the distress of the people of this place, I left on Monday for Nicholl's Town and issued provisions as before stated. On the way to Nicholl's Town I called in at Lowe Sound and found the people in great distress, twenty three houses having been blown down, and four damaged and the people in great want of food. I therefore landed two barrels of flour and one barrel of grits for distribution. I was informed by Charles Sherman and others that they had buried eight bodies that had been washed up. I sailed from Nicholl's Town on Wednesday 23rd for Mastic Point. I landed at Mr. Chamberlain's Wharf and walked from there to the settlement, about a mile distant. On the way I inspected and made a list of the houses that had been damaged and blown down during the storm. The information gathered from this settlement was given me by Mr. Bernice Albury, the Public School Teacher, and was on par with what I had received with regard to the destruction of property, etc., at the other places. I supplied him with three barrels of flour and three barrels of grits, for distribution to the people of the two districts in this settlement. At this place quite a number of vessels were capsized but there was no loss of life. The place had been flooded by the sea during the NE wind. The crops at this place are also destroyed.

Leaving Mastic Point on Thursday morning, I arrived at Staniard Creek at 10am of the same day, where I met Mr. K.G. Malcolm, who was distributing provisions. The people at this place were in a most destitute condition. The damage done by the storm in every particular, it appeared to me, was much greater than at any of the other places that I had visited. The sea had flooded the entire settlement, houses were blown away completely, trees uprooted and blown across houses, some of the occupants of which narrowly escaped with their lives. I immediately landed the remaining six barrels of provisions that I had with me and handed them over to Mr. Malcolm who undertook to supply them to the people. All the crops at this place were destroyed but there was no loss of life.

I left Staniard Creek with the intention of reporting myself to the Resident Justice, who I heard was at Fresh Creek. Upon my arrival there I found he had gone to Mangrove Cay. From this place I walked to Calabash Bay; neither of those places appeared to have suffered very much from the storm. Some houses had been blown down, several vessels had been capsized, but there had been no loss of life...."

This account of the storm was written by an unnamed person living at Clarence Town, Long Island on August 12, 1899 just after the storm. This was taken from the Nassau Guardian Newspaper on Wednesday, September 30, 1899.

Sir,

Sweet is the breath of morn, writes Milton, and after all is passed over, on this morning with a clear azure sky on which begins to forget the anxiety and terror experienced on the 10th of this month.

For some time past you could hear the weather-wise mariners saying "I don't like the looks of the weather! Here we are in the month of August with the wind blowing from the Northeast and so cool indoors, but hot outside."

Well at 6pm on the 10th things began to bear a suspicious aspect, wind E by N, and a drizzly rain. The barometer began to fall very gradually, but by 10 o'clock the sky was overcast, and looked gloomy and the wind increase much. The sloop 'Lucy Ann' had dragged ashore high on the beach, and the waves were running high on the shore. The next few minutes the schooner Brave was beached, and the wind now in small gusts tells us without referring to the barometer that the hurricane was on us. A fall of nearly 3-10ths of an inch in the barometer confirmed it, and hammers could be heard everywhere. As the wind hauled eastwardly and inclined southward, I was satisfied that the centre of the cyclone was to the south of us. Yet it blew terribly. This kept up with continual rain until 4am on the 11th, when we began to realize that its force was much lessened, and all appearances of better times coming. The weather remained unsettled until about 8pm on the 11th, when fair weather begun to dawn on us again, which continued to improve up to this time.

It was severe but not to be compared with the hurricanes of '66 and '83, yet it has done some damage on shore. Five houses have been blown down or so much damaged as to cause them to be untenantable, and 9 others are seriously damaged, but can be lived in in fair weather. As most of our homes are of thatched roofs, all suffered from being flooded with rain, and the tanks are nearly filled with water. None of the Government buildings suffered from the storm, and the vessels ashore are very little injured. The 'Lucy' Ann suffered nothing to speak of, and the' Brave' a few sheets of metal are rubbed off, and her rudder displaced and spindles bent or broken. The schooner 'Addie' is expected but not heard from; the 'Hattie H. Roberts' also; all we can hear of her, or supposed to be of her, is that early on Thursday morning a large schooner was seen passing Burrows Harbour. If it be her I fear she has had it bad. The lower portion of the land on the northern districts are under water, and large trees have been thrown across the roads so as to make them impassable, which prevents us hearing from Deadman's Cay until the debris is removed. The local Board of Works has the work in hand, and labourers are employed to clear away. Not one accident has occurred to any person to my knowledge, nor one animal injured so far as heard from. Should any further news come in from the North it will come to you.

THE LOSS OF THE SCHOONER ADDIE-THE TALE OF THE CAPTAIN

On Wednesday the 9th, at 5pm we were anchored in Hog Cay Cut; the weather looked queer and we thought we would lay there until the morrow which we did sailed for home (Long Island) on the morning of the 10th. Our Barometer reading was 30.10 inches. Between 10 and 11am with moderate weather before, we now find it changing, a high sea running and squalls passing in gusts of wind, and although the barometer was the same we thought it advisable to turn back to the Cut. We got safely again into this cut. We got safely again into the Cut at 1:30pm. Between 12 midnight and 1am on the 11th the barometer fell to 29.95 inches and the schooner commenced dragging. We took to anchor and were forced in a strong gale to scud down the Exuma shore. The barometer falling and the gale increasing we thought of beaching the schooner but it was so dark we could not see where to put her so we kept on scudding at the mercy of the wind and sea. Presently we brought up on a bar near a projecting point of the land and lay there from 4pm on the land until 4am the following morning. The tide was running so strongly around this point that it prevented us from getting ashore at the next point to fasten a hawser to a projecting rock to keep us there. The wind now shifting to the SE blew us of the bar. I then noticed the barometer was 29.40 inches. We brought up again on the next point of land to leeward where she lay until 6am when the wind shifted to the SW. We took to the boat to save our lives, loading her with those who could not swim. Three of the crew with the mate volunteered for safe landing to swim, holding on the gunwale of the boat which we sculled ashore to the land that was overflowed with the extra high tide. Our boat got under the lee of some mangroves which we held to until 2pm.

The weather moderating, we made for the mainland which we found to be the Pond at Exuma and we went to the house of Mr. Knowles, Mr. Brice's overseer, who took us in and sheltered us. On the next day we went to the schooner to save what cargo we could and did so to the extent of 22 barrels, some goods, 2 boxes of Tobacco, 2 tins of Kerosene, 1/2 barrel of beef, 1 tin of Lard, a few other articles, some clothing of the passengers and crew. I went to Rolle Town engaged the schooner 'Dial' put in the freight and passengers with the crew and some of the schooner's materials and arrived here yesterday afternoon. The people of the place acted very unchristian like. They got almost deliriously drunk with the liquor they stole from our cargo and acted in such a way that upon rising the schooner to inspect her bottom we were afraid to go under her fearing that they would let up and crush us. They seem to think that this vessel and her cargo was a godsend to them and barrels could be found all through the bushes broken open and their contents taken away. The old clothing of the crew lying on deck was taken away before our eyes although we sanctioned them not to take them. Everything they could lay their hands on they took and converted to their own use. I regret that such things could occur to distressed vessels in our Islands especially. The port planks of the schooner are broken but she can be repaired and floated although she is 200 feet from the sea over a ridge of sand.

Captain William Bethel of the schooner 'Excel' left for Nassau to be repaired, reported to me while at Exuma it was wrecked and that he was in the schooner 'Raven' on which he was a passenger; that the 'Raven' was lost at Soldier's Cay, no loss of life but everything else with the vessel and also that a sponger with eleven hands on board had been lost at Rocky Point and only five saved. The schooner 'Celeste' on which I freighted some cargo in Nassau, to the extent of 32 barrels and other things was last heard of on Tuesday pm when she landed some passengers at the 'Cottage' on Exuma and then left there for the North End of this Island. I have not heard anything further of her yet, nor have I heard of the 'Hattie Darling' which sailed from Nassau on Wednesday the 9th. I have heard from others of several losses but I cannot say they are authentic enough to speak of.

This account of the Great Abaco Hurricane of 1932 was written by a Nassau Guardian Reporter as told to him by a boat Captain Mr. Holland as he arrived at Abaco to render assistance to the people of Abaco just after the storm. This account was taken from the Nassau Guardian Newspaper on Saturday, September 10, 1932.

CAPTAIN HOLLAND'S STORY

In an interview with a Nassau Guardian reporter Captain Holland told the following story:

"We were heading for Green Turtle Cay, but as we neared Bluff Point, 15 miles this side of our destination, we saw that the settlement was in a state of ruins. Sheets were hanging high up on trees as distress signals and a Red Ensign could be seen floating upside-down on a flagstaff. The entire population, numbering about 250, was clustered together in large groups and the general atmosphere was one of complete bewilderment. Six persons had been badly injured and almost everyone had minor injuries. There was no food of any kind in the settlement and as a last resort water was obtained from small puddles. Every boat had been destroyed and it was not

possible, therefore, to catch any fish. The seas had swept right over the settlement destroying every building and all vegetation.

We then continued to Green Turtle Cay where we discovered an equally bad state of affairs. Six persons had been killed and 26 badly injured. Very little food or water was to be had. Mr. W. A. Kendrick, who acts in a medical capacity around the settlements of Abaco, worked untiringly night and day among the injured. Disinfectants were very badly needed. Almost every house had been swept away.

At Great Guana Cay, ten miles below, only four houses were left standing. Fifteen persons had been injured and one killed. The seas swept over this settlement also and had taken its toll on the people and the town. At Marsh Harbour, extensive damage had been done and all the crops were destroyed. There were fortunately no deaths or injuries in this settlement. Hope Town met the same fate. The wireless station was completely destroyed and the Church among other buildings was completely demolished. Again, there was no loss of lives. Cooper's Town was wiped out but Cherokee Sound sustained little damage. Elbow Cay was said to have had a terrific wind velocity estimated by some at 150 miles per hour. It seems that the very height of the storm raged over this part." Captain Holland concluded.

Mr. Alexander Reckley, Schoolmaster at Bluff Point, gave the Nassau Guardian a most graphic description of the Great Abaco Hurricane of 1932 as he experienced the peak and the after effects of the storm. This account was taken from the Nassau Guardian Newspaper on Saturday, September 10, 1932.

SCHOOLMASTER AT BLUFF POINT RECORDS PITIFUL STORY

As early as 2 o'clock on the morning of Monday, 5th September, Mr. Reckley and his wife and four children were up and dressed watching the weather, their two-storey wooden house being securely battened up, except for one small aperture.

Twelve hours later, between 2 and 3 in the afternoon the storm was at its worst, the wind blowing from the north. When they saw the weather increasing they said their prayers. "Then" said Mr. Reckley, "We waited to see what the Lord would do." Just then they heard ominous creaks in the timbers of the house. "Then the Spirit led

me, my wife and four children to the nearest neighbouring shelter."
This was an outside-kitchen, 8x10. "Every house on Bluff Point," he
continued, "Was almost down. Then the wind fell off, there was ten
minutes of calm and the wind blew fierce from the south. Just after
dark every house was down."

In the kitchen where a fire was kept burning until the storm
abated in the early hours of Thursday morning, round about 100
people collected, attracted by the glow and warmth. Here they passed
the time singing hymns and praying. "The Lord heard us and kept
the roof on, though it nearly came off."

Already the people lived on young canes, which are sour, and
rotten and bruised pears. All the chickens were drowned, except two
roosters which found shelter in the kitchen.

Mr. Reckley, who came in the Ethel B. on Monday is wearing his
only suit of clothes left, the jacket of which he found in a pond. He
hopes to take back with him tonight food and clothes for the people.

This account of the Great Abaco Hurricane of 1932 was written
by a Nassau Guardian Reporter as told to him by an Anglican Bishop
as he arrived at Abaco to render assistance to the people of Abaco just
after the storm. This account was taken from the Nassau Guardian
Newspaper on Saturday, September 17, 1932.

THE BISHOP'S VISIT TO ABACO-ALTAR IN RUINED CHURCH
INTACT.

"I left Nassau at 2am on Wednesday in the 'Malola' for Green Turtle
Cay. The weather was very rough at first and there were heavy
squalls of rain."

"I arrived at Green Turtle Cay about 5pm and was met at the
dock by the Catechist and the principle people of the place. I then
proceeded to go round the settlement. Enough has already been said
of the absolute ruin to the place. The church, a solid building built of
quarried stone, is completely destroyed, the stone work having fallen
inwards. Yet I noticed that in the middle of all the ruin the altar is
standing uninjured and has still one candlestick with the candle in
place while the chalice and paten which were in the church when it
collapsed are quite undamaged."

"The Rectory, a well built two storey wooden house, was lifted completely off its pins and set gently down again about 12 feet back where it stands as a building. I was able to walk upstairs and one of the windows which is glazed had only one small pane broken. The school too is quite destroyed."

"I then walked around the settlement calling on the sick and bereaved and just as it was growing dark I gathered the people around me by the new graves in the church yard and held a short service."

" I then went back to the motor boat and early next morning said a Mass for the people in one of the rooms of the Rectory as I had brought all requisites for the service with me and gave Communion. I then saw some more sick folks but had to hurry on board as the 'Malola' was ready to leave for Nassau."

"It is to be realized that a number of people have literally lost all they once had. They have no houses or clothes or crockery or cooking utensils and many have no shoes. Gifts in kind would be very acceptable."

" It was a great disappointment to be unable to visit Blackwood Point situated on the main land six miles to the west of Green Turtle Cay. There they are in a very bad way indeed and are short of everything. All I could do was to leave behind the 200lbs of grits I brought with me and to ask that they might be sent over from Green Turtle Cay. This they gladly promised to do. I brought the grits for the people of Green Turtle Cay but they themselves suggested that Blackwood Point was in even a worse condition than they were. This seemed to me an appealing instance of very fine generosity. All of the people appreciated my visit whether belonging to the Church of England or not."

"The impossibility of visiting Blackwood Point affected the Bishop very much as there is a very faithful band of Church people. The instance demonstrates the necessity of the Bishop having his own yacht. Subscriptions towards a new one have already been received towards the cost which is estimated to be about £1500 and Mr. Cox of Messers Cox and Stevens has consented to prepare the plane free of cost. The boat will be an auxiliary motor boat."

CHAPTER THIRTEEN
Hurricane Preparedness

BE PREPARED BEFORE THE HURRICANE SEASON

- Know the storm surge history and elevation of your area.
- Learn safe routes inland and try not to wait until the last minute to begin your evacuation.
- Learn locations of official Hurricane Shelters.
- Review needs and working conditions of emergency equipment such as flashlights, battery-powered radios and cell phones (ensured that before the hurricane the battery is charged to 100% capacity).
- Ensure that non-perishable foods, can goods and water supplies are on hand and are sufficient to last for at least two weeks.
- Obtain and secure materials necessary to secure your home properly, such as plywood and plastic.
- Know the hurricane terms *Hurricane Alert, Hurricane Warning* and *Hurricane Watch* well in advance of an approaching storm and develop a clear and concise evacuation plans for your home, school, office or business in the event a hurricane threatens your area.
- Check your home for loose and clogged rain gutters and downspouts.
- Keep trees and shrubbery trimmed. Cut weak branches and trees that could fall or bump against the house and damage it in

a hurricane. When trimming, try to create a channel through the foliage to the center of the tree to allow for airflow.

- Determine where to move your boat in an emergency.
- Obtain and store material, such as plywood, which are necessary to properly secure your windows and doors.
- Review your insurance policy to ensure that it provides adequate coverage and try not to wait until the hurricane season to take out or renew your policy because some insurance companies will not cover your home or business if the policy is taken out just before a storm and in most cases it takes some time for the policy to become effective but this varies from company to company so check with your individual company about this aspect of the policy.
- Take pictures of your home, inside and out to bolster insurance claims.
- Individuals with special needs should contact the local office of NEMA (Office of Emergency Management).
- For information and assistance with any of these items, contact your local meteorological office, office of emergency management, or the Bahamas Red Cross Society.

WHEN A HURRICANE ALERT IS ISSUED

- Monitor radio, television, and hurricane hotline numbers frequently for official bulletins of the storm's progress (such as the local 915 weather by phone).
- You should now begin your preparations for the approaching storm.
- Learn the location of official hurricane shelters
- Know the hurricane risks in your area, eg. determine whether you live in a potential flood zone.
- Find out where official hurricane shelters are located.
- Develop a family action plan.
- Review working condition of emergency equipment, such as flashlights and battery-powered radios.
- Ensure you have enough non-perishable food and water supplies on hand.
- Buy plywood or shutters to protect doors and windows.
- Clear loose and clogged rain gutters and downspouts.

- Determine where to move your boat in an emergency.

WHEN A HURRICANE WATCH IS ISSUED

- Be prepared to take quick action.
- Monitor radio, television, and hurricane hotline numbers frequently for official bulletins of the storm's progress (such as the local 915 weather by phone).
- Fuel and service family and business vehicles.
- Inspect and secure all business and homes.
- Prepare to cover all window and door openings with shutters or other shielding materials.
- Secure unanchored garbage cans, building materials, garden-tools and patio furniture immediately.
- Take down television, radio, and satellite antennae.

CHECK FOOD AND WATER SUPPLIES

- Have clean, airtight containers on hand to store at least a two-week supply of drinking water (about 14 gallons per person).
- Stock up on canned provisions.
- Get a camping stove with fuel.
- Keep a small cooler with frozen gel packs handy for packing refrigerated items.
- Check prescription medicines; obtain at least ten days to two weeks' supply.
- Stock up on extra batteries for radios, flashlights, and lanterns.
- Prepare to store and secure outdoor lawn furniture and other loose, lightweight objects, such as garbage cans, garden tools, and potted plants, which can be used as projectiles and missiles during the storm.
- Check and replenish first aid supplies.
- Have an extra supply of cash on hand.

WHEN A HURRICANE WARNING IS ISSUED

- Closely monitor radio, TV, or hurricane hotline telephone numbers for official bulletins.

- Follow instructions issued by local officials and leave immediately if ordered to do so.
- Complete preparation activities, such as putting up storm shutters and securing loose objects.
- Evacuate areas that might be affected by storm surge flooding such as coastal and low lying areas.
- If and when evacuating, leave early (if possible, in daylight).
- Notify neighbours and family members outside the warning area of your evacuation plans.

EVACUATION

PLAN TO EVACUATE IF YOU:

- Live on a coastline, on an island waterfront or in an area prone to flooding.
- Live in a high rise such as a hotel or office building. Hurricane winds are stronger at higher elevations. Glass doors and windows may be blown out of their casings and weaken the structure.

WHEN YOU LEAVE:

- Stay with friends or relatives or at low-rise inland hotels or motels outside the flood zones.
- Leave early to avoid heavy traffic, road blocked by early floodwaters, and bridges impassable due to high winds.
- Put food and water out for your pets if you cannot take them with you or take them to the local humane society for safekeeping. Public shelters do not allow pets, and nor do most motels/hotels.
- Go to a hurricane shelter if you have no other place to go. Shelters may be crowded and uncomfortable, with no privacy and no electricity. Do not leave your home for a shelter until government officials announce on radio or television that a particular shelter is open. If you must leave your home for a shelter or to a family or friends, remember turn off the main electricity switch and cut off your gas supply, as these can become fire hazards during the storm.

WHAT TO BRING TO A SHELTER:

- First aid kit, medicine, baby food and diapers, playing cards, games and books for entertainment purposes, toiletries, battery-powered radio, flashlights (one per person), extra batteries, blankets or sleeping bags, identification, valuable papers (insurance and passport), and cash.

IF STAYING AT HOME:

- Reminder: Only stay in a home if you have not been ordered to leave. If you are told to leave, do so immediately!
- Store water. Fill sterilized jugs and bottles with water for a two-week supply of drinking water. Fill bathtub and large containers with water for sanitary purposes.
- Turn refrigerator to maximum cold, and open it only when necessary.
- Turn off utilities if told to do so by authorities. Turn off propane tanks.
- Unplug small appliances.
- Stay inside a well-constructed building. Examine the building and plan in advance what you will do if winds become strong. Strong winds can produce deadly missiles and structural failure.

IF WINDS GROW STRONG:

- Stay away from windows and doors, even if they are covered. Take refuge in a small interior room, closet, or hallway. Take a battery-powered radio and flashlight with you to your place of refuge.
- Close all interior doors. Secure and brace external doors, particularly double inward-opening doors and garage doors.
- If you are in a two-story house, go to the basement, an interior first floor room such as a bathroom or closet, or under the stairs.
- If you are in a multi-story building and away from the water, go to the first or second floor and take refuge in a hall or interior room, away from windows. Interior stairwells and the areas around elevator shafts are generally the strongest part of a building.

- Lie on the floor under a table or another sturdy object.
- Be alert for tornadoes, which often are spawned by hurricanes.
- **If the 'Eye' of the hurricane should pass over your area, be aware that the improved weather conditions are only temporary. The storm conditions will return with winds coming from the opposite direction, sometimes within just a few minutes and usually within an hour so it is important that you stay indoors until the weather officials give the 'All-Clear!!!'**

AFTER THE STORM PASSES

- Stay in your protected area until announcements are made on the radio or television that the dangerous winds have passed.
- If you have evacuated, do not return home until officials announce that your area is ready. Remember, proof of residency may be required in order to re-enter evacuated zones.
- If your home or building has structural damage, do not enter until officials check it.
- Avoid using candles and other open flames indoors.
- Beware of outdoor hazards.
- Avoid downed power lines and any water in which they may be lying. Be alert for weakened bridges and washed-out roads. Watch for weakened limbs on trees and/or damaged overhanging structures.
- Do not use the telephone unless absolutely necessary. The system usually is jammed with emergency calls during and after a hurricane.
- Guard against spoiled food. Use dry or canned food. Do not drink or prepare food with tap water until you are certain it is not contaminated.
- When cutting up fallen trees, use caution, especially if you use a chain saw. Serious injuries can occur when these powerful machines snap back or when the chain breaks.

CONCLUSION

A hurricane's immense power is capable of killing thousands of people. It also captures the imagination of people all around the world, even those who never expect to experience such a storm. The complex interaction of the forces that create hurricanes and similar storms makes them even more fascinating to those who want to learn a little about how nature works. News images and reports of the recent and historical hurricanes physical and human devastation to many areas of the Bahamas demonstrated to the world not only the power of strong hurricanes, but also the consequences both to individuals and to society of not being prepared to cope with such storms despite ample warnings. While a hurricane lives, the transaction of energy within its circulation is immense. A couple of facts help illustrate the power of hurricanes; first the average hurricane precipitates a trillion gallons of water a day and second, the condensation heat energy released by a hurricane in one day can be equivalent of the energy released by the fusion of 400 20-megaton bombs. To demonstrate this fact, one day's released energy, converted to electricity, could supply the United States' electrical needs for about six months. Hurricane Andrew in 1992 had the equivalent power of an atomic bomb exploding every minute when it made landfall in here in the Bahamas. Hurricanes are neither the largest nor strongest storms, but their combination of size and strength definitely makes them the deadliest and most destructive storms on earth.

From the time of Christopher Columbus, hurricanes have shaped the patterns of settlement in the Caribbean and the structures of maritime commerce. Their effects challenged governments to respond, and those that failed revealed their weakness and lost their legitimacy. Revolts and upheavals have sometimes followed the storms. Some storms actually determined or contributed to the outcome of individual military engagements and imperial struggles as well as the competition for markets. The hurricanes caused populations to rethink the role of God and nature in human affairs. People have sought the technology of communications and prediction to answer the threat. Above all, hurricanes and their effects have served as prisms through which societies can be seen and judged. The luck of hurricanes missing the Bahamas won't hold forever, meteorologists think weather cycles have changed and we've entered a period when more hurricanes are likely to be forming every summer. In fact, as a meteorologist I have noticed that there are clear indications that Bahamian residents for the last few years have fallen into a false sense of security because of the lack of intense and deadly hurricanes to hit the Bahamas in the recent years. It is my hope that these two deadly hurricanes act as a catalyst for us to change our mentality when it comes to preparing for these storms. Furthermore, it is my hope and desire that when the next hurricane arrives over the Bahamas, we will be fully prepared and ready for the worse it can inflict upon us as a people. That can only come with education, knowledge and preparation.

Hurricanes present a variety of opportunities for weather historians such as me. They are natural phenomena, but they are not necessarily natural disasters for only when a storm encounters dense concentrations of people or property and create massive destruction does it become a catastrophe. Here in the Bahamas, the location of populations along the coastlines, the development of beach front homes and hotels, failure to impose proper hurricane planning and improved building codes: all have contributed to increasing the destructiveness of the Bahamian and Caribbean storms. We confront a seeming anomaly. Despite technological and scientific advances in the forecasting and prediction of these storms, the destructive effects of natural disasters have increased considerably since 1930s when the last of these two storms struck the Bahamas. The average annual worldwide mortality due to disasters increased from 23,000 per year to 143,000 between the 1930s and 1970s, but property damage has increased even more. But property values aside, the Southeast Asian Tsunami of 2004 and Hurricane Katrina of 2005 underline the fact that those in human terms, by far the worst sufferers of the effects of "climatic" disasters have been poor people and poor countries. In the contemporary world, "natural disasters" like hurricanes have been socially selective, and they have probably been so in the past.

Historians of hurricanes need to ask how natural disasters have shape politics and social relations, and how political and social structures create the contexts for the impact of those phenomena. How did explanations for and understandings of the storms reflect changing conceptualizations of God, nature, science, and human abilities? Then too, there is yet another level of analysis that awaits attention. What have been the long-term cumulative effects of repeated natural disasters on the Bahamas? To what extent have these storms contributed to the national problems of growth or development? Such issues have never been calculated or estimated. The Bahamas might lend itself particularly well to such an analysis although information is spotty and the formula for calculation will be extremely complex. The writing of the history of Bahamian hurricanes like that of much environmental history begins with a problem. For all their power and destructive potential, the history of the hurricanes is, because of their frequency, almost inherently boring. Unlike volcanoes or earthquakes, the great storms are somewhat dependable. Almost every year some island or coast is inundated or devastated. While for individual islands or cities or stretches of shoreline, hurricanes may be spaced decades apart, in a regional sense, the phenomenon is repetitious and the results expected.

The scenes of destruction are all too common and all too similar: shattered homes and shattered lives, boats piled up on the beaches or carried far inland, destruction of homes and businesses in all directions, downed trees and power lines and later on, scenes of relief and aid amidst a backdrop of ruin. The individual stories may be poignant, but their repetition is numbing. Accounts seem to vary only in the level of destruction, the amount of loss, or the level of the force of the winds or storm surge. If the story to be told is only that of the storms themselves, then the repetitiveness is inherent.

The variations from one storm to the next may be interesting from a meteorological perspective, but have less significance from a historical one. Moreover, as acts of nature or the handiwork of God, the hurricanes are beyond human control and are therefore outside of history, this explains why they have been ignored as a theme in themselves. Storms are the classic deus ex machina that we as weather historians and social scientists are admonished to avoid like the plague. But, at the same time, because of their ubiquity and regularity, we can also fall into the opposite error of seeing them as the explanation of everything. Almost every event, battle, revolt, revolution or election in the Caribbean region in the past has been preceded by one or several hurricanes and in many cases it changed the course of history. To find the balance between explaining too much and too little in the history of Bahamian hurricanes is a tricky business at best.

From the time of Christopher Columbus, hurricanes shaped the patterns of settlements here in the Bahamas and the structure of maritime commerce. Their effects challenged the Bahamas government to respond, and those that failed revealed their weakness and lost their legitimacy. Revolts and upheavals have sometimes followed the storms. The storms determined or contributed to the outcome of individual military engagements and imperial struggles as well as the competition for markets. The hurricanes caused populations to rethink the role of God and nature in human affairs and to seek in the technology of communications and prediction as ways to answer the threat. And above all, these two hurricanes and their effects have served as prisms through which societies can be seen and future storms can be measured.

The Great Bahamian Hurricanes of 1899 and 1932 were two particularly interesting examples of notable Bahamian storms. These storms had different impact on the various islands of the Bahamas. Many Bahamian islands in the south received very little damage from both of these storms but those in the most northern islands received the brunt of these storms. They allowed us to see the ways in which local conditions contextualized the same natural threat. Leadership in both individual societies had a vision of an ideal future and they were willing to use the disaster as a tool to implement that vision.

In the southeast Bahamas, damages and immediate mortality were relatively low for both storms, but on many of these islands the only damage that occurred was to the lucrative salt raking industry pan and unharvested salt. However in the northwest Bahamas it was the complete opposite where the death toll was significant and many islands reported massive devastation.

SOURCES

- *"HURRICANE!"A Familiarization Booklet by NOAA, April, 1993.*
- Chris Landsea, et al. (2003). *"Documentation of Atlantic Tropical Cyclones Changes in HURDAT: 1896-1900"*. NHC-Hurricane Research Division. http://www.aoml.noaa.gov/hrd/hurdat/metadata_1896-00.htm#1899_3.
- Chris Landsea, et al. (2003). *"Raw Observations for Hurricane #3, 1899"* (XLS). Hurricane Research Division. http://www.aoml.noaa.gov/hrd/hurdat/excelfiles_centerfix/1899/1899_3. XLS. E.B. Garriott (August 1899). *"Monthly Weather Review"* (PDF). U.S. Weather Bureau. http://www.aoml.noaa.gov/hrd/hurdat/mwr_pdf/1899.pdf.
- Chris Landsea, et al. (2011). *"Raw Observations for Hurricane #4, 1932"* (XLS). Hurricane Research Division.
- Chris Landsea, et al. (2011). *"Documentation of Atlantic Tropical Cyclones Changes in HURDAT: 1932 Hurricane Season"*. NHC-Hurricane Research Division.
- *The Hurricane of San Ciriaco: Disaster, Politics, and Society in Puerto Rico, 1899-1901*, Stuart B. Schwartz, Hispanic American Historical Review 72:3, by Duke University Press.
- *The Governor's Dispatches-CO-23 January-December, 1899, pgs 80,81,82,83,84,95,97,98*
- *The Governor's Dispatches-CO-23 August-December, 1932.*
- *Votes of the House of Assembly-1899-1900 & 1932.*
- *The Bahamas Journal of Science Vol. 6 No.1 Historic Weather at Nassau-*Ronald V. Shaklee, Media Publishing Ltd.

- *The Bahamas Journal of Science Vol. 5 No.1 Historical Hurricane Impacts on The Bahamas, Part I: 1500-1749* Ronald V. Shaklee, Media Publishing Ltd.
- *The Bahamas Journal of Science Vol. 5 No.2 Historical Hurricane Impacts on The Bahamas, Part II: 1750-1799* Ronald V. Shaklee, Media Publishing Ltd.
- *The Bahamas Journal of Science Vol. 8 No.1 Historical Hurricane Impacts on The Bahamas: Floyd on San Salvador & Early Nineteenth Century Hurricanes 1800-1850* Ronald V. Shaklee, Media Publishing Ltd.
- *The Bahamas in the late Nineteenth Century 1870-1899 Booklet-Department of Archives Exhibition 2-28 February, 1987. Pgs 1-45.*
- *The Sponging Industry Booklet-Department of Archives Exhibition 18-22 February, 1974. Pgs 1-31.*
- *A Columbus Casebook-A Supplement to "Where Columbus Found the New World" National Geographic Magazine, November 1986.*
- *The Nassau Guardian-Lifestyles Section, February 17, 2005 'The historic development of the 'City of Nassau'-Part I & II Early Developments & Loyalist Impact.'* By Dr. Gail Saunders.
- *The Nassau Guardian-Lifestyles Section, November, 2005 'The historic development of the 'City of Nassau'-Part III Modern Developments.'* By Dr. Gail Saunders.
- *The Nassau Guardian, Monday, August 14, 1899 pg 1-'The Hurricane,' 'Missing Vessels' & 'Casualties to Shipping.'*
- *The Nassau Guardian, Wednesday, August 16, 1899 pgs 1&2- 'Our Visitation.' 'The Hurricane' & 'The loss of the schooner Jane.'*
- *The Nassau Guardian, Saturday, August 19, 1899 pgs 1&2- 'Hurricane Notes.'*
- *The Nassau Guardian, Wednesday, August 23, 1899 pg 1-'The Hurricane' & 'Harbour Island Notes.'*
- *The Nassau Guardian, Saturday, August 26, 1899 pg 1-'The Hurricane.'*
- *The Nassau Guardian, Wednesday, August 30, 1899 pgs 1&2- 'The Hurricane-Long Island' & 'The loss of the schooner Addie-The tale of the Captain.'*

- *The Nassau Guardian, Saturday, September 02, 1899 pg 1-'The Hurricane.'*
- *The Nassau Guardian, Wednesday, September 06, 1899 pg 1-'The Hurricane.'*
- *The Nassau Guardian, Saturday, September 23, 1899 pg 1-'The Hurricane.'*
- *The Nassau Guardian, Wednesday, October 11, 1899 pg 1-'The Hurricane.'*
- *The Nassau Guardian, Wednesday, November 22, 1899 pg 1-'Government Notice.'*
- *The Nassau Guardian, Saturday, September 03, 1932 pg 2-'The Hurricane Season.' & 'The Barometer'*
- *The Nassau Guardian, Wednesday, September 07, 1932 pgs 1&2-'Storm passes to North of Nassau' & 'Being Prepared.'*
- *The Nassau Guardian, Saturday, September 10, 1932 pgs 1&2-'Arrival of Relief Ship at Abaco.'& 'His Excellency visits Abaco.'& 'Suffering Abaco.'*
- *The Nassau Guardian, Wednesday, September 14, 1932 pgs 1&2-'Hurricane News from Grand Bahama.' 'American Visitors Experience Hurricane' 'Personal Experiences at Abaco' 'The Epic of Abaco' & 'Hurricane Relief'*
- *The Nassau Guardian, Saturday, September 17, 1932 pg 1-'The Bishop's visit to Abaco.' 'Successful Concert for Hurricane Relief Fund' 'Government's Action to help Abaco.'*
- *The Nassau Guardian, Wednesday, September 21, 1932 pg 1-'Abaco Relief Fund.'*
- *The Nassau Guardian, Saturday, December 31, 1932 pg 2-'A Hurricane-Terrance Keogh's Description.'*
- *The Nassau Daily Tribune, Saturday, September 03, 1932 pg 1-'The Latest News of the Storm.'*
- *The Nassau Daily Tribune, Tuesday, September 06, 1932 pgs 1&2-'Second Hurricane Passes by Nassau.'*
- *The Nassau Daily Tribune, Wednesday, September 07, 1932 pg 1-'Effects of the Storm at Harbour Island.'*
- *The Nassau Daily Tribune, Friday, September 09, 1932 pg 1-'11 Killed, 30 Injured at Abaco.'*
- *The Nassau Daily Tribune, Saturday, September 10, 1932 pg 1-'Administrator Opens Abaco Fund.'&'Governor's Wife Dresses wounds of Abaco Injured.'*

- *The Nassau Daily Tribune, Tuesday, September 12, 1932 pg 1-'Relief Boat Sent to Grand Bahama-Sections Suffered from Hurricane.'*
- *The Nassau Daily Tribune, Tuesday, September 13, 1932 pg 1-'Tragedy of the Abaco Hurricane-Death and Destruction-First Hand Stories.'*
- *The Nassau Daily Tribune, Wednesday, September 14, 1932 pg 1-'An Appeal to the People of Nassau.' 'Effects of the Storm at Harbour Island.'*
- *The Nassau Daily Tribune, Friday, September 16, 1932 pg 1-'Abaco Relief Expedition Organized.'*
- *The Nassau Daily Tribune, Saturday, September 17, 1932 pg 1-'Governor Outlines Plans for Abaco.'*
- *The Tribune-Features Section, September 19, 2007 'Here's to the Bootleggers of the Bahamas!'* By Larry Smith.
- *Bahamas Gazette 1784-1815, John Wells, Editor. Nassau, Bahamas.*
- *Florida Historical Society: The Florida Historical Quarterly volume 65 issue 3*
- Ahrens, D. (2000) *Meteorology Today, An Introduction to Weather, Climate, and The Environment*, USA, Brooks/Cole Publishing.
- Albury, P. (1975) *The Story of The Bahamas*, London, Macmillan Education Ltd. Pgs. 163-169.
- Allaby, M. (2000) *DK Guide to Weather-A Photographic Journey Through The Skies,* London, Dorling Kindersley Ltd.
- Barnes, J. (2007) *Florida's Hurricane History*, Chapel Hill, The University of North Carolina Press.
- Barratt, P. (2003) *Bahama Saga-The Epic Story of the Bahama Islands*, Indiana, Authorhouse Publishers.
- Buker, G. (1993) *Blockaders, Refugees, and Contrabands: Civil War on Florida's Gulf Coast, 1861-1865*, University of Alabama Press.
- Burroughs, Crowder, Robertson, et al. (1996) *The Nature Company Guides to Weather*, Singapore, Time-Life Publishing Inc.
- Butler, K. *The History of Bahamian Boat Builders from 1800-2000*, Unpublished.

- Butler, E. (1980) *Natural Disasters*, Australia, Heinemann Educational Books Ltd.
- Challoner, J. (2000) *Hurricane and Tornado*, Great Britain, Dorling Kindersley.
- Clarke, P., Smith, A. (2001) *Usborne Spotter's Guide To Weather*, England, Usborne Publishing Ltd.
- Craton, M. (1986) *A History of The Bahamas*, Canada, San Salvador Press. Pgs 236-238, 250-254.
- Davis, K. (2005) *Don't Know Much About World Myths*, HarperCollins Publishers.
- Domenici, D. (2008) *The Aztecs-History and Treasures of an Ancient Civilization*, White Star Publishing.
- Douglas.S.M. (1958) *Hurricane,* USA, Rinehart and Company Inc.
- Duedall, I., Williams, J. (2002) *Florida Hurricanes and Tropical Storms 1871-2001,*USA, University Press Of Florida._
- Durschmied, E. (2001)_*The Weather Factor-How Nature has changed History*, New York, Arcade Publishing, Inc.
- Elekund, R.B. Jackson J.D., Thornton, M. (2004) *The Unintended Consequences' of Confederate Trade Legislation.* Eastern Economic Journal, Spring 2004.
- Emanuel, K. (2005) *Divine Wind-The History and Science of Hurricanes,* New York, Oxford University Press.
- Fitzpatrick, J.P. (1999) *Natural Disasters-Hurricanes,* USA, ABC-CLIO, Inc.
- Green, J., MacDonald, F., Steele, P. & Stotter, M. (2001) *The Encyclopedia of the Americas*, London, South Water Publishing.
- Gore, A.,(2006) *An Inconvenient Truth*, New York, USA, Rodale Books.
- Hairr, J. (2008) *The Great Hurricanes of North Carolina*, United Kingdom, The History Press. Pgs 81–104.
- Henry, J, Portier, K. & Coyne, J.(1994) *The Climate and Weather of Florida*, USA, Pineapple Press Inc. Pgs, 169-192.
- Horatio, L.W. (1898) *The Blockade of the Confederacy*, Century Magazine, LVI pgs 914-928.
- Horvitz, A.L. (2007) *The Essential Book of Weather Lore*, New York, The Reader's Digest Association, Inc.

- J.D. Jarrell, Max Mayfield, Edward Rappaport, & Chris Landsea *NOAA Technical Memorandum NWS TPC-1 The Deadliest, Costliest, and Most Intense United States Hurricanes from 1900 to 2000(And Other Frequently Requested Hurricane Facts)*.
- Jones W. (2005) *Hurricane-A Force of Nature*, Bahamas, Jones Communications Intl Ltd. Publication.
- Kahl, J. (1998) *National Audubon Society First Field Guide To Weather*, Hong Kong, Scholastic Inc.
- Keegan, W., (1992) *The People Who Discovered Columbus-The Prehistory of the Bahamas*, Tallahassee, University Press of Florida.
- Kindersley, D., (2002) *Eyewitness Weather*, London, Dorling Kindersley Ltd.
- Lauber, P. (1996) *Hurricanes: Earth's Mightiest Storms*, Singapore, Scholastic Press.
- Lawlor, J& A., (2008) *The Harbour Island Story*, Oxford, Macmillan Caribbean Publishers Ltd, pgs 154-177, 203-226.
- Lightbourn, G. R. (2005) *Reminiscing I & II-Photographs of Old Nassau*, Nassau, Ronald Lightbourn Publisher.
- Lloyd, J. (2007) *Weather-The Forces of Nature that Shape Our World*. United Kingdom, Parragon Publishing.
- Ludlum, D. M., (1989) *Early American Hurricanes 1492-1870*. Boston, MA: American Meteorological Society.
- Lyons, A.W. (1997) *The Handy Science Weather Answer Book*, Detroit, Visible Ink Press.
- MacPherson, J. (1967) *Caribbean Lands-A Geography Of The West Indies*, 2nd Edition, London, Longmans, Green and Co Ltd.
- Malone, S. and Roberts, R. *Nostalgic Nassau-Picture Postcards-1900-1940*.
- Millas C.J. (1968) *Hurricanes of The Caribbean and Adjacent Regions 1492-1800*, Edward Brothers Inc/ Academy of the Arts and Sciences of the Americas Miami, Florida.
- Pearce, A.E., Smith G.C. (1998) *The Hutchinson World Weather Guide*, Great Britain, Helicon Publishing Ltd.
- Phillips, C. (2007) *The illustrated Encyclopedia of the Aztec & Maya*, London, Lorenz Books.

- Redfield; W.C., 1846, *On Three Several Hurricanes of The Atlantic and their Relations To the Northers of Mexico and Central America*, New Haven.
- Reynolds, R., (2000) *Philip's Guide To Weather*, London, Octopus Publishing Group Ltd.
- Rouse, I., (1992) *The Tainos-The rise and decline of the people who greeted Columbus*, New Haven, Yale University Press.
- Saunders, A. (2006) *History of Bimini Volume 2*, Bahamas, New World Press.
- Saunders, G. (1983) *Bahamian Loyalists and Their Slaves*, London, MacMillan Education Ltd, pg 2.
- Saunders, G. (2010) *Historic Bahamas*, Bahamas, D. Gail Saunders. Pgs 85-87.
- Saunders, G, and Craton, M. (1998*) Islanders in the Stream: A History of the Bahamian People Volume 2,* USA, University of Georgia Press. Pgs 43-44, 79.
- Schwartz S. *The 1928 Hurricane and the Shaping of the Circum-Caribbean Region,* ReVista-Harward Review of Latin America. Winter 2007.
- Triana, P.(1987) San Salvador-The Forgotten Island, Spain, Ediciones Beramar.
- Williams, P.,(1999) *Chronological Highlights in the History of the Bahamas 600 to 1900*, Nassau, Bahamas Historical Society. Pgs 1,54.
- www.noaa.gov
- www.nasa.gov
- www.weather.unisys.com
- www.wunderground.com
- www.wikipedia.org
- www.paperspast.natlib.govt.nz
- www.colorado.edu
- www.hurricanecity.com
- www.nationalgeographic.com
- www.weathersavvy.com
- http://agora.ex.nii.ac.jp/digital-typhoon/help/world.html.en

The writing of this book has been a highly satisfying project, made so not only by the subject itself but also by the people who have helped and assisted me in some way or the other, so here are the persons I wish to thank: -

My Father and Mother Lofton and Francita Neely
Mr. Coleman and Diana Andrews and family
The late Mrs. Joanna Gibson
Ms. Deatrice Adderley
Professor William Gray
Ms. Stephanie Hanna
Mrs. Darnell Osborne
Mr. Ray Duncombe
Mr. Ethric Bowe
Mr. Peter Graham
Ms Janett Jackson
Mr. Leroy Lowe
The late Mr. William Holowesko
The Hon. Glenny's Hanna-Martin
Mr. Murrio Ducille
Mr. Charles and Eddie Carter
Dr. Gail Saunders
Mr. Joshua Taylor and family
Mrs. Patrice Wells
Mr. Brett Archer
Mrs. Ivy Roberts
Mrs. Jan Roberts
Ms. Jaffar Gibson
Mrs. Shavaughn Moss
Ms. Kristina McNeil
Mr. Ronald V. Shaklee
Mrs. June Maura
The late Mrs. Macushla Hazelwood
Mrs. Suzette Moss-Hall
Mr. Rodger Demeritte
Mr. Michael and Phillip Stubbs
Mr. Orson Nixon
Mr. Neil Sealey
Mrs. Patricia Beardsley Roker
Dr. Myles Munroe
Dr. Timothy Barrett

Rev. Theo and Blooming Neely and family
Staff and Management of The Nassau Guardian Newspaper
Staff and Management of Media Enterprises
Staff and Management of The Tribune Newspaper
Staff of IslandFM Radio Station
Staff of the Broadcasting Corporation of The Bahamas (ZNS)
Staff of the Cable12 News
Staff of the Department of Archives
Staff of the Department of Meteorology
Staff of Gemini Printing in Florida
Staff of NOAA and National Hurricane Center in Miami
Mr. Christopher Landsea
Mr. Phil Klotzbach
Mr. Bryan Norcross
Mr. Jack and Karen Andrews
Mrs. Margaret Jeffers

The good people of the Bahamas who opened their doors, hearts and minds to assist me with this project and provided me with overwhelming research materials, and many others too numerous to mention who gave me their take on these two hurricanes.

Contact Information:

Mr. Wayne Neely
P.O. Box EE-16637
Nassau, Bahamas
E-Mail:
wayneneely@hotmail.com
wayneneely@yahoo.com

Since I first started writing these books on notable Bahamian hurricanes and Bahamian history, there have been several companies who stood with me side by side in seeing that these books are not only published, but also placed in our local schools here in the Bahamas. My and their goal is a simple one, and that is to see that future generations of Bahamians can read about these great storms and the significant impact that they had on our society as a whole. If you can, please support these companies if and whenever you can because your support of these companies helps make this book possible. I would like to sincerely thank each one of these sponsors below, both individual and corporate who assisted me financially and in other ways in making this book project a reality. Without them, this book would have not been possible, so from the bottom of my heart I thank each and every one of them.

Serving you is all we do

Insurance Company of the West Indies (Bahamas) Ltd
Suite # 2 Fort Nassau Centre
The British Colonial Hilton
West Bay Street
Nassau, Bahamas
Telephone: 242-323-4004 Fax 242-322-6715
E-Mail: jojackson@icwi.com
www.icwi.com

34 Collins Ave.
P.O. Box N-8337
Nassau, Bahamas
Tel: 242-322-2341
E-Mail: info@jsjohnson.com
www.jsjohnson.com

Insurance Company of the Bahamas Ltd.
Collins Ave.
Nassau, Bahamas
Tel: 242-326-3100/3130/3144 Fax: 326-3132
E-Mail: dosborne@icbbahamas.com
www.icbbahamas.com

Crawford St. Oakes Field
P.O. Box N-8170
Nassau, Bahamas
Tel: 242-323-5171
E-Mail: rduncombe@cavalierbahamas.com
www.bobcatbahamas.com

East Bay Street
P.O. Box SS-5004
Nassau, Bahamas
Tel: 242-393-6054
Reservations: U.S. Toll Free (800) 398-DIVE
bahdiver@coralwave.com
www.bahamadivers.com

P.O. Box N-3039
Nassau, Bahamas
Phone: 242-361-5220-4
Fax: 242-361-5583
E-Mail: svfsltd@batelnet.bs

HIGHBOURNE CAY
EXUMA • BAHAMAS

P.O. Box SS-6342
Nassau, Bahamas
Phone: 242-355-1008
Fax: 242-355-1003
E-Mail: highborne@earthlink.net

#432 East Bay Street
P.O. Box CR-54288 | Nassau, N.P. Bahamas
Tel: 242-322-6735 | 242-322-6736 | Fax: 242-322-6793
Email: admin@afsbahamas.com| Facebook: AFSBahamas | Twitter@AFSBahamas

#120 Mermaid Blvd. West
P.O. Box CR-54288 | Nassau, N.P. Bahamas
Tel: 242-341-7575 | 242-341-3670 | Fax: 242-341-2018
Email: admin@atelbahamas.com

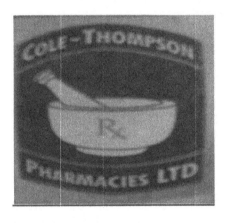

Cole-Thompson Pharmacy
P.O. Box SS-5366
Bay & Charlotte Streets
Nassau, Bahamas
Tel: 242-322-2062 or 242-322-2301
Fax: 242-356-3140
Email: colethompsonpharmacy@gmail.com

WEATHER DEFINITIONS

Advisory
Official information issued by a meteorological office describing all tropical cyclone watches and warnings in effect along with details concerning tropical cyclone locations, intensity and movement, and precautions that should be taken. Advisories are also issued to describe: (a) tropical cyclones prior to issuance of watches and warnings and (b) subtropical cyclones.

Air
This is considered the mixture of gases that make up the earth's atmosphere. The principal gases that compose dry air are Nitrogen at 78.09%, Oxygen at 20.95%, Argon at 0.93, and Carbon Dioxide at 0.033%. One of the most important constituents of air and most important gases in meteorology is water vapour.

All Clear
All Clear simply means that the hurricane has left the affected area and all the Alerts, Warnings, and Watches are lifted but the residents in that area should exercise extreme caution for downed power lines, debris, fallen trees, flooding etc.

Aneroid Barometer
An instrument used for measuring the atmospheric pressure. It registers the change in the shape of an evacuated metal cell to measure variations on the atmospheric pressure. The aneroid is a thin-walled metal capsule or cell, usually made of phosphorus bronze or beryllium copper which

expands and contracts with air pressure changes. The scales on the glass cover measure pressure in both inches and Millibars.

Anemometer
An instrument used to measure the wind speed or force of the wind.

Anemograph
An instrument used to measure the wind speed and direction.

Atmosphere
The envelope of gases that surround a planet and are held to it by the planet's gravitational attraction. The earth's atmosphere is mainly nitrogen and oxygen.

Atmospheric Pressure
The pressure exerted by the atmosphere at a given point. It measurements can be expressed in several ways. One is Millibars, another is Hector Pascal's and another is in inches or millimeters of Mercury.

Barograph
A continuous-recording barometer. It normally consists of a rotating drum, a sensor and a chart to measure the atmospheric pressure on a continuous basis and typically the chart consisted of a daily or weekly chart or graph.

Barometer
A weather instrument used for measuring the pressure of the atmosphere. The two principle types are aneroid and mercurial.

Beaufort wind scale
A system of estimating and reporting wind speed originally based on the effect of various wind speeds on the amount of canvas that a full-rigged nineteenth century frigate could carry. Typically in 1899 this was the most common way to estimate the wind speeds by most fishermen and spongers.

Best Track
A subjectively-smoothed representation of a tropical cyclone's location and intensity over its lifetime. The best track contains the cyclone's latitude,

longitude, maximum sustained surface winds, and minimum sea-level pressure at 6-hourly intervals. Best track positions and intensities, which are based on a post-storm assessment of all available data, may differ from values contained in storm advisories. They also generally will not reflect the erratic motion implied by connecting individual center fix positions.

Calm
Atmospheric conditions devoid of wind or any other air in motion and where smoke rises vertically. In oceanic terms, it is the apparent absence of the water surface when there is no wind.

Cape Verde Islands
A group of volcanic islands in the eastern Atlantic Ocean off the coast of West Africa. A Cape Verde hurricane originates near here.

Cape Verde Type Hurricane
A hurricane system that originated near the Cape Verde Islands just west of the west coast of Africa.

Center
Generally speaking, the vertical axis of a tropical cyclone, usually defined by the location of the minimum wind or minimum pressure. The cyclone center position can vary with altitude.

Central Pressure
The central pressure is sometimes referred to as the 'minimum central pressure' and this is the atmospheric pressure at the center of a high or low. It is the highest pressure in a high and lowest pressure in a low, referring to the sea level pressure of the system on a surface chart.

Climate
The historical record and description of average daily and in seasonal weather events that help describe a region. Statistics are generally drawn over several decades. The word is derived from the Greek klima, meaning inclination, and reflects the importance early scholars attributed to the sun's influence.

Cold Front
The boundary created when a cold air mass collides with a warm air mass.

Cyclone
An area of low atmospheric pressure, which has a closed circulation, that is cyclonic (counterclockwise in northern hemisphere and clockwise in southern hemisphere). It is a particularly severe type of tropical storm with very low atmospheric pressure at the centre and strong winds blowing around it. Violent winds and heavy rain may affect an area of some hundreds of miles. The name applies to such storms in the Indian Ocean. 'Typhoons' and 'hurricanes' are other names applied to the same phenomena in the Pacific and Atlantic Oceans respectively.

Depression
It is a region where the surface atmospheric pressure is low. A distinctive feature on a weather map and the opposite of an anticyclone. Usually associated with clouds and rain and sometimes-strong winds. A less severe weather disturbance than a tropical cyclone.

Disturbance
This has several applications. It can apply to a low or cyclone that is small in size and influence. It can also apply to an area that is exhibiting signs of cyclonic development. It may also apply to a stage of tropical cyclone development and is known as a tropical disturbance to distinguish it from other synoptic features.

Doppler radar
An advanced kind of radar that measures wind speed and locates areas of precipitation. It is like conventional radar in that it can detect areas of precipitation and measure rainfall intensity. But a Doppler radar can do more-it can actually measure the speed at which precipitation is moving horizontally toward or away from the radar antenna. Because precipitation particles are carried by the wind, Doppler radar can peer into a severe storm and reveal its winds.

Easterlies
Usually applied to the broad patterns of persistent winds with an easterly component, such as the easterly trade winds.

El Niño
A Spanish term given to a warm ocean current, and to the unusually warm and rainy weather associated with it, which sometimes occurs for a few weeks off the coast of Peru (which is otherwise an extremely dry and cool region of the tropics). Several years may pass without this current appearing.

Equator
The ideal or conceptual circle at 0 degrees latitude around the Earth that divides the planet into the northern and southern hemispheres.

Extratropical
A term used in advisories and tropical summaries to indicate that a cyclone has lost its "tropical" characteristics. The term implies both pole ward displacement of the cyclone and the conversion of the cyclone's primary energy source from the release of latent heat of condensation to baroclinic (the temperature contrast between warm and cold air masses) processes. It is important to note that cyclones can become extratropical and still retain winds of hurricane or tropical storm force.

Eye
A region in the center of a hurricane (tropical storm) where the winds are light and skies are clear to partly cloudy.

Eyewall
This is a wall of dense thunderstorms that surrounds the eye of a hurricane.

Feeder Bands
These are the lines or bands of thunderstorms that spiral into and around the center of a tropical system. Also known as outer convective bands, a typical hurricane may have several of these bands surrounding it. They occur in advance of the main rain shield and are usually 40 to 80 miles apart. In thunderstorm development, they are the lines or bands of low level clouds that move or feed into the updraft region of a thunderstorm.

Flood
Overflowing by water of the normal confines of a stream or other body of water, or accumulation of water by drainage over areas that are not normally submerged.

Forecast

A statement of expected future occurrences. Weather forecasting includes the use of objective models based on certain atmospheric parameters, along with the skill and experience of a meteorologist.

Fresh gale

Wind with a speed between 34 and 40 knots (39 and 46 mph); Beaufort scale number 8.

Front

The transition or boundary between two air masses of different densities, which usually means different temperatures. The several types of fronts bring distinct weather patterns.

Gale

A gale is a very strong wind. There are conflicting definitions of how strong the winds must be to classify it as a gale. The U.S. Government's National Weather Service defines a gale as 34–47 knots (39–54 miles per hour) of sustained surface winds. Forecasters typically issue gale warnings when winds of this strength are expected. Other sources use minimums as low as 28 knots and maximums as high as 90 knots. Through 1986, the National Hurricane Center used the term gale to refer to winds of tropical storm force for coastal areas, between 33 knots and 63 knots. The 90-knot definition is very non-standard. A common alternative definition of the maximum is 55 knots. Typically in 1899 whenever a storm or significant bad weather was approaching the Bahamas most people said that 'Gale was travelling' which had no relation at the time to the true meaning of the word but essentially meaning that there will be severe weather from a hurricane to be experienced over that area to which they referred.

Gale warning

A warning for marine interest for impending winds from 34 to 47 knots.

High

The center of an area of high atmospheric pressure, usually accompanied by anticyclonic and outward wind flow. Also known as an anticyclone.

Hurricane

This the term used in the North Atlantic Region and in the eastern North Pacific Ocean to describe a severe tropical cyclone having winds in excess of 64 knots (74mph) and capable of producing widespread wind damage and heavy flooding. The same tropical cyclone is known as a typhoon in the western Pacific and cyclone in the Indian Ocean.

Hurricane Alert

A hurricane alert indicates that a hurricane poses a threat to an area (often within 60 hours) and residents of the area should start to make any necessary preparations.

Hurricane Season

The part of the year having a relatively high incidence of hurricanes. The hurricane season in the North Atlantic runs from June 1 to November 30.

Hurricane Warning

A formal advisory issued by forecasters in the North Atlantic Region when they have determined that hurricane conditions are expected in a coastal area or group of islands within a 36 hour period. A warning is used to inform the public and marine interests of the storm's location, intensity, and movement. At this point residents should have completed the necessary preparations for the storm.

Hurricane Watch

A formal advisory issued by forecasters in the North Atlantic Region when they have determined that hurricane conditions are a potential threat to a coastal area or group of islands within 48 hour period. A watch is used to inform the public and marine interest of the storm's location, intensity, and movement and residents of the area should be in the process of being prepared.

Knot

The unit of speed in the nautical system; one nautical mile per hour. It is equal to 1.1508 statute miles per hour or 0.5144 meters per second.

Landfall
The intersection of the surface center of a tropical cyclone with a coastline. Because the strongest winds in a tropical cyclone are not located precisely at the center. It is possible for a cyclone's strongest winds to be experienced over land even if landfall does not occur. Similarly, it is possible for a tropical cyclone to make landfall and have its strongest winds remain over the water.

Low
An area of low barometric pressure, with its attendant system of winds. Also called a depression or cyclone.

Meteorologist
A scientist who studies and predicts the weather by looking at what is happening in the atmosphere.

Meteorology
The study of the atmosphere and the atmospheric phenomena as well as the atmosphere's interaction with the Earth's surface, oceans, and life in general.

Millibar
A unit of pressure, which directly expresses the force exerted by the atmosphere. Equal to 1000 dynes/cm^2 or 100Pascals.

Moderate gale
Wind with a speed between 28 and 33 knots (32 and 38 mph); Beaufort scale number 7.

National Hurricane Center
The National Weather Service office in Coral Gables, Florida, that tracks and forecasts hurricanes and other weather in the Atlantic, Gulf of Mexico, Caribbean Sea, and parts of the Pacific.

NOAA
National Oceanic and Atmospheric Administration.

Precipitation
Any and all forms of water particles, liquid or solid, that falls from the atmosphere and reach the ground.

Radar
Acronym for **RA**dio **D**etection **A**nd **R**anging. An electronic instrument used to detect objects (such as falling precipitation) by their ability to reflect and scatter microwaves back to a receiver.

Rainfall
The amount of precipitation of any type, primarily liquid. It is usually the amount that is measured by a rain gauge.

Rain gauge
Instrument for measuring the depth of water from precipitation that is assumed to be distributed over a horizontal, impervious surface and not subject to evaporation and measured during a given time interval. Measurement is done in hundredths of inches (0.01").

Reconnaissance Aircraft
This is an aircraft, which flies directly into the eye of a hurricane to make a preliminary survey to gain information about a hurricane using advanced meteorological instruments.

Recording rain gauge
A rain gauge that automatically records the amount of precipitation collected, as a function of time.

Saffir-Simpson Damage-Potential Scale
A scale relating a hurricane's central pressure and winds to the possible damage it is capable of inflicting and it was first introduced in 1971 by Herbert Saffir and Robert Simpson.

Satellite
Any object that orbits a celestial body, such as a moon. However, the term is often used in reference to the manufactured objects that orbit the earth, either in geostationary or a polar manner. Some information that is gathered by weather satellites, such as GOES9, includes upper air, temperatures and humidity, recording the temperatures of cloud tops,

land, and ocean, monitoring the movement of clouds top determines upper level wind speeds, tracing the movement of water vapour, monitoring the sun and solar activity, and relaying data from weather instruments around the world.

Satellite Images
Images taken by weather satellite that reveal information, such as the flow of water vapour, the movement of frontal systems, and the development of a tropical system.

Schooner
A typically 2-masted fore-and-aft rigged vessel with a foremast and a mainmast stepped nearly amidships.

Severe Weather
Generally, any destructive weather event, but usually applies to localized storms, such as blizzards, intense thunderstorms, or tornadoes.

Severe Thunderstorm
A thunderstorm with winds measuring 50 knots (58 mph) or greater, ¾ inch hail or larger, severe thunderstorms may also produce torrential rain and frequent lightning.

Shower
Precipitation from a cumuliform cloud. Characterized by the suddenness of beginning and ending, by the rapid change in intensity, and usually by a rapid change in the condition of the sky. The solid or liquid water particles are usually bigger than the corresponding elements in other types of precipitation and usually lasts less than an hour in duration.

Small Craft Advisory:
When a tropical cyclone threatens a coastal area, small craft operators are advised to remain in port or not to venture into the open sea. It is an advisory issued for marine interests, especially for operator of small boats or other vessels. Conditions include wind speeds between 20 knots (23 mph) and 34 knots (39 mph).

Sponging
This was an industry of the Bahamas in the mid to late 1800s thru the mid-1900s. This industry was the number industry in the Bahamas for many years before over-sponging; the introduction of synthetic sponges and sponge diseases killed it off in the mid-1900s. The fishermen went to harvest the sponges from the seabed and then sold them to the sponge exchange in Nassau.

Storm
An individual low pressure disturbance, complete with winds, clouds, and precipitation. Wind with a speed between 56 and 63 knots (64 and 72 mph); Beaufort scale number 11.

Storm Surge
This is the mound or rise in ocean water drawn up by the low pressure below a hurricane; it causes enormous waves and widespread damage if the hurricane reaches land.

Storm tide
The actual level of sea water resulting from the astronomic tide combined with the storm surge.

Strong gale
Wind with a speed between 41 and 47 knots (47 and 54 mph); Beaufort scale number 9.

Swell
Ocean waves that have travelled out of their generating area. Swells characteristically exhibits a more regular and longer period and has a flatter wave crests than waves within their fetch.

Thunderstorm
A local storm produced by cumulonimbus clouds and always accompanied by lightning and thunder.

Tornado
The name given to a very strong and damaging whirlwind with a clearly visible dark, snake-like funnel extending from a thundercloud to the

ground. The track of a tornado at the ground level is rarely very wide, but buildings, trees, and crops may be totally devastated.

Tropics
The region of the Earth located between the Tropic of Cancer, at 23.5 degrees North latitude, and the Tropic of Capricorn, at 23.5 degrees South latitude. It encompasses the equatorial region, an area of high temperatures and considerable precipitation during part of the year.

Tropical depression
A mass of thunderstorms and clouds generally with a cyclonic wind circulation between 20 and 34 knots.

Tropical disturbance
An organized mass of thunderstorms with a slight cyclonic wind circulation of less than 20 knots. It is a moving area of thunderstorms, which maintains its identity for 24 hours or more.

Tropical storm
Once a tropical depression has intensified to the point where its maximum sustained winds are between 35-64 knots (39-73 mph), it becomes a tropical storm.

Tropical Wave
An inverted, migratory wave-like disturbance or trough in the tropical region that moves from east to west, generally creating only a shift in winds and rain. The low level convergence and associated convective weather occur on the eastern side of the wave axis. Normally it moves slower than the atmospheric current in which it is embedded and is considered a weak trough of low pressure. Tropical waves occasionally intensify into tropical cyclones. They are also called Easterly Waves.

Tropical Storm Watch
A tropical Storm Watch is issued when tropical storm conditions, including winds from 39 to 73 mph (35 to 64 knots) pose a possible threat to a specified coastal area within 48 hours.

Tropical Storm Warning
A tropical storm warning is issued when tropical storm conditions, including winds from 39 to 73 mph (35 to 64 knots) are expected in a specified coastal area within 36 hours or less.

Typhoon
The name given in the Western Pacific and particularly in the China Sea to violent tropical storms or cyclones with maximum sustained winds of 74 miles per hour or higher. This same tropical cyclone is known as a hurricane in the eastern North Pacific and North Atlantic Ocean, and as a cyclone in the Indian Ocean.

Weather
The state of the atmosphere, mainly with respect to its effects upon life and human activities. As distinguished from climate, weather consists of the short-term (minutes to months) variations of the atmosphere.

Willy Willies
A colloquial Australian term for a violent tropical storm or cyclone affecting the coasts of northern Australia.

Wind
Air in motion relative to the surface of the Earth. Almost exclusively used to denote the horizontal component.

Wind speed
Rate of wind movement in distance per unit time.

Wind vane
An instrument used to indicate wind direction.

World Meteorological Organization (WMO)
This is the governing sub-body for meteorology within the United Nations made up of 185 member states and territories. It succeeded the International Meteorological Organization, which was founded in 1873. It is the United Nations system's authoritative voice on the state and behaviour of the Earth's atmosphere, its interaction with the oceans, the climate it produces and the resulting distribution of water resources.

Printed in the United States
by Baker & Taylor Publisher Services